INTERNATIONAL ORIGINS OF SOCIAL AND POLITICAL THEORY

POLITICAL POWER AND SOCIAL THEORY

Series Editor: Julian Go

Recent Volumes:

Volume 13:	1999
Volume 14:	2000
Volume 15:	2002
Volume 16:	2004
Volume 17:	2005
Volume 18:	2006
Volume 19:	2008
Volume 20:	2009
Volume 21:	2010
Volume 22:	Rethinking Obama: 2011
Volume 23:	2012
Volume 24:	Postcolonial Sociology: 2013
Volume 25:	Decentering Social Theory: 2013
Volume 26:	The United States in Decline: 2014
Volume 27:	Fields of Knowledge: Science, Politics and Publics in the Neoliberal Age: 2014
Volume 28:	Patrimonial Capitalism and Empire: 2015
Volume 29:	Chartering Capitalism: Organizing Markets, States, and Publics: 2015
Volume 30:	Perverse Politics? Feminism, Anti-Imperialism, Multiplicity
Volume 31:	Postcolonial Sociologies: A Reader

POLITICAL POWER AND SOCIAL THEORY VOLUME 32

INTERNATIONAL ORIGINS OF SOCIAL AND POLITICAL THEORY

EDITED BY

TARAK BARKAWI
GEORGE LAWSON
London School of Economics and Political Science, London, UK

emerald PUBLISHING

United Kingdom – North America – Japan
India – Malaysia – China

Emerald Publishing Limited
Howard House, Wagon Lane, Bingley BD16 1WA, UK

First edition 2017

British Library Cataloguing in Publication Data
A catalogue record for this book is available from the British Library

ISBN: 978-1-78714-267-1 (Print)
ISBN: 978-1-78714-266-4 (Online)
ISBN: 978-1-78714-724-9 (Epub)
ISBN: 978-1-83867-922-4 (Paperback)

ISSN: 0198-8719 (Series)

CONTENTS

LIST OF CONTRIBUTORS

Tarak Barkawi	The London School of Economics and Political Science, London, UK
David L. Blaney	Macalester University, St. Paul, MN, USA
Samuel A. Chambers	Johns Hopkins University, Baltimore, MD, USA
Ricarda Hammer	Brown University, Providence, RI, USA
Beate Jahn	University of Sussex, Brighton, UK
Helen M. Kinsella	University of Wisconsin, Madison, WI, USA
George Lawson	The London School of Economics and Political Science, London, UK
Daniel J. Levine	University of Alabama, Tuscaloosa, AL, USA
Jeppe Mulich	The London School of Economics and Political Science, London, UK
Patricia Owens	University of Sussex, Brighton, UK
Aleksandra Thurman	Independent Researcher, Hong Kong

SENIOR EDITORIAL BOARD

STUDENT EDITORIAL BOARD

EDITORIAL STATEMENT

Political Power and Social Theory is a peer-reviewed annual journal committed to advancing the interdisciplinary understanding of the linkages between political power, social relations, and historical development. The journal welcomes both empirical and theoretical work and is willing to consider papers of substantial length. Publication decisions are made by the editor in consultation with members of the editorial board and anonymous reviewers. For information on submissions, please see the journal website at www.emeraldgrouppublishing.com/tk/ppst

SERIES EDITOR'S INTRODUCTION

It is with great honor that I present this special volume of PPST, *International Origins of Social and Political Theory*. Based upon a workshop held at the London School of Economics and Political Science in 2016, this volume offers fresh insights on the hitherto under-examined relations between international history and social theory. Thanks to co-editors Tarak Barkawi and George Lawson for putting this volume together and to the authors for their eye-opening contributions.

Julian Go
November 2016
Boston, MA

THE INTERNATIONAL ORIGINS OF SOCIAL AND POLITICAL THEORY

Tarak Barkawi and George Lawson

ABSTRACT

This article introduces the main themes that animate this special issue: the necessary entanglement of theory and history, the cortical relationship between theory and practice, and the transboundary (i.e., international) relations that help to constitute systems of both thought and practice. We integrate the contributions to the special issue within these overarching themes and identify their main contributions. We make three core arguments: first, all theory is situated knowledge, derived in and through historical context; second, theory-practice is a single field in which theory arises out of and acts upon historical experience; and third, both social and political theory have international origins, arising from transboundary encounters.

Keywords: History; theory; practice; social theory; political theory; international relations

---

International Origins of Social and Political Theory
Political Power and Social Theory, Volume 32, 1–7

ISSN: 0198-8719/doi:10.1108/S0198-871920170000032001

INTRODUCTION

What is the relationship between history and theory? Most of the time, theory seems to stand apart from history. Social scientists apply theories to historical events, seeing history as a testing bed or as a site of "operationalization" for their theoretical schemas (e.g., Elman and Elman, eds., 2001; for a critique, see Lawson, 2012). Others, among them historians of thought, see theory as speech acts either rooted in their particular time and place (Skinner, 1988), or, alternately, as reflections of broader social forces (Vitalis, 2016). On either account, theory (as intellectual systems) and history (as events, experiences, and practices) appear as distinct domains. This special issue takes a different view: the relations between history and theory are better conceived as co-constitutive. Theory is made in history, and it helps to make history. Understanding theory, and understanding history, requires inquiry attuned to the entwinement of theory and history.

The authors in the special issue develop this insight in two distinctive directions. Firstly, they do so through a focus on "transboundary" (i.e., international) encounters and the ways in which they generate and shape theorizing. Secondly, they direct attention to the immersion of theorists and theory in practice. In this introduction, we say a little more about what we mean by a co-constitutive approach to history and theory, and about each of these distinctive directions. We also comment briefly on the articles that follow.

HISTORY/THEORY

What does it mean to say that theory is made in history, and that it helps to make history? It means that theories arise historically, formed amid encounters between theorists and the events and practices they experience and take part in. Haiti's revolutionary slaves informed Hegel's thinking on masters and slaves (Buck-Morss, 2000). Napoleon's France schooled Clausewitz by defeating him in battle and making him a prisoner (Strachan, 2007, p. 46). Marx studied in the hothouse of Europe's 1848 uprisings. Historical "happenings" – often unexpected and even shocking to contemporaries – help to generate, frame, and shape theory. To take just one example explored in depth in this special issue, Hannah Arendt's lived experiences of totalitarianism and exile fundamentally informed her political action as well as her theorizing (Owens, 2017).

Theories are not only formed historically, but they are also refracted through ongoing encounters; theories are reconceived in different times and places. Mulich (2017) shows how theorists have wrongly interpreted the postcolonial order in the New World at the turn of the 19th century as a radical break from the past, laying the groundwork for an international order centered on nation-states. Seen in the context of the time, the Western Hemisphere was mainly the site of creative, but limited, experimentation in existing notions of divided sovereignty and composite polities – imperialism remained the principal source of political authority throughout the 19th century, and the only really radical experiment in the New World – Haiti – was overlooked by political theorists until recently. Similarly, Blaney (2017) shows how contemporary disciplinary divisions between economics and political theory obscure the central role played by Alfred Marshall, a leading political economist in late Victorian Britain, in constituting both the ideas and practices that helped to shape British imperialism (also see Bell, 2007). Both Mulich and Blaney make clear that theoretical interpretations are recrafted as they encounter new histories, new times, and new places. As Levine (2017) also shows in his contribution to this volume, the historical contexts that form the crucible in which theorizing is produced are often forgotten by later actors and thinkers operating in different contexts. Theory is not something "out there," removed from history, even retrospectively. Rather, theories are assessed and reassessed, made and remade through ongoing encounters with history.

Theory, then, is made historically. At the same time, theory informs practice, shaping events and processes, governments and economies, and wars and revolutions. Equally, thinkers immersed in practice produce the theories that help to make history. Often, the boundaries between theory and practice characteristic of the contemporary professionalized academy have obscured their co-constitutive interaction. David Ricardo, to take one example, brokered stocks and manipulated markets while developing ideas that shaped, and continue to shape, economies. Clausewitz was an officer and commander, a staff college lecturer and an instructor of princes. Kinsella (2017) demonstrates how former guerrilla fighters became legal theorists at the meetings leading to the 1977 Additional Protocols to the Geneva Conventions, forcing alterations in the laws of war that accorded with their experiences in anticolonial, nationalist struggles. Neither Kinsella's guerrilla fighters, nor figures like Ricardo and Clausewitz, much less Marx, Freud, Hayek, and Keynes, can be restricted to realms of either "thought" *or* "practice"; rather, their work arose from the conjoining of thought *with* practice. Much of this work went on to inform both theorizing and action in ways that vastly exceed both the achievements of the specialized scholarship of the academy and of contemporary "policy relevant" knowledge. The point is not that theory *should* be more practice- or policy-oriented. Rather, the contributions to this special issue stress the cortical relationship between theory and practice that has been lost in the valorization and, from other quarters, condemnation, of theory as a realm distinct from practice.

This special issue also draws attention to the "transboundary" encounters that have generated and shaped theorizing. By "transboundary" (which we use synonymously with "international"), we mean the histories that interconnect people across borders, whether these borders represent groups, states, regions, empires, or other entities. Thinking about government, society, and economy owes profound debts to such encounters. Historiography begins as the stories of wars and travels (Herodotus, 1987 [c.440 BC]). The conquest of the Americas, and contemporary representations of its peoples, provided Hobbes with his vivid embodiment of the "condition of warre" in the state of nature (Hobbes, 1996 [1651], p. 89). Grotius generated his ideas about the law of the sea from the practices of the Indian Ocean system (Alexandrowicz, 1967; Steinberg, 2001), just as trade between Britain and India helped to form Adam Smith's ideas about free trade (Erikson, 2017), and utilitarian thought was forged in the imperial encounters between Britain and India (Chatterjee, 2012; Mehta, 1999; Stokes, 1959). The tradition of "reason of state," thinking about strategy and war, and treatises on diplomacy and the education of princes, take as given a world of competing sovereigns and other armed entities, their conflicting (and common) interests and policies, and their often violent encounters with one another. One of the most extreme transboundary encounters of all – war – casts a shadow over many systems of thought. As a number of contributions to this special issue show, imperial encounters have been fundamental to the generation of systems of both thought and practice, from serving as the leitmotif to the thinking of Frantz Fanon and Stuart Hall (Hammer, 2017) to understanding symbolic mourning rituals in 17th century Korea (Thurman, 2017).

In sum, this project is animated by the insight that theory arises in and through historical encounters. These encounters are iterative and, often, international. The relationship between history and theory is not something that can be reduced to a footnote, introductory note, or biographical detail. Rather, establishing the generative relationship between history and theory should be the starting point for any assessment of theoretical systems. And it should also be the starting point for analyses of the histories that theoretical systems help to shape. History is an archive of events and experiences that leads to theorizing, often by practitioners participating in those very events.

If theories arise historically, these theories are subsequently abstracted from historical events, experiences, and practices – in effect, the tracks in which a theory are formed are subsequently covered up. Theories become seen as more or less consistent abstractions removed from the historical encounters through which they emerged. Collectively, the articles in this volume seek to uncover some of these hidden tracks and, along with them, some of the constitutive relations between history and theory. Jahn (2017) shows how the "world crisis" (Bayly, 1989) of the late 18th and early 19th centuries helped to forge a modern "episteme" that, in turn, produced a divide between disciplinary history and the social sciences, a divide that has been maintained – and reinforced – ever since. Chambers (2017) repositions the Labor Theory of Value as a capitalist fairy tale, a story known to be false. Far from intending to offer an ahistorical theory of value (later dismissed as unworkable by modern economists), Marx was in fact showing how questions of value were addressed in the concrete historical context of capitalist society. Resurrected as a false theory, the Labor Theory of Value now functions both to dismiss Marx, while reifying the idea of theory as ahistorical.

WHY THIS MATTERS

There are three main consequences that flow from the interventions made in this special issue. First, the articles envisage a relationship between theory and history in which the former is no longer seen as outside of and/or applied to, the latter. Rather, all theory is situated knowledge, derived in and through history. The second consequence concerns establishing a distinctive notion of theory and practice. As with the theory–history relationship, it posits not theory *and* practice, but *theory-practice* as a single field constituted by the productive tension between how participants make sense of historical experiences and the ways in which these experiences shape policy and practice. Finally, the contributors see international encounters as constitutive of theory. Theories are not forged by individuals living within distinct – and discrete – "local" environments. Rather, theory is forged through ongoing encounters between "here" and "there," "home" and "abroad," the "domestic" and the "foreign." Both social and political theory have international origins.

REFERENCES

Alexandrowicz, C. H. (1967). *An introduction to the history of the law of nations in the East Indies: 16th, 17th, and 18th centuries*. Oxford: Clarendon.

Bayly, C. A. (1989). *Imperial meridian. The British Empire and the world, 1780–1830*. London: Longman.

Bell, D. (2007). *The idea of Greater Britain: Empire and the future of world order 1860–1900*. Princeton, NJ: Princeton University Press.

Blaney, D. (2017). Late-Victorian worlds: Alfred Marshall on competition, character, and Anglo-Saxon civilization. In T. Barkawi & G. Lawson (Eds.), *International origins of social and political theory* (Vol. 32). Political Power and Social Theory. Bingley: Emerald Publishing Limited.

Buck-Morss, S. (2000). Hegel and Haiti. *Critical Inquiry*, *26*(4): 821–865.

Chambers, S. (2017). The labor theory of value as a capitalist fairytale: Marx as genealogist in Zur Kritik. In T. Barkawi & G. Lawson (Eds.), *International origins of social and political theory* (Vol. 32). Political Power and Social Theory. Bingley: Emerald Publishing Limited.

Chatterjee, P. (2012). *The black hole of empire: History of a global practice of power*. Princeton, NJ: Princeton University Press.

Erikson, E. (2017). The global origins of economic theory. In J. Go & G. Lawson (Eds.), *Global historical sociology*. Cambridge: Cambridge University Press.

Hammer, R. (2017). Epistemic ruptures: History, practice and the anticolonial imagination. In T. Barkawi & G. Lawson (Eds.), *International origins of social and political theory* (Vol. 32). Political Power and Social Theory. Bingley: Emerald Publishing Limited.

Herodotus. (1987). *The history* (D. Grene, Trans.). Chicago, IL: The University of Chicago Press [c.440B.C.].

Hobbes, T. (1996 [1651]). *Leviathan*. R. Tuck (Ed.). Cambridge: Cambridge University Press.

Jahn, B. (2017). The imperial origins of social and political thought. In T. Barkawi & G. Lawson (Eds.), *International origins of social and political theory* (Vol. 32). Political Power and Social Theory. Bingley: Emerald Publishing Limited.

Kinsella, H. (2017). Superfluous injury and unnecessary suffering: National liberation and the laws of war. In T. Barkawi & G. Lawson (Eds.), *International origins of social and political theory* (Vol. 32). Political Power and Social Theory. Bingley: Emerald Publishing Limited.

Lawson, G. (2012). The eternal divide? History and international relations. *European Journal of International Relations*, *18*(2): 203–226.

Levine, D. J. (2017). "These Days of Shoah": History, habitus, and realpolitik in Jewish Palestine, 1942–1943. In T. Barkawi & G. Lawson (Eds.), *International origins of social and political theory* (Vol. 32). Political Power and Social Theory. Bingley: Emerald Publishing Limited.

Mehta, U. S. (1999). *Liberalism and empire: A study in nineteenth-century British liberal thought*. Chicago, IL: The University of Chicago Press.

Mulich, J. (2017). Empire and violence: Continuity in the age of revolution. In T. Barkawi & G. Lawson (Eds.), *International origins of social and political theory* (Vol. 32). Political Power and Social Theory. Bingley: Emerald Publishing Limited.

Owens, P. (2017). The international origins of Hannah Arendt's historical method. In T. Barkawi & G. Lawson (Eds.), *International origins of social and political theory* (Vol. 32). Political Power and Social Theory. Bingley: Emerald Publishing Limited.

Skinner, Q. (1988). Meaning and understanding in the history of ideas. In J. Tully (Ed.). Meaning and context: Quentin skinner and his *critics*. Princeton, NJ: Princeton.

Steinberg, P. (2001). *The social construction of the ocean*. Cambridge: Cambridge University Press.

Stokes, E. (1959). *The English utilitarians and India*. Oxford: Oxford University Press.

Strachan, H. (2007). *Clausewitz's "On War."* New York, NY: Grove Press.

Thurman, A. (2017). The sovereign society: Historical rupture and the emergence of the "domestic" seventeenth century Europe and East Asia. In T. Barkawi & G. Lawson (Eds.), *International origins of social and political theory* (Vol. 32). Political Power and Social Theory. Bingley: Emerald Publishing Limited.

Vitalis, R. (2016). *White world order, black power politics*. Ithaca, NY: Cornell University Press.

THE IMPERIAL ORIGINS OF SOCIAL AND POLITICAL THOUGHT

Beate Jahn

ABSTRACT

The attempt to recover the international origins of social and political thought is motivated by the unsatisfactory fragmentation of modern knowledge – by its failure to account for the intimate connections between theory and history in general and its international dimension in particular – and seeks to overcome these divides. This article provides an analysis of the theory/history divide and its role for the fragmentation of modern knowledge. Theoretically, it shows, this divide is rooted in, and reproduced by, the epistemic foundations of modern knowledge. Historically, the modern episteme arises from a crisis of imperial politics in the 18th century. This analysis suggests that theory, history, and the international are products rather than origins of modern social and political thought. These historical origins thus do not provide the basis for more integrated forms of knowledge. They do, however, reveal how the fragmentation of knowledge itself simultaneously serves and obscures the imperialist dimension of modern politics.

Keywords: History; theory; international relations; episteme; empire

International Origins of Social and Political Theory
Political Power and Social Theory, Volume 32, 9–35

ISSN: 0198-8719/doi:10.1108/S0198-871920170000032002

INTRODUCTION

The project of recovering the international origins of social and political thought is motivated by the glaring disjuncture between the everyday experience of intimate connections between theory and history, domestic and international politics on the one hand and their separation in scientific knowledge production on the other. Bridging these gaps thus promises "better" knowledge: theories that are rooted in and sensitive to the historical context; histories conscious of their theoretical assumptions; "theory-practice as a single field"; and international relations as an integral dimension of theory *and* history (Barkawi & Lawson, 2017). Such knowledge, in turn, is expected to provide the basis for "better" political practice. A return of universal history, for example, is expected to generate "a sense of human solidarity or global citizenship" (Christian, 2010, pp. 7, 8, 19, 25, 26).

Yet, fragmentation does not just affect the relations between history, theory, and the international. It has long been identified as a problem of the modern sciences in general and social and political thought in particular, leading to almost ubiquitous demands for interdisciplinarity and inspiring the development of new fields, or approaches, like historical sociology, political economy, biochemistry, or universal history that aim to bridge the gap between neighboring fields or even between the humanities and the natural sciences at large (Christian, 2010, p. 24). Such projects are often successful in institutionalizing new fields of study, but they do not satisfactorily resolve the problem of fragmentation. Despite its rich contributions to our understanding of the modern world, historical sociology, for example, has failed to convince mainstream sociology of the need for a historical approach, is criticized by historians for not meeting the methodological requirements of history, is itself internally fragmented, and has a history of excluding relevant dimensions of social and political life, such as culture or race (Adams, Clemens, & Orloff, 2005, pp. 10, 11, 25–27, 30, 32). This fate is by no means specific to historical sociology but rather a characteristic of attempts to cross disciplinary divides, and it thus calls for a general analysis of the dynamics of fragmentation in the modern sciences. This article provides such an analysis, focusing on the example of History and International Relations (IR).[1]

I will begin by analyzing previous attempts to bridge the gap between history and (international) theory, which fall into two broad strategies. The first seeks to build on common features of these disciplines. It tends to fail because it overlooks that the separation is embodied in their very constitution. Consequently, the second strategy seeks to reconceptualize history and/or theory but fails to take into account the necessary historical context.

Responding to these lacunae, the second section provides a theoretical account of the constitution of modern disciplines in general, and History and IR in particular. Following Foucault's archeological approach, I argue that the fragmentation of knowledge has its roots in the modern episteme. Reconstructing the nature and dynamics of the modern episteme explains why systematic attempts to overcome disciplinary divisions simply tend to reproduce fragmentation.

The third section locates the historical origins of this modern episteme in the "age of revolutions." It shows that politics at the time was characterized by empires and that the modern episteme and its distinction between theory and history, domestic and international politics, is a response to, rather than the root of, a political crisis of empire. On the one hand, historical analysis, therefore, cannot lead back to a time when the international and domestic, historical and theoretical, dimensions of politics were integrated and could therefore provide the basis for less fragmented forms of knowledge today. On the other hand, this historical analysis draws attention to the fact that epistemic and disciplinary fragmentation provided a "solution" to the crisis of imperial politics. It thus highlights that the distinction between theory and history, domestic and international politics today serves as the continuation of imperialist power politics precisely by obscuring them.

In conclusion, this article suggests that bridging the gap between history and (international) theory is bound to fail: theoretically, because each of these fields is constituted through the separation from the other, and historically, because their origins lie in imperial rather than international politics, a distinction I will discuss in depth in the section "Historicizing the History/Theory Divide." However, the analysis of these theoretical dynamics and historical origins of the fragmentation of modern knowledge does reveal its performative role in making the reproduction of imperialist policies possible. If not overcoming the fragmentation of modern knowledge as such, therefore, this analysis nevertheless opens up particular functions of this fragmentation to critique.

BRIDGING THE GAP BETWEEN HISTORY AND IR

The fragmentation of modern knowledge is seen as a problem both in History and in International Relations. Historians and IR scholars have thus explored the possibilities of bridging the gap between the two disciplines. Broadly, two different strategies, I will show, characterize these efforts – but both tend to fail. Analyzing these strategies, I will argue that both miss a crucial dimension – theoretical in one case and historical in the other – of the root of the problem.

In many ways, History and IR are inextricably linked (Isacoff, 2002, p. 603; Jenkins, 1991, p. 5; Smith, 1999, pp. 1, 8; Walker, 1989). History and the social sciences, including IR, emerged from a common discourse in the 19th century (Sewell, 2005, p. 2). Early IR scholars were often trained as historians and/or approached the problematique of international politics through historical investigations. Despite particularly the behaviorist challenges, historical approaches were never entirely replaced in IR. And since the end of the Cold War, there has been renewed interest in historical approaches and even the suggestion of a "historical turn" in the discipline (Bell, 2001; Hobden, 2002, p. 56; Lawson, 2012; Teschke, 2003, pp. 1–2; Vaughan-Williams, 2005, p. 116).

Furthermore, IR cannot escape history in the sense of "the past" or "past events." Its subject matter, international politics, itself consists of historical events and the data used to substantiate even the most ahistorical and abstract IR theory are "historical facts." Conversely, historians regularly use social science concepts, categories, metaphors, and theories not only explicitly, as in the case of the Annales school, but also as a matter of course (Revel, 2008, pp. 397–398; Sewell, 2005, pp. 1, 2, 5; Wright, 2008, p. 114).

Despite this intimate connection, however, the constitution of separate academic disciplines "utterly transformed the Edenic intellectual landscape" (Sewell, 2005, p. 2). While the differences between these disciplines are not absolute or exclusive (Smith, 1999, p. 9), they are real enough and widely recognized: historians aim to explain particular events (the idiographic approach), while IR scholars (and other social scientists) search for general laws (the nomothetic approach); historians adopt a chronological concept of causation, while ahistorical concepts of causation dominate in IR; historians focus on agency, while IR scholars are interested in structure and unintended consequences; historians highlight the moral choices of particular actors, while IR scholars are interested in the nature of things; and historians tend to integrate their theoretical assumptions into historical narratives, while IR scholars separate theoretical and empirical material (Christian, 2010, p. 20; Elman and Elman, 2001, pp. 12–23, 25–27; Lawson, 2012, p. 204; Sewell, 2005, pp. 3, 6, 9, 10; Smith, 1999, pp. 23–25; Steinmetz, 2008, pp. 536–537).

These distinctions are widely seen as affecting the quality of work in both disciplines. Thus, while historians borrow theoretical concepts from social scientists and even change or develop these concepts further in light of their historical expertise, they rarely engage in theoretical debates

(Sewell, 2005, pp. 4–5). This entails the danger, first, of leaving theoretical assumptions embedded in the concepts imported from other disciplines unexamined (Revel, 2008, pp. 402–403). Second, historians are likely to overlook structures and processes beyond particular historical cases (Lawson, 2012, p. 205; Lebow, 2001, p. 112). The absence of theoretical debate, third, means that historians often fail to feed their own theoretical insights back to social scientists (Sewell, 2005, p. 5).

Social scientific scholars, meanwhile, tend to treat the output of historians as a trove of facts and data, of empirical material that provides building blocks for the construction of theories or evidence substantiating them (Elman & Elman, 2001, p. 36; Smith, 1999, p. 1). Hence, they overlook that historical material is itself only the highly contested product of the narratives that individual historians have created around "traces of the past" usually in response to particular problems in the present and against similar narratives developed by other historians (Jenkins, 1991; Lawson, 2012, p. 205). In other words, by treating "ambiguous historical evidence unambiguously" (Smith, 1999, p. 11) social scientific theories based on such material resemble castles built on sand.

In short, while history and theory are always co-implicated, either time or structure tends to be hegemonic (Walker, 1989, p. 168), and this imbalance undermines the quality of their respective output. Scholars on both sides of the divide thus argue that "a deeper theoretical engagement ... could be mutually enlightening," that structure and historical conceptions of temporality need to be combined, that each discipline would better be able to achieve its own goals if it learned from the other (Levy, 2001, p. 82; Puchala, 2003; Sewell, 2005, pp. 1, 15; Steinmetz, 2008, p. 549).

In pursuit of this goal, two main approaches can be identified. The first consists of building on common interests, assumptions, and methods. This narrows the potential for cooperation down to scholars with qualitative, interpretive, or case study approaches (since the core assumptions of mainstream social scientists are incompatible with those of historians) and traditional historians interested in diplomatic or military affairs (Elman & Elman, 2001, p. 1; Sewell, 2005, p. 13). Establishing cooperation on such shared grounds, moreover, implies that the differences of method, sensibility, and aesthetics between History and social science are in fact of "secondary" importance while common assumptions, methods, or concerns provide "shared ground" (Lawson, 2012, p. 221). Such commonalities include attention to context – both textual and socio-political – and hence also a limitation of the truth claims of either discipline (Lawson, 2012, p. 216). Both historians and case studies researchers in IR use "process tracing" which is based on the assumption that events always have a synchronic and diachronic dimension and thus "*historical* events enable *social* formations to emerge, reproduce, transform and, potentially, break down" (Bennett & George, 2001, pp. 137, 145; Lawson, 2012, p. 217). Further, narrative emplotment is used as a method of establishing order, meaning, and explanation in history and the social sciences (Lawson, 2012, p. 219). Finally, the use of ideal types or typological theory – simplified maps of historical reality – is found in both disciplines and promises a sensitivity to historical particularity and complexity as well as a commitment to systematic inquiry (Bennett & George, 2001, pp. 138, 157; Lawson, 2012, p. 220). One strategy of addressing the gap between theory and history thus lies in building on such shared assumptions and practices.

And yet, scholars in both disciplines have long adopted such common strategies without producing a body of work that successfully transcends the division. Even projects that explicitly aim to bridge the gap by building on such common practices ultimately fail (Elman & Elman, 2001, p. 1). While historians, for example, use process tracing in order to explain particular cases, social scientific scholars tend to use it to develop and test generalizable theories (Bennett & George, 2001, p. 145). This suggests that the separation between history and theory is not "secondary" but fundamental. Hence, scholars argue that the separation itself is fruitful, indeed constitutive, of their disciplines. It is "essential for our work that historians remain experts on particular historical eras, events, or regions" because only then will there be "historical case studies to draw upon and historical experts to critique our work" (Bennett & George, 2001, pp. 165–166). In other words, the very possibility of social scientific scholarship depends upon the existence of *historical* expertise and vice versa. Identifying common ground is ultimately a tool for "tacking" more effectively between separate disciplines (Lawson, 2012, p. 206) rather than for merging them. The fate of these projects suggests, then, that shared assumptions, methods, and concerns do not constitute common ground but similar means to achieve separate ends and that these separate ends are embodied in the very constitution of academic disciplines.

This insight provides the starting point for the second strategy of dealing with the divide between History and IR – reconceptualizing the fields themselves. Given that historians themselves have begun to fundamentally question the meaning of "history" (Vaughan-Williams, 2005, p. 117), that "history cannot escape its own process" and will "therefore always be rewritten" (Isacoff, 2002, p. 608), that there is "no international 'history', only 'histories'" (Reus-Smit, 2008, p. 401), IR scholars set out to develop alternative conceptions of history. Following Derrida, Vaughan-Williams (2005, pp. 134, 136, 129) argues that instead of importing history, IR should import the problem of history, thereby making "the undecidable infinity of possible truths" its object of analysis. Inspired by Dewey, Isacoff (2002, pp. 608, 616) conceives history as an intersubjectively shared or settled understanding of the world that offers the opportunity for acting within it.

Essentially, these approaches accept the "problem of history" as constitutive and thus turn it into a theoretical issue, into a question of adjudication between competing truth claims. While the Derridean approach accepts their undecidability, for the Deweyan approach "democratic processes" or the "consensus of community" are decisive (Isacoff, 2002, pp. 605, 620), and constructivists follow Skinner in lowering the criteria for truth claims from infallibility to plausibility (Reus-Smit, 2008, p. 405). Yet, such "theories" themselves continue to rely on "historical" claims and narratives which, in the absence of independent criteria, gain a "solidity" that contradicts claims of more or less radical contingency (Isacoff, 2002, p. 619; Smith, 1999, p. 171). Moreover, toning down the truth claims of historical narratives fundamentally affects their role in the construction of theory – and thus requires a redefinition of theory itself (see also Lawson, 2012, p. 216). Hence, Smith calls for a more supple and less monolithic conception of theory in accordance with its ancient Greek meaning of contemplation and speculation outside of fixed forms of thought (Smith, 1999, pp. 183–184).

These attempts to reconceptualize history show, first, that history and theory are indeed constituted in relation to each other. Redefining one of these concepts necessarily impacts on the definition of the other. Second, attempts at redefining history and/or theory have themselves a long history. Debates about the nature and meaning of history are part and parcel of the discipline's development just as debates on what constitutes theory are an integral part of the history of other disciplines like IR. Yet, while such debates are productive of a variety of conceptions of history and/or theory and do inspire fruitful work, none of these alternatives has generated a body of work that satisfactorily addresses the "problem of history." The dynamic of disciplinary divisions produces "an illusion of progress from a reality of tradition": Marx, Freud, Weber, Durkheim, and others "erected a vision of the social world that has not changed in any foundational sense since their time" (Abbott, 2001, pp. 26, 27, 147, 152). This suggests that conceptions of history and theory are themselves historically grounded and require a particular historical context to flourish. It highlights that "once upon a time" the struggle between time and structure did not exist (Walker, 1989, pp. 168–169).

The analysis of these attempts to address the gap between theory and history, in sum, shows that neither strategy satisfactorily conceptualizes the space in which the separation occurs. This space, as the attempt to build on commonalities shows, needs to be located outside the individual disciplines. And its logic, as projects of reconceptualization show, must be relational. Finally, this analysis suggests that the space of separation is itself historical. What is missing from these strategies to overcome the history/theory divide, in short, is its theorization and its historicization.

THEORIZING THE HISTORY/THEORY DIVIDE

Projects to overcome disciplinary divides tend to reproduce fragmentation. In order to explain this contradictory dynamic, this section provides a theoretical account of the fragmentation of modern knowledge in general and the divide between history and (international) theory in particular. To this end, I will follow Foucault's archeological approach because it addresses the three requirements identified above: it identifies a common epistemic ground for different fields of knowledge, analyzes its logical dynamic, and locates it within a historical context.[2] The modern episteme, I will show, generates the fragmentary dynamics of modern knowledge in general and the history/theory divide in particular.

Foucault argues that all substantive knowledge rests on a deeper layer, the episteme, which describes a particular way of "ordering things," a "structure of thought," that is "common to all branches of knowledge" and that "men in a particular period cannot escape" (1972, p. 191; 1970, p. xxi). This assumption explicitly addresses the three dimensions found wanting in existing strategies to bridge the gap between history and theory: the common foundations of different disciplines, their relational logic, and historical specificity. Foucault describes three concrete epistemes: the first underpinned Renaissance knowledge in the 16th century (Foucault, 1970, pp. 30–34); the second, the classical episteme or "science of order," reigned from the 17th century and Locke to the Englightenment and the Idéologues (Foucault, 1970, pp. 71, 329, 346); and the third emerges at the end of the 18th and the beginning of the 19th century and constitutes the modern sciences (Foucault, 1970, pp. 220, 221, 346).[3]

In order to highlight the implications of the shift to the modern episteme, I will begin with a brief description of its predecessor: the classical episteme. Under the classical episteme, knowledge was produced by positing an abstract philosophical principle – often in the form of the state of nature,[4] which was then used to mechanically link different elements together into a composite whole, leading to a rational account of creation and its laws (Foucault, 1970, p. 346). In light of the fact that reality often deviated considerably from such rational orders, Enlightenment histories were designed to provide an historical explanation for these deviations and advocated a return to the proper laws (for a concrete example, see Jahn, 2013, pp. 41–53). This classical way of "ordering things," however, gave way to the modern episteme at the turn of the 19th century. Instead of deriving a composite whole from universal philosophical principles, the modern episteme endows individual phenomena with their own internal nature. Now, knowledge is concerned with "the interior time of an organic structure which grows in accordance with its own necessity and develops in accordance with autochthonous laws" (Foucault, 1970, pp. 226, 265). Yet, by endowing individual phenomena with their own internal nature, the modern episteme severs the relations between these elements – they are no longer part of the same space, subject to the same pressures, operating according to the same laws – and thus constitutes "new sciences and techniques with unprecedented objects" (Foucault, 1970, pp. 226, 253; Ross, 2008, p. 205). Where classical histories had been concerned with establishing the relations between different phenomena leading to universal laws governing humanity, the modern discipline of History explores the internal development of individual actors (Woolf, 2011, p. 362).

The extent of this rupture is debated among historians. While some authors argue that 19th century historians were united by their antipathy to and rejection of Enlightenment rationalism (White, 1973, pp. 38–39), others hold that modern conceptions of history "flowed directly from" and built on Enlightenment work (Reill, 1975, p. 220). Yet, Foucault's distinction between the epistemic and the substantive levels of knowledge was developed precisely to explain the simultaneity of rupture and continuity. Hence, 19th century historians were deeply invested in history as "the key to unlock the meaning of life" and as a "necessary prologue to meaningful reform" (Reill, 1975, p. 214; see also Iggers, 1986). But they also held that "the concept of progress and its accompanying optimism has *not yet* been provided with adequate cognitive justification" (White, 1973, p. 47). Modern historians, in other words, pursued the same goals as their Enlightenment predecessors, but in radically different ways. And these embody and reflect the dynamics of the modern episteme.

Modern historians departed from the universal time governing individual phenomena in Enlightenment histories. Instead, they located time within individual phenomena. Thus, Herder, for example, held that every nation followed its own organic historical development (White, 1973, pp. 67, 75). Modern history thus moved away from grand theories and speculative world histories, from histories of and for humanity as a whole, and focused on agency and the (heroic) individual, whether in the form of state, society, or culture (Armitage, 2013, p. 17; Christian, 2010, pp. 12–13; Smail, 2011, pp. 21–22; White, 1973, p. 62; Woolf, 2011, pp. 352–354). This reorientation had profound implications for the treatment of historical evidence. For Enlightenment historians, only evidence in line with their philosophical principles was valid and they rejected much – especially local, particular, imaginative – evidence as representing unreason, ignorance, prejudice, and superstition. In contrast, such particular evidence was valuable for modern historians exploring the internal processes of particular entities and they believed that by directly looking at empirical evidence they could work out its inner meaning (White, 1973, pp. 51, 52, 64; Woolf, 2011, p. 394). This attitude toward the careful gathering and critical evaluation of empirical evidence, systematically developed by Leopold von Ranke, became one of the core characteristics of modern historiography. Modern histories thus build bigger pictures from the ground up instead of from philosophical principles down (Woolf, 2011, pp. 352, 353, 370, 371).

Moreover, history that conceives of individual actors – nations, states, cultures, individuals – as developing in accordance with their own internal nature does not view any present either as "demented coinage of a nobler age" or as "incomplete anticipation of an age yet to come" (White, 1973, p. 78). While Enlightenment history sat in judgment over people, modern history is characterized by "empathy" and plays a socializing role (White, 1973, p. 38; Woolf, 2011, p. 394). Hence, the 19th century historical narratives of the nation were used in schools and in the training of civil servants – playing an important role for national integration (Christian, 2010, p. 14; Woolf, 2011, p. 346; Wright, 2008, p. 123).

Despite substantive continuities, therefore, the shift from the classical to the modern episteme gave rise to a new empirical, particular, organicist, empathetic instead of speculative, universalist, rationalist, mechanistic, and didactic conception of history. More importantly, however, the epistemic logic underpinning this conception of history accounts for the fragmentation of modern knowledge in general and the theory/history divide in particular. By establishing the internal organic time of singularities, the modern episteme fractured the conception of universal time (White, 1973, pp. 39, 78, 79) and with it the essential unity of history and knowledge. This does not imply that tensions between history and theory were not already present in Enlightenment thought. As mentioned above, Enlightenment authors struggled with the disjuncture between their universal "theories" and historical particularity. The argument is, rather, that the modern episteme responded to this tension by providing the foundations for a radically different conception of theory and history – for a conception of knowledge that builds bridges between fundamentally different phenomena rather than positing universal axioms that deny these differences (Abbott, 2001, p. 5).

First, it led to the substantive fragmentation of the modern discipline of History. By endowing individual phenomena with their own internal time, universal history dissolved into a myriad histories with every individual phenomenon requiring its own historical investigation: diplomatic history, political history, institutional history, ecclesiastical history, intellectual history, military history, economic history, legal history, administrative history, art history, colonial history, social history, agricultural history, and so on (Revel, 2008, p. 402; Smith, 1999, p. 185; White, 1973, p. 39). This process of fragmentation, moreover, develops dynamically. Narrating the history of a particular nation as the result of its internal development, for example, ignores the role of its external relations that then calls for a new field of study, such as diplomatic history. The modern episteme is thus the source of the problem of "tunnel history," of a continuous tunnel linking the present to the past in a particular field but "sealed off from contact with or contamination by anything that was going on in any of the other tunnels" (Hexter cited in Smith, 1999, p. 185; Löwith, 1949, p. 19).[5]

Second, the dissolution of universal time leads to theoretical and methodological fragmentation. When the overarching religious or cosmological context disappears, individual historical facts suddenly become meaningless and thus require the creation of meaning (Löwith, 1949, p. 10). Hence, the middle of the 19th century was characterized by sustained attempts on the part of historians like Michelet, Ranke, Tocqueville, and Burckhardt to systematically develop and apply historical theory. These attempts, however, culminated in a number of "equally comprehensible and plausible, yet apparently mutually exclusive, conceptions of the same sets of events" and thus led to the crisis of historicism at the end of the 19th and the beginning of the 20th century (White, 1973, pp. 41, 432; Wright, 2008) – that is, to the recognition that the theoretical ground for choosing an interpretative strategy was lacking. The discipline of History thus developed theoretical and methodological divisions between romantic, idealist, positivist history, history as science and history as literary masterpiece (White, 1973, p. 39; Woolf, 2011, pp. 377, 378). This theoretical fragmentation continues to haunt the discipline of History and underpins the frequently recurring debates among historians (Vaughan-Williams, 2005, pp. 133, 134; see also Smail, 2011, p. 35).

Third, this dissolution of Theory into theories and the integration of the latter into particular historical narratives constitutes the modern separation of history and theory and its institutionalization in the fragmentation of the modern sciences. Having abandoned the concept of universal time, historians were unable to fulfill their desire to pull the disparate histories together. They provided historical material, individual "historical facts," that could only be drawn together and made sense of by the application of theory – that is, by abstracting from their concrete and particular individual nature and linking them, across time and space, to similar entities. It was thus no accident that the grand theories of the time tended to be produced by nonhistorians like Hegel, Comte, Marx (Woolf, 2011, pp. 354, 379). History, in other words, developed into a master discipline that provided historical material, "historical facts," to other disciplines and fields of knowledge from literary fiction, the collection and display of nature, to comparative philology, sociology, economics, anthropology, IR and, in turn, borrowed theoretical concepts from them (Revel, 2008, pp. 397, 398, 403; Woolf, 2011, p. 378). These other disciplines, meanwhile, filled the gap that History had left behind: they set out to link the disparate "historical facts." In short, they supplied theory.

The development, and fragmentation, of the modern sciences at large follows precisely this logic. The modern, or internal, conceptualization of economy, for example, excluded its political dimension which led to the development of a discipline of Political Science whose internal definition, in turn, led to the emergence of International Relations addressing external political relations (Bannister, 2008; Farr, 2008; Long & Schmidt, 2005; Morgan, 2008; Schabas, 2008). And each of these sciences, disciplines, and fields of study is itself – just like the discipline of History – subject to dynamic fragmentation and hence internally divided in terms of issue areas, methods, and theoretical approaches (Jahn, 2016). The most fundamental of these divides within the modern sciences at large – that between the natural and social sciences – was in fact triggered by historians in the 19th century who argued that nature and history were driven by entirely different internal logics and their analysis hence required fundamentally different tools (Wright, 2008, pp. 117, 119). And it is this division between history and the natural sciences that attempts to revive universal history today aim to overcome (Christian, 2010, p. 24).

The modern episteme thus provides the common ground for the modern sciences in general and for History and International Relations in particular. Key to understanding the failure of attempts to overcome this history/theory division, however, is the fact that the modern episteme constitutes them *in relation to each other*. The modern understanding of theory as explaining the dynamics of interaction between different phenomena – states, markets, social groups, cultures, genders, individuals – presupposes the prior establishment of these entities as particular units with their own internal nature and history. The very possibility of IR and its pursuit of nomothetic theories, in other words, are dependent on the ideographic conception of history which produces the gaps that nomothetic theories must fill (Woolf, 2011, p. 387). This is why even scholars interested in closer cooperation between History and IR ultimately come to the conclusion that the separation between these disciplines is "essential" (Bennett & George, 2001, pp. 165–166). Neither the modern conception of history nor that of (international) theory could exist without their separation.

More generally, it is the recognition that modern knowledge is always only "partial" knowledge (Foucault, 1970, p. 373) that leads to the almost ubiquitous pursuit of interdisciplinarity. Yet, because modern knowledge cannot help but establish the internal coherence of such new fields, interdisciplinarity ironically contributes to the dynamic reproduction of fragmentation (Abbott, 2001, p. 147; Foucault, 1970, pp. 357, 358; Ross, 2008, pp. 227, 235). It manages to overcome existing boundaries only by erecting new ones around the internal coherence of newly integrated fields. This theorization of the history/theory divide thus explains not only the failure of bridge-building attempts, but it also explains why such projects themselves become a source of fragmentation.

HISTORICIZING THE HISTORY/THEORY DIVIDE

The failure of alternative conceptions of these fields to gain historical traction, meanwhile, requires a historicization of this divide. The modern episteme and hence modern social and political thought, I will suggest, arises in response to a crisis of imperial rather than international politics. Epistemic foundations of knowledge are therefore historically constituted and cannot be changed at will. The imperial nature of their historical origins nevertheless highlights the "imperialist" function of the modern notion of international relations and lays it open to critique.

Foucault himself was not interested in exploring the link between the historical context and the emergence of the modern episteme but focused instead on the analysis of the type of knowledge to which it gave rise. Nevertheless, he held that particular historical events might provide "a determined set of circumstances" or "precise questions" that shape the development of knowledge (1970, p. 345). He also located the emergence of the modern episteme at the end of the 18th and the beginning of the 19th century and went so far as to provide exact dates for the outer limits of this process: 1775–1825 (1970, pp. 221, 233, 234).[6] In line with other scholars, he thus placed the emergence of the modern episteme squarely in "the age of revolution" (Armitage, 2013, p. 37; Hobsbawm, 1962, pp. 336–358; Löwith, 1949, pp. 193–194; Wright, 2008, p. 113).

The age of revolution was conventionally associated with the American, French, Industrial, and (much more rarely) Haitian Revolutions. These revolutions were interpreted as the result of domestic developments in (mostly) European or Western societies that gave birth to the modern nation state and modern conceptions of politics that subsequently spread across the globe (Hobsbawm, 1962; Palmer, 1959). This narrative is now highly contested and debates range from the "chronological definition of the Age of Revolutions" through its causes and consequences, to its meaning and scope (Armitage & Subrahmanyam, 2010, p. xviii). The conventional conception is accused of being "strikingly Eurotropic, if not quite Eurocentric" (Armitage & Subrahmanyam, 2010, p. xxx; Hunt, 2010) and revisions highlight global rather than domestic causes, the continuity of empire rather than the establishment of nation states (Mulich, 2016a), and the diversity of influences and comparative developments in the non-European world (Armitage & Subrahmanyam, 2010, pp. xix, xxxi–xxxii). Though following this revisionist literature, I will nevertheless focus on European actors since this is the geographical context in which the modern sciences were institutionalized.

At first glance it appears as if international politics played a crucial role for the development of modern social and political thought. There is a widespread agreement now that the 18th century saw the first "world wars" and was more generally characterized by a "world crisis" or "world conflict" (Armitage & Subrahmanyam, 2010, pp. xiv, xxiii; Bayly, 1989, pp. 95, 164; Bayly 2010, p. 216). These "world" crises and wars, I want to suggest, however, cannot be equated with "international" politics. The polities that populated Europe during the 18th century (and many other parts of the world as well) were empires and the nature of imperial politics defies the modern distinction between domestic and international politics. Hence, scholars regularly apply terms like "global," "cosmopolitan," "transboundary" (Armitage, 2013, pp. 33–45), or "transnational" (Bayly, 2010, p. 216) to the politics of that time.

Empires can be defined as large and expansionist political units that incorporate, "usually coercively," a variety of different populations and govern these groups differently (Burbank & Cooper, 2010, p. 8; Go, 2011, pp. 6–7). Consequently, empires are "politically fragmented, legally differentiated, and encased in irregular, porous, and sometimes undefined borders" with "areas of partial or shared sovereignty within larger spheres of influence or rule" (Benton, 2010, p. 2). Modern nation states, in contrast, are based "on the idea of a single people in a single territory constituting itself as a unique political community" (Burbank & Cooper, 2010, p. 8). Politics in an imperial age is thus characterized by internal diversity, fuzzy borders, and fluid and expansive policies, while politics in the age of nation states is characterized by internal homogeneity (ideally, if not in practice), external diversity, and a clear inside/outside distinction (Walker, 1993). The latter gives rise to two different types of politics – domestic and international – neither of which existed during the 18th century.

From the 16th to the 18th century, European powers extended their rule dramatically across space to America, Africa, and Asia, as well as over territories and populations within Europe. During the 18th century, hence, all the major actors in Europe were empires. These empires included enclave trading colonies, plantation colonies, settlement colonies in addition to older conquests within Europe. The British Empire, for example, entailed Scotland, Ireland, Wales, settler colonies in North America, plantation colonies in the Caribbean, trading posts in India. These entities were home to a wide variety of people and peoples: indigenous peoples, slaves, English-speaking creoles, trading corporations, land speculators, peasant farmers, virtually self-governing settlers, and local elites (Bayly, 1989, p. 76). Each of these groups, moreover, was subjected to a different type of rule. While the Scottish elite was represented in parliament, the Irish was not (Bayly, 1989, p. 88); while the English were taxed highly and subject to close control by the government, the settlers in the American colonies paid very few taxes and enjoyed considerable political autonomy (McFarlane, 1994, p. 254); while slaves in the sugar islands had no rights, their white masters made their voices heard in Parliament (Bayly, 1989, p. 80); and while the North American colonies were ruled by governors, the East India Company relied on indigenous rulers (Burbank & Cooper, 2010, pp. 242–243). Indeed, delegated legal authority carried by "ship captains, leaders of reconnaissance voyages, trading companies, municipalities, colonial governors or viceroys, and garrison commanders" and the resulting "layered sovereignties" were a defining feature of empire (Benton, 2010, p. 31).

This diverse internal make-up of empires made anything resembling domestic politics impossible. While British common law was restricted to England, the legal authority of the King and English subjecthood was projected to other areas of the empire. Similarly, the Spaniards limited ecclesiastical authority and developed new institutions for (American) Indian subjects. Generally, "anomalous legal zones were so common that they came to be regarded as integral and expected elements of empire" (Benton, 2010, pp. 29–30). Conversely, the principle of "occupation" that is now regarded as a major feature of international law was not employed in the context of equal relations between sovereign states but between dominant and dependent parts of the globe (Fitzmaurice, 2014, p. 16).

The diverse internal make-up of empires also implied fuzzy borders. When, after the Seven Years War, Britain took over the French colonies in North America, for example, it guaranteed the laws, customs, legal systems, and religious life of the Quebecois. This fed the suspicions of the original British settlers that the Western lands were to be settled with Catholics and ruled despotically (McFarlane, 1994, pp. 253, 259). Moreover, having lost their French allies, indigenous tribes were suddenly confronted with the expansionist interests of British settlers. In order to reduce friction, Britain established the Proclamation Line that was supposed to keep these groups apart. Maintaining such a boundary, however, proved impossible. The line was "difficult to locate and impossible to police" (Benton, 2010, p. 14); both parties lived on both sides of the line and it fed the resentment of the settlers against the government (McFarlane, 1994, pp. 253–254). In other cases, relatively clearly defined boundaries did not prevent local actors from cooperating with each other. In the Leeward Islands white planters from islands belonging to different empires established security cooperation across borders in the face of slave revolts (Benton, 2010, p. 37; Mulich, 2016b). And in yet other cases control in border regions constantly shifted from one power to the other (Benton, 2010, p. 37). Such fluid boundaries made it difficult to determine what was inside and what outside.

Moreover, these examples show that the expansionist policies of empires were driven by a variety of actors like trading companies, planters, settlers, and governments (Benton, 2010, p. 3; Burbank & Cooper, 2010, p. 170), by private agents seeking "wealth, virtue or religious redemption" (Darwin, 2009, p. 3) and not by a clearly defined foreign policy of the metropole. The different interests within these empires created powerful pressures for expansion and hence for geopolitical competition within and outside Europe

(Bayly, 1989, p. 95). Already at the beginning of the 18th century, Britain participated in the War of the Spanish Succession (1702–1713) partly because a rising influence of France in the Americas would have threatened the strategic security of its North American colonies (McFarlane, 1994, p. 220). With the boundaries between British and French colonies in North America unsettled, the need to protect British settlers from impending French expansion also led to the participation of Britain in the Seven Years War (1756–1763). White planters on the sugar islands were dependent on imperial protection in the face of potential slave revolts, Spanish and French competition, and for the supply of basic necessities that were not produced in plantation economies (Bayly, 1989, pp. 91–92; McFarlane, 1994, p. 261). Irish dairy and pastoral products were excluded from the English market in order to protect English farmers and hence particularly dependent on export to the colonies (Bayly, 1989, p. 87). Similarly, poor Scots emigrated in large numbers to the overseas colonies, joined the East India Company, and the military that fought the Seven Years War and the War of American Independence (Bayly, 1989, p. 86). Conversely, the collapse of the South Sea Company produced a serious political crisis in London and thus ensured that the government subsequently guaranteed, however grudgingly, British interests abroad (Bayly, 1989, p. 80).

The fact that these empires were made up of a ragtag of different populations, forms of rule, and fuzzy borders thus led not only to expansionist pressures, but it also turned interimperial rivalries into "world wars" fought out in all corners of the globe. Already the War of the Spanish Succession at the beginning of the 18th century was fought not just in Europe but also in North and South America. Theaters of the Seven Years War – by some accounts "rightly seen as the first truly transnational war in history" (Bayly, 2010, p. 216) – could be found in Europe, North America, Central America, West Africa, India, and the Philippines (Burbank & Cooper, 2010, p. 220). Even the War of American Independence was not just fought between the settlers and the British government but included Spain and France. And yet, these wars were not "international" in the sense of pitching clearly defined domestic or national interests represented by imperial governments against each other. They were driven, instead, by a conglomerate of reasons ranging from dynastic competition through private economic interests to local conflicts and intraimperial tensions.

The cost of these "world wars," however, played a crucial role in bringing about the upheavals of the age of revolutions. Not only, as Kant noted, did imperial policies furnish soldiers for wars in Europe but also their financing through debt seriously harmed the population (1957, pp. 6, 23).

Generally, imperial governments tried to cover the cost of these wars by increasing taxation – and this led to widespread resistance (Bayly, 2004, p. 86; Darwin, 2009, p. 18; Fitzmaurice, 2014, p. 5). France's attempt to raise additional revenue ultimately led to the Franco-Haitian Revolution (Burbank & Cooper, 2010, p. 220; Lawson, 2015, pp. 308–309; McFarlane, 1994, p. 302; Skocpol & Kestnbaum, 1990, p. 17). Britain's repeated attempts to raise taxes in its North American colonies and in India resulted eventually in North American independence (Burbank & Cooper, 2010, p. 220). Spain tightened control over its colonies and thus upset intermediaries and triggered resistance (Burbank & Cooper, 2010, p. 247). While the outcome of these tensions and struggles differed from case to case (Blaufarb, 2007, p. 761; Burbank & Cooper, 2010, pp. 225, 227, 247; McFarlane, 1994, pp. 258, 274), they were consistently triggered by the increase of taxes and central control in order to cover the cost of war.

The crisis that culminated in the age of revolutions at the end of the 18th century thus had its roots in the nature and weaknesses of imperial politics rather than in international or domestic politics. "National" identity or "democratic" aspirations were not the source of the crisis but rather its product. There was no clearly articulated American nationalism in the British colonies before 1765 and it was only in the context of resistance against the British that poorer men began to join the committees and transformed American political life (McFarlane, 1994, pp. 258, 272, 274). Similarly, in France the Jacobin clubs initially mobilized the propertied and educated elites and only later, in the context of war, began to serve as recruitment agencies for national administrative and military efforts and hence wider participation (Skocpol & Kestnbaum, 1990, pp. 19–20). And the slaves of St Domingue, too, were initially not fighting for "national" independence but rather for freedom within the empire (Burbank & Cooper, 2010, p. 227).

The outcome of these political struggles was therefore not the constitution of nation states. Instead, it was an uneasy and volatile mixture between new political ideas revolving around freedom and old imperial politics. On the one hand, the age of revolution gave rise to new forms of thinking about politics, new forms of "claim-making," new conceptions of the role of the state and the nature of international order, and new ideas about popular rights (Bayly, 1989, p. 100; Bayly, 2010, pp. 212–213) and led to the fragmentation of empires, particularly in the Americas (Armitage, 2013, pp. 215–216). On the other hand, they generally resulted in a continuation of imperial politics albeit in different constellations. Spain managed to strengthen its control over the American colonies between 1783 and 1796 (McFarlane, 1994, p. 302). The result of the French Revolution was the crowning of Napoleon as emperor and his pursuit of empire building both within and, less successfully, outside Europe. Citizenship rights, moreover, were ultimately neither extended equally to the population of St Domingue nor to the various populations conquered in Europe (McFarlane, 1994, pp. 272, 274). American independence led to an "empire of liberty" that included slavery and rightless indigenous populations (McFarlane, 1994, p. 281). Upon independence from Portugal, Brazil set itself up as an empire in its own right continuing differential political rule (Burbank & Cooper, 2010, pp. 220–221). Threatened by the military and ideological challenge of the French Revolution and fearful of social upheaval, Britain entered a new phase of imperial expansion (McFarlane, 1994, p. 306). The crisis of empire and fear of domestic revolt led creole elites to line up behind the government (Bayly, 1989, p. 99). Despite the loss of the North American colonies, Britain gained new territories in the Caribbean, strengthened its hold over Canada and hardened its control of India (McFarlane, 1994, p. 285). Indeed, the principle of layered sovereignty, which is so characteristic of empire was confirmed in the Berlin Conference as late as the end of the 19th century (Fitzmaurice, 2014, p. 8, 27). Nineteenth century politics, in sum, was characterized by the contradictory political principles of freedom and imperialism (Benton, 2010, p. 4; Mulich, 2016a) and the idea of an international order based on nation states was only codified in 1948 in the UN Charter, and largely realized in the 1970s after decolonization (Armitage, 2013, p. 21; Burbank & Cooper, 2010, p. 183).

It was to this tension between freedom and empire and its fragmentary potential that the modern episteme provided a "solution." As the second part of the 18th century unfolded, schism and severance, conflict and suffering increased and widened the gap between the universalist structure of thought and the lived experience of people (White, 1973, p. 62). The modern episteme naturalized this fragmentation by providing different people and peoples with their own internal nature and individual – national – histories. "Herder's acceptance of every totality as inherently possessing its own rule of articulation could be extended to a contemporary society, as well as to past social orders, in a spirit acceptable to both the Conservative and Liberal ranges of the spectrum of political ideology" (White, 1973, p. 78; see also Bayly, 2010, p. 212). Consequently, tensions between these groups did not appear any longer as the result of a dysfunctional political order but as rooted in their diverse natures and developmental differentials. The national histories of the 19th century thus played a crucial role in ameliorating the social and political tensions of the revolutionary era, and they were indeed used, in education systems and the training of civil servants (Christian, 2010, p. 14; Woolf, 2011, p. 346; Wright, 2008, p. 123), as guiding principles for the establishment of national unity in the crisis-ridden and fragmented societies emerging from the age of revolution.

This invention of the modern concept of the nation as a political community with its own internal nature and independent history, moreover, simultaneously implied the existence of an international sphere in which these independent nations interacted with each other. The concept of sovereignty developed by 19th century lawyers encapsulated and codified precisely this freedom and independence of individual nations from others, while providing the basis for the modern conception of international relations as the interaction of free and formally equal "like units." Hence, it was no accident that the term "international" was first used by Bentham in the 1780s with reference to the legal relations between independent communities (Armitage, 2013, pp. 42, 70).

These concepts completely obscured, however, that historically these sovereign nation-states-in-the-making had not developed independently from each other but were constituted by and through the messy and hierarchical relations within and between empires of which most of them were still a part. And it was precisely by hiding these constitutive relations between individual communities that the modern episteme facilitated the continuation of empire. It allowed 19th century international lawyers, political theorists, and practitioners to present the right to freedom – sovereignty – as a natural property of the internal characteristics of a nation. By the same token, however, the denial of sovereignty to other communities was not depicted as the result of power politics but rather as the natural consequence of (lacking) internal – cultural, religious, racial, or political – achievements. As John Stuart Mill famously argued, barbarians had no rights as a nation (Mill, 1984, p. 119). Nineteenth century international law is, in fact, characterized by the (ultimately unsuccessful) attempt to elaborate objective criteria for the recognition or denial of sovereignty rights based on the internal characteristics of particular communities (Anghie, 2007). The modern episteme thus allowed political actors to endorse the universal principle of freedom even while they engaged in imperialist power politics.

Similarly, the 19th century imperialism of free trade, combining freedom and oppression, was made possible by this internalist conception of politics and economics and their separation. Imperialism of free trade entails the use of economic means to establish, maintain, and expand political inequality and informal empire within the international system (Gallagher & Robinson, 1953). Yet, such practices were not considered "imperialism" because they simply followed the generally valid internal logic of economics – free trade; just as the resultant hierarchies were not "imperialism" because they did not entail formal political rule of a dominant over a dependent community. In contrast to the 18th century empires in which politics and economics were intimately linked and the metropole was forced to deal with the political consequences of its economic policies (such as revolutions as a result of increasing taxes), the empire of free trade could distance itself from the political fall-out of its economic policies (such as the destruction of indigenous industries) and leave this responsibility to formally independent indigenous governments. It thus facilitated the continuation of imperialism not just ideologically but materially.

Finally, as Vitalis (2015) has recently shown, even the establishment of the discipline of International Relations in the United States was driven to a considerable extent by the desire to defend, maintain, and expand the dominance of the white over other races (see also Bell, 2014). Yet, these roots of the discipline have remained hidden for almost a century behind the modern conception of international relations as relations between sovereign states, and hence divorced from anxieties about race that crossed the domestic/international divide and concerned the "natural" properties of different groups rather than the "relations" between them.

The modern episteme, in sum, structures thought by providing individual phenomena with an independent nature and thus separating them from others. This structure underpins the modern political concepts – nation, international, sovereignty, politics, economics, etc. – that came to play a crucial role in facilitating the continuation of imperialism during the 19th century. It provides three crucial political functions: it naturalizes and thus depoliticizes fragmentation, including social and political tensions; it provides the guiding principles for internal integration, including national integration; and it hides the constitutive role of relations between different entities and thus accommodates contradictory principles, including those of the domestic and international, economics and politics, power and freedom, sovereignty and imperialism.

CONCLUSION

This special issue explores the possibilities of bridging the gap between theory, history and the international with a view to producing more integrated and hence also more useful knowledge. Since previous attempts to address the fragmentation of modern knowledge have remained unsuccessful, this article has taken a step back from these bridging projects and provided a theorization and historicization of the fragmentation of modern knowledge in general and the history/theory divide in particular.

It shows that this fragmentation has its roots in the modern episteme that endows individual phenomena with their own internal nature and thus severs their relations to each other. This structure underlying modern thought constitutes particular historical "facts" that then require "theories" to link them with each other and provide them with meaning. Overcoming these fragmentary dynamics would thus require new epistemic foundations of knowledge. Yet, epistemic change, I have argued, is triggered by specific historical circumstances – in this case a "crisis of empire" (McFarlane, 1994, p. 252) in the 18th century. New conceptions of history or theory thus fail to gain traction, I suggest, because they lack the requisite historical foundations that could sustain them. Yet, tracing the origins of modern social and political thought does not just identify the historical nature of epistemic change. In addition, it challenges a widely shared assumption that also motivates this particular project: the idea that identifying the historical nature of particular institutions allows us to change them, that anything that is the result of human practices can be unmade – purposely destroyed, altered, neglected, forgotten, or radically reconstructed – by human practices (Sewell, 2005, p. 10; see also White, 1973, p. 434).

The modern episteme that underpins the fragmentation of modern knowledge certainly is the result of human practices – specifically, I have argued, of the crisis of empire in the 18th century. Yet, while recovering this history shows that things could have been different and thus allows us to discover our agency, it "does not provide us with a warrant to engage in fantasies of omnipotence" (Kratochwil, 2006, p. 8). The crisis was the result of the conjunctural and unintended consequences of a myriad of individual events; practices spread across the entire globe. It was a *general* crisis that gave rise to a *general* structure of knowledge beyond the reach of any particular purposeful human agency. Indeed, the very conception of politics that holds that human beings "can, in principle, master all things by calculation" (Weber, 1948, p. 139) is itself the product of the modern episteme, of the fragmentation of knowledge into a myriad "things."

More constructively, the search for the roots of modern social and political thought draws attention to the fact that its architecture "is inherently disposed towards empire or inherently disposed towards Western interests and values"; it unveils the "liberal myth … that the instruments of political thought are objective or neutral standards" (Fitzmaurice, 2014, pp. 11, 12). It shows that modern social and political thought provided a "solution" to the 18th century crisis of empire by accommodating both freedom and imperialism. And it draws attention to the fact that the very same function still operates today. Just as in the 19th century, the denial of sovereignty rights through sanctions and interventions is depicted as the natural result of the internal shortcomings of particular societies: their failure to protect human rights; their lack of good government; and free trade policies are imposed on weaker economies with reference to the nature of economics. Missing from these accounts are the power relations between the different parties. And it is these power relations embedded in and hidden by modern social and political thought that the search for its international origins brings to light and lays open to critique.

NOTES

1. I will distinguish the academic discipline of History with capital letters from history in the sense of the past. IR denotes the academic discipline studying international relations/politics.
2. Alternative approaches tend to cover one or two but not all three of these requirements. Comparative and philosophical approaches, as the previous section shows, fail to provide an account of the common foundations of modern disciplines and their relations to each other, respectively. Sociological and historical analyses, meanwhile, identify common foundations of modern knowledge in the historical context but fail to account for the relations between different disciplines. For a comparison between the sociology, history, and philosophy of knowledge on the one hand and the archeology of knowledge on the other, see Foucault (1972, pp. 192, 206).
3. The modern sciences here refer to the establishment of modern academic disciplines and not to the scientific revolution that is widely associated with substantive developments particularly in the "natural sciences" starting in the 16th century with Copernicus.
4. For these conceptions of the state of nature, the "discovery" of America and its indigenous population played an important role. But "man" was under the classical episteme still an integral part of a cosmology. Only under the modern episteme did "man" become an individual governed by its own internal nature.
5. The equivalent in theory are "theoretical silos" (Buzan and Lawson, 2016).
6. See Michon (2002) for a general discussion of time in Foucault's work.

ACKNOWLEDGMENTS

I would like to thank Tarak Barkawi and George Lawson for the invitation to contribute to this project and for a wonderfully constructive and interesting workshop. Aleksandra Thurman, David Blaney, Helen Kinsella,

Jan Tattenberg, Daniel Levine, Oliver Kessler, Patricia Owens, Ricarda Hammer, and Samuel Chambers all provided excellent ideas and feedback. Particular thanks to Jeppe Mulich for the many useful references. I am also grateful to two anonymous reviewers for their engagement, enthusiasm, and very helpful suggestions for improvement.

REFERENCES

Abbott, A. (2001). *Chaos of disciplines*. Chicago, IL: The University of Chicago Press.

Adams, J., Elisabeth, S. C., & Orloff, A. S. (Eds.). (2005). *Remaking modernity. Politics, history, and sociology*. Durham, NC: Duke University Press.

Anghie, A. (2007). *Imperialism, sovereignty, and the making of international law*. Cambridge: Cambridge University Press.

Armitage, D. (2013). *Foundations of modern international thought*. Cambridge: Cambridge University Press.

Armitage, D., & Subrahmanyam, S. (2010). Introduction: The age of revolutions, c. 1760–1840 – Global causation, connection, and comparison. In D. Armitage & S. Subrahmanyam (Eds.), *The age of revolutions in global context* (pp. xii–xxxii). Basingstoke: Palgrave.

Bannister, R. C. (2008). Sociology. In T. M. Porter & D. Ross (Eds.), *The Cambridge history of science* (pp. 329–353). Cambridge: Cambridge University Press.

Barkawi, T., & Lawson, G. (2017). The international origins of social and political theory. In T. Barkawi & G. Lawson (Eds.), *International origins of social and political theory* (Vol. 32). Political Power and Social Theory. Bingley: Emerald Publishing Limited.

Bayly, C. A. (1989). *Imperial meridian. The British Empire and the World, 1780–1830*. London: Longman.

Bayly, C. A. (2004). *The birth of the modern world 1780–1914*. Oxford: Blackwell.

Bayly, C. A. (2010). The age of revolutions in global context: An afterword. In D. Armitage & S. Subrahmanyam (Eds.), *The age of revolutions in global context* (pp. 209–217). Basingstoke: Palgrave.

Bell, D. (2001). International relations: The dawn of a historiographical turn? *British Journal of Politics and International Relations*, *3*(1), 115–126.

Bell, D. (2014). Before the democratic peace: Racial Utopianism, Empire and the abolition of war. *European Journal of International Relations*, *20*(3), 647–670.

Bennett, A., & George, A. L. (2001). Case studies and process tracing in history and political science: Similar strokes for different foci. In C. Elman & M. F. Elman (Eds.), *Bridges and boundaries. Historians, political scientists, and the study of IR* (pp. 137–166). Cambridge, MA: The MIT Press.

Benton, L. (2010). *A search for sovereignty: Law and geography in European Empires, 1400–1900*. New York, NY: Cambridge University Press.

Blaufarb, R. (2007). The western question: The geopolitics of Latin American independence. *The American Historical Review*, *112*(3), 742–763.

Burbank, J., & Cooper, F. (2010). *Empires in world history. Power and the politics of difference*. Princeton, NJ: Princeton University Press.

Buzan, B., & Lawson, G. (2016). Theory, history, and the global transformation. *International Theory*, *18*(3), 502–522.
Christian, D. (2010). The return of universal history. *History and Theory*, *49*(4), 6–27.
Darwin, J. (2009). *The empire project. The rise and fall of the British World System, 1830–1970*. Cambridge: Cambridge University Press.
Elman, C., & Elman, M. F. (Eds.). (2001). *Bridges and boundaries. Historians, political scientists, and the study of IR*. Cambridge, MA: The MIT Press.
Farr, J. (2008). Political science. In T. M. Porter & D. Ross. *The Cambridge history of science* (pp. 306–328). Cambridge: Cambridge University Press.
Fitzmaurice, A. (2014). *Sovereignty, property, empire, 1500–2000*. Cambridge: Cambridge University Press.
Foucault, M. (1970). *The order of things. An archeology of the human sciences*. London: Tavistock.
Foucault, M. (1972). *The archeology of knowledge*. London: Tavistock.
Gallagher, J., & Robinson, R. (1953). The imperialism of free trade. *The Economic History Review*, *6*(1), 1–15.
Go, J. (2011). *Patterns of empire. The British and American Empires, 1688 to the present*. Cambridge: Cambridge University Press.
Hobden, S. (2002). Historical sociology: Back to the future of international relations? In S. Hobden & J. Hobson (Eds.), *Historical sociology of international relations* (pp. 42–59). Cambridge: Cambridge University Press.
Hobsbawm, E. (1962). *The age of revolution, 1789–1848*. London: Cardinal.
Hunt, L. (2010). The French revolution in global context. In. D. Armitage & S. Subrahmanyam (Eds.), *The age of revolutions in global context* (pp. 20–36). Basingstoke: Palgrave.
Iggers, G. (1986). *The German conception of history*. Middletown: Wesleyan University Press.
Isacoff, J. B. (2002). On the historical imagination of international relations: The case for a 'Deweyan Reconstruction'. *Millennium. Journal of International Studies*, *31*(3), 603–626.
Jahn, B. (2013). *Liberal internationalism. Theory, history, practice*. Basingstoke: Palgrave.
Jahn, B. (2016). Theorizing the political relevance of international relations theory. *International Studies Quarterly*. doi:10.1093/isq/sqw035
Jenkins, K. (1991). *Re-thinking history*. London: Routledge.
Kant, I. (1957). *Perpetual peace*. In L. W. Beck (Ed.). London: Macmillan.
Kratochwil, F. (2006). History, action and identity. Revisiting the 'Second' great debate and assessing its importance for social theory. *European Journal of International Relations*, *12*(1), 5–29.
Lawson, G. (2012). The eternal divide? History and international relations. *European Journal of International Relations*, *18*(2), 203–226.
Lawson, G. (2015). Revolutions and the international. *Theory and Society*, *44*(4), 299–319.
Lebow, R. N. (2001). Social science and history: Ranchers versus farmers? In C. Elman & M. F. Elman (Eds.), *Bridges and boundaries. Historians, political scientists, and the study of IR* (pp. 111–135). Cambridge, MA: The MIT Press.
Levy, J. S. (2001). Explaining events and developing theories: History, political science, and the analysis of international relations. In C. Elman & M. F. Elman (Eds.), *Bridges and boundaries. historians, political scientists, and the study of IR* (pp. 39–83). Cambridge, MA: The MIT Press.

Long, D., & Schmidt, B. C. (Eds.). (2005) *Imperialism and internationalism in the discipline of international relations*. Albany, NY: State University of New York Press.
Löwith, K. (1949). *Meaning in history*. Chicago, IL: The University of Chicago Press.
McFarlane, A. (1994). *The British in the Americas, 1480–1815*. London: Longman.
Michon, P. (2002). Strata, blocks, pieces, spirals, elastics and verticals. Six figures of time in Michel Foucault. *Time and Society*, *11*(2/3), 163–192.
Mill, J. S. (1984). A few words on non-intervention. In J. M. Robson (Eds.), *The collected works of John Stuart Mill* (Vol. 21, pp. 109–124). Toronto: University of Toronto Press.
Morgan, M. S. (2008). Economics. In T. M. Porter & D. Ross (Eds.), *The Cambridge history of science* (pp. 275–305). Cambridge: Cambridge University Press,.
Mulich, J. (2016a). Empire and violence: Continuity in the age of revolution. Political power and social theory. In T. Barkawi & G. Lawson (Eds.), *International origins of social and political theory* (Vol. 32). Political Power and Social Theory. Bingley: Emerald Publishing Limited.
Mulich, J. (2016b). *Imperial order: Colonial configurations as hierarchical networks.* Unpublished manuscript.
Palmer, R. R. (1959). *The age of the democratic revolution. A political history of Europe and America, 1760–1800*. Princeton, NJ: Princeton University Press.
Puchala, D. J. (2003). *Theory and history in international relations*. New York, NY: Routledge.
Reill, P. H. (1975). *The German enlightenment and the rise of historicism*. Berkley, CA: University of California Press.
Reus-Smit, C. (2008). Reading history through constructivist eyes. *Millennium Journal of International Studies*, *37*(2), 395–414.
Revel, J. (2008). History and the social sciences. In T. M. Porter & D. Ross (Eds.), *The Cambridge history of science* (pp. 391–404). Cambridge: Cambridge University Press.
Ross, D. (2008). Changing contours of the social science disciplines. In T. M. Porter & D. Ross (Eds.), *The Cambridge History of Science* (pp. 205–237). Cambridge: Cambridge University Press.
Schabas, M. (2008). British economic theory from Locke to Marshall. In T. M. Porter & D. Ross (Eds.), *The Cambridge History of Science* (pp. 171–182). Cambridge: Cambridge University Press.
Sewell, W. H. Jr. (2005). *Logics of history. Social theory and social transformation*. Chicago, IL: The University of Chicago Press.
Skocpol, T., & Kestnbaum, M. (1990). Mars unshackled: The French revolution in world historical perspective. In F. Feher (Eds.), *The French revolution and the birth of modernity* (pp. 13–29). Berkeley, CA: University of California Press,.
Smail, D. L. (2011). Genealogy, ontology, and the narrative arc of origins. *French Historical Studies*, *34*(1), 21–35.
Smith, T. W. (1999). *History and international relations*. London: Routledge.
Steinmetz, G. (2008). "Logics of History" as a framework for an integrated social science. *Social Science History*, *32*(4), 535–553.
Teschke, B. (2003). *The myth of 1648: Class, geopolitics, and the making of modern international relations*. London: Verso.
Vaughan-Williams, N. (2005). IR and the 'Problem of History'. *Millennium: Journal of International Studies*, *34*(1), 115–136.

Vitalis, R. (2015). *White world order, black power politics. The Birth of American international relations*. Ithaca, NY: Cornell University Press.

Walker, R. B. J. (1989). History and structure in the theory of international relations. *Millennium: Journal of International Studies*, *18*(2), 163–183.

Walker, R. B. J. (1993). *Inside/outside: International relations as political theory*. Cambridge: Cambridge University Press.

Weber, M. (1948). Science as a vocation. In H. H. Gerth & C. W. Mills (Eds.), *From Max Weber. Essays in sociology* (pp. 129–156). London: Routledge.

White, H. (1973). *Metahistory. The historical imagination in nineteenth century Europe*. Baltimore, MD: The Johns Hopkins University Press.

Woolf, D. (2011). *A global history of history*. Cambridge: Cambridge University Press.

Wright, J. K. (2008). History and historicism. In T. M. Porter & D. Ross (Eds.), *The Cambridge History of Science* (pp. 113–130). Cambridge: Cambridge University Press.

THE INTERNATIONAL ORIGINS OF HANNAH ARENDT'S HISTORICAL METHOD

Patricia Owens

ABSTRACT

This article examines the multiple ways in which Hannah Arendt's thought arose historically and in international context, but also how we might think about history and theory in new ways with Arendt. It is commonplace to situate Arendt's political and historical thought as a response to totalitarianism. However, far less attention has been paid to the significance of other specifically and irreducibly international experiences and events. Virtually, all of her singular contributions to political and international thought were influenced by her lived experiences of, and historical reflections on, statelessness and exile, imperialism, transnational totalitarianism, world wars, the nuclear revolution, the founding of Israel, war crimes trials, and the war in Vietnam. Yet, we currently lack a comprehensive reconstruction of the extent to which Arendt's thought was shaped by the fact of political multiplicity, that there are not one but many polities existing on earth and inhabiting the world. This neglect is surprising in light of the significant "international turn"

International Origins of Social and Political Theory
Political Power and Social Theory, Volume 32, 37–62

ISSN: 0198-8719/doi:10.1108/S0198-871920170000032003

in the history of thought and intellectual history, the growing interest in Arendt's thought within international theory and, above all, Arendt's own unwavering commitment to plurality not simply as a characteristic of individuals but as an essential and intrinsically valuable effect of distinct territorial entities. The article examines the historical and international context of Arendt's historical method, including her critique of process- and development-oriented histories that remain current in different social science fields, setting out and evaluating her alternative approach to historical writing.

Keywords: Arendt; historical method; international relations

INTRODUCTION

> [T]his system of relationships established by action, in which the past lives on in the form of a history that goes on speaking and being spoken about, can only exist within the world produced by man, nesting there in the stones until they too speak and in speaking bear witness, even if we must first dig them out of the earth.
>
> Arendt (2005 [1955], pp. 161–162)

Few twentieth-century political thinkers exemplify more than German-American Jewish political theorist Hannah Arendt the extent to which international encounters are productive of theorizing and how theory arises historically. Virtually all of Arendt's singular and enduring contributions to political and international thought were constituted in and through her lived experiences of, and historical reflections on, statelessness and exile, imperialism, transnational totalitarianism, world wars, the founding of Israel, war crimes trials, and the war in Vietnam. She insisted that political thought be grounded in historical knowledge. Otherwise, as she told students in 1955, "we don't know what we do and what we are talking about" (Arendt, 1955, p. 5). To be sure, Arendt most often described herself as a political theorist and she should not be read as a conventional historian of imperialism, totalitarianism, and revolution, though she wrote significant books on these subjects. Yet, Arendt approached even the most philosophical of questions historically. Some of her earliest scholarly writing engaged with philosophies of history; she consistently sought to establish the historical grounds for her political theory; and she actively embraced and sought to theorize the role of historical experience on political and historical thought. She argued that thought and historical writing is not only bound *to* time, but also the character *of* the times governs the possibility of thinking the relationship of the past to the present in a fully historical and political manner. These seemingly simple avowals have profound implications for the task of considering the relation between history and theory, especially historical-theoretical sensibility and method. Given the enormity of Arendt's contributions to twentieth-century political thought, it is thus surprising that only recently have political theorists and historians of thought begun to place her historical writings at the center of her work (Hoffmann, 2010; Honohan, 1990; Kang, 2013; Keedus, 2015; King and Stone, 2007; Novák, 2010; Yaqoob, 2014a).

It is commonplace to situate Hannah Arendt's political and historical thought as a response to totalitarianism (Benhabib, 2000; Canovan, 1992; Villa, 1999; Young-Bruehl, 2004 [1982]) and war (Owens, 2007). However, far less attention has been paid to the influence of other specifically and irreducibly *international* experiences and events on Arendt's life and work and, more specifically, her approach to historical epistemology. We currently lack a comprehensive reconstruction of the extent to which the context and content of Arendt's thought was shaped by the fact of political multiplicity, that there are not one but many polities existing on earth and inhabiting the world, to adapt Arendt's understanding of plurality (Arendt, 1958, p. 7). This neglect is surprising in light of the significant "international turn" in the history of thought and intellectual history (Sluga, 2015), the growing interest in Arendt's thought within international theory (Hayden, 2009; Lang and Williams, 2005; Owens, 2007), and, above all, Arendt's own unwavering commitment to political plurality not simply as a characteristic of individuals but as an essential and intrinsically valuable result of distinct territorial entities. As Arendt wrote in the 1961 preface to *Between Past and Future*, "thought itself arises out of incidents of living experience and must remain bound to them as the only guideposts by which to take its bearings" (Arendt, 1968a, p. 14). Given the considerable extent to which international encounters form the incidents of lived experience then serious thinking about Arendt's thought, and of course the international itself, must remain bound to them. Of course, "thought itself is historic" (Arendt, 1994b [1954], p. 431). But this history is not fully understood if we neglect its international conditions. Hence, we need a fuller examination of the international origins of Arendt's historical method.

The first part of this article places Arendt's earliest political activism and intellectual development in the context of Jewish statelessness in 1930s Europe. Arendt was involved in practical action and intellectual debates on the course of the Second World War, the British Mandate in Palestine, the political organization of Jewish people, and the postwar reconstruction of Europe and its empires. These political and intellectual commitments shaped the content and structure of Arendt's most historical work, her monumental study, *The Origins of Totalitarianism* (1966 [1951]). Arendt's decisive influence on the historiography of the period was her insistence that the roots of European fascism were not German, or even European. They were fundamentally imperial and international. Crucially, totalitarian domination represented a rupture in the continuity of historical time, and were thus incomprehensible to conventional historical and sociological approaches predicated upon this continuity. Accordingly, the second part analyzes the highly unconventional historical approach that Arendt adopted in *Origins*, first published in 1951. Later, in an effort to develop a political response to the absolute novelty of the death factories, and by now a citizen of Cold War America, Arendt reflected on the character of historical thought in the more immediate context of another new reality that encompassed the whole of humanity and could destroy all life on earth. Hence, the third part examines Arendt's still prescient critique of process- and development-oriented understandings of history in response to the invention of the atomic bomb. The final part examines Arendt's post-totalitarian alternatives to the grand, sweeping historical sociological generalizations about global "processes" and historical development still so current across several social science fields. This historical counterpart to Arendt's novel theory of politics centered on identifying the basic phenomenological conditions of historical experience since the possibility of politics itself is bound to individual and collective experiences of time; understanding the fragmentary and discontinuous character of the remembered past; seeking to grasp phenomena and events in their singularity and particularity; and identifying the new and unexpected, including through the exemplary lives of historical persons. Hannah Arendt points us toward a method for international history that is grounded in "lived incidents" as guideposts for thinking, while accepting the fragmentary character of understanding given its rootedness in the plurality not only of persons but also polities.

"THOUGHT ITSELF IS HISTORIC"

Hannah Arendt's position as a secular middle-class Jewess in interwar Germany – an *international* position "from the very beginning" as modern anti-Semitism "functioned as an International" (1994c [1945], p. 141) – profoundly shaped her earliest political activity and writing. In 1929, before she became active against Nazism, Arendt began researching a biography of the writer and influential salon hostess, Rahel Varnhagen (1771–1833), based on Varnhagen's papers collected at the Manuscript Division of the Prussian State Library. This was before the Gestapo arrested Arendt in 1933 and imprisoned her for also researching anti-Semitic propaganda. *Rahel Varnhagen*, first published almost three decades later, is not a straightforward historical biography, but an experimental attempt to "narrate the story of Rahel's life as she herself might have told it" (Arendt, 1974 [1957], p. xv). The narrative centers on Varnhagen's initial striving for acceptance in German gentile society through marriage, Christian conversion, and Enlightenment emancipation, but ultimately her eventual acceptance of her Jewish and pariah status. Except in its unconventionality and concern with the "Jewish Question," this "life of a Jewish woman" does not sit easily within the rest of Arendt's *oeuvre*. And yet, as others have suggested, to a great extent, the biography becomes semi-autobiography, as well as a prescient historical and political analysis of the seeds of the coming catastrophe faced by millions of European Jews (Young-Bruehl, 1982/2004).

Arendt was more politically active as a stateless and rightless Jew between 1933 and 1951 than at any other period of her life: arrested and imprisoned in Germany; escaping without papers to Geneva where she briefly worked as an administrator at the League of Nations; then to France where she worked to send children to Palestine; interred by the Vichy regime at the camp in Gurs; escaping before many of its inmates were sent to Auschwitz; and arriving in the United States (Young-Bruehl, 1982/2004, pp. 106–107). The central purpose of Arendt's writing in these decisive years was to historicize anti-Semitism and politicize Jews. Assimilation had failed, but so too would any Zionist embrace of pseudo-biological essences, the notion of Jewish identity as emanating from "an eternal organic body, the product of inevitable natural growth of inherent qualities" or any notion of an eternal anti-Semitism (2007a [1944], p. 367). To the extent that Jewish identity was to be political it had to be understood as worldly and historical. Yet, if attacked as Jews, Arendt insisted, they ought to embrace political and military resistance *as Jews*: "you cannot say,"Excuse me, I am not a Jew; I am a human being." That is silly," she wrote. To defend oneself as anything else would have been "nothing but a grotesque and dangerous evasion of reality" (Arendt, 1968b, p. 18). Arendt's intense support for the creation of a Jewish army, especially through 1942, went beyond chipping in to the military effort. She envisioned the organization and mobilization of units of armed Jewish men and women as a founding act of Jewish political organization. But, contra Clausewitz and the tradition of political realism, this participation in reciprocal violence was not to be understood as the quintessence of politics itself, though exemplary political action could occur in wartime (Arendt, 1970a; Owens, 2007).

It is abundantly clear that several of Hannah Arendt's major contributions to political theory were shaped by her active involvement in the struggle over the new order in Palestine. One of the earliest and still most influential "post-Zionists," she offered concrete proposals to undermine the establishment of a monoethnic/religious Jewish state to prevent Palestinians suffering a similar fate as European Jews. Exclusive national sovereignty in the State of Israel could only be a kind of Jewish pseudo-sovereignty (2007b [1948], p. 401). "A home that my neighbor does not recognize and respect is not a home ... but an illusion – until it becomes a battlefield" (Arendt, 2007c [1945], p. 235). Eventually, Arendt came to endorse a bi-national state since the vast majority of Arabs and Jews rejected multiethnic/religious federation. The influence of socialist Zionism on Arendt's writings on Israel/Palestine, and much of her mature political thought, is clear (Ashcroft, 2015). It has also been noted that "Arendt's strategies of historical representation shared profound affinities with the urgent and engaged historical thinking of her German-Jewish contemporaries," including Walter Benjamin (Curthoys, 2010, p. 107). Less well-known is how Arendt's signature contribution to international historiography in *The Origins of Totalitarianism* was shaped by her involvement in pan-European debates on the future of postwar world order among wartime resistance movements.

Hannah Arendt vehemently opposed "German" readings of totalitarianism, as the result of some deeply rooted authoritarianism within its history or character. First, she insisted that, to a great extent, Nazism arose "from the vacuum resulting from an almost simultaneous breakdown of *Europe's* social and political structures .... The truth was that the class structure of European society could no longer function; it simply could no longer work either in its feudal form in the East or in its bourgeois form in the West" (Arendt, 1994d [1945], p. 111, emphasis added). Second, the germ of fascism was *international*, not just European: its "roots are strong and they are called – Anti-Semitism, Racism, Imperialism" (Arendt, 1994d [1945], p. 150). To center totalitarianism within German, or even European history, was not simply historically dubious. It legitimized the return to national sovereign states after German fascism was overcome. To prevent the reemergence of a new fascist *international* it was not enough to limit German sovereignty. Those elements of totalitarianism "do not cease to exist," she wrote, "with the defeat of one or all totalitarian governments" (Arendt, 1994a [1954], p. 324). Citing what she claimed was the dominant view among the underground resisters – as distinct from the governments-in-exile – Arendt argued that European and eventually worldwide federation was the only real antidote to the "walking corpse" of the sovereign state (Arendt, 1994c [1945], p. 143). Hannah Arendt's *political* conviction regarding the necessity of federally organized commonwealths, rooted in international encounters and personal experiences, contributed directly to the central historical argument of her path-breaking transnational history of totalitarianism. As Selinger has recently made clear, Arendt (2016, p. 418) saw "the historiography of Nazism as profoundly connected with the future reconstruction of Europe."

The Origins of Totalitarianism (1966 [1951]) is "one of the constitutive books of postcolonial studies," prefiguring claims by leading scholars of race and empire about the colonial origins of European fascism (DuBois, 2015 [1947], p. 23; Grosse, 2006, p. 36). Central to this status is a series of historical distinctions Hannah Arendt drew between Jew-hatred and anti-Semitism; race thinking and rac*ism*; and settler colonialism and the "new imperialism" of the late nineteenth century. "In historical inquiries," she wrote, "it is not important to arrive at ready-made definitions, but constantly to make distinctions, and these distinctions must follow the language we speak and the subject matter we deal with" (Arendt, 1994h [1953], p. 385). Ordinary Jew-hatred became radicalized and ideological as the institutions and economies of European states collapsed. Race thinking, which had always accompanied European expansion, was transformed into rac*ism* when race was propagated as "the new key to history" (Arendt, 1966 [1951], p. 170). The governments established under settler colonialism and traditional empire building had no counterpart in the age of the "new imperialism." Instead, the amalgamation of bureaucracy and racism served as a replacement for government, rationalizing the massacre and administration (or both – "administrative massacres") of subject peoples. Arendt's formative role in postcolonial scholarship is grounded on her claim that this substitution of a racial for political order was normalized and transported back to Europe. "African colonial possessions," she wrote, "became the most fertile soil for the flowering of what later was to become the Nazi elite. Here, they had seen with their own eyes how peoples could be converted into races and how ... one might put one's own people into the position of the master race" (Arendt, 1966 [1951], p. 206). From "the wild murdering" of Carl Peters in German Southeast Africa, to the ideology of "expansion for expansion's sake," "the stage seemed to be set," she wrote, "for all possible horrors. Lying right under anybody's nose were many of the elements which gathered together could create a totalitarian government on the basis of racism" (Arendt, 1966 [1951], pp. 185, 221).

Hannah Arendt's version of the boomerang thesis, the unintended consequences of imperial blowback, has been central to all subsequent historical studies of the links between Imperial Germany's conduct in Africa and Nazi conduct on the Eastern front (Arendt, 1966 [1951], pp. xvii, 155, 206, 223; Hull, 2005; Zimmerer, 2004). However, in Arendt's own analysis, British, French and even German imperial practices played an *indirect* role in Europe's further descent into twentieth-century total war. In *Origins*, the most significant precursor to totalitarianism was not overseas imperialism, but the *continental* imperialisms of the pan-German and pan-Slav Leagues. These imperialist pan-movements were the real templates for totalitarian rule with their disdain for constitutional politics and existing institutions. Mobs replaced classes and the party system, organized around the basis of class interests, was overwhelmed. The *immediate* predecessor of totalitarianism was continental imperialism. And yet several of the ideological rationalizations and forms of thought that accompanied overseas imperialism – obedience to the laws of nature or history, the role of impersonal and world historical "processes" and necessities – were fundamental to totalitarianism.

The profound originality and relevance of Hannah Arendt's work in this context is not simply her decentered, international, and transnational history of what she took to be the central phenomenon of the twentieth century, nor is it that *Origins* was shaped by Arendt's international experiences and wartime political commitments, significant though they are. The political, historiographical, and philosophical stakes are even higher. For while the discussion thus far has centered on Arendt's formative role as the "godmother" of the boomerang thesis (Kühne, 2013, p. 341), more significant is her insistence on the *unprecedented* character of totalitarianism. Hannah Arendt is best read not simply as an historian of the imperial roots of totalitarianism, but also for how and why she violated and reworked conventional historical narrative of cause and effect, that is, as a theorist of history. For Arendt, totalitarianism marked a fundamental rupture in the presumed continuity of history with enormous implications for the experience of historical time and the practice of historical writing. The event of totalitarian domination, she wrote, "marks the division between the modern age – rising with the natural sciences in the seventeenth century, reaching its political climax in the revolutions of the eighteenth, and unfolding its general implications after the Industrial Revolution of the nineteenth – and the world of the twentieth century, which came into existence through the chain of catastrophes touched off by the First World War" (Arendt, 1968c, pp. 26–27). This is not any vulgar notion of one century being somehow more important than another. Rather, as we now discuss, what led up to and happened in the Nazi death factories radically transformed the continuity of historical time and with it the conditions of historical thought. "We can no longer afford to take that which was good in the past and simply call it our heritage, to discard the bad and simply think of it as a dead load which by itself time will bury in oblivion. The subterranean stream of Western history has finally come to the surface" (Arendt, 1966 [1951], p. ix).

"ANALYSIS IN TERMS OF HISTORY"

It is a cliché to observe that Hannah Arendt's writing does not correspond to any traditional school of thought or academic field. The distance between her work and conventional approaches to political science and historical method is well known (Luban, 1983; Vollrath, 1977). "One of the difficulties of the book," Arendt later wrote about *Origins*, "is that it does not belong to any school and hardly uses any of the officially recognized or officially controversial instruments" (Arendt, 1994e [1953], p. 402). She not only "saw herself at odds with the entire disciplinary matrix of her epoch" (Baehr, 2002, p. 804); she actively broke many of the rules of historical and political science. As Benhabib (2000, p. 63) has observed, *Origins* "is too systematically ambitious and overinterpreted to be a strictly historical account; it is too anecdotal, narrative, and ideographic to be considered social science, and although it has the vivacity and stylistic flair of a work of political journalism, it is too philosophical to be accessible to a broad public." But this is not just a question of an iconoclast shunning orthodoxy. Arendt believed that conventional historical narrative and social science could not adequately comprehend the industrial production of corpses. The Nazi "extermination camps ... must cause social scientists and historical scholars to reconsider their hitherto unquestioned fundamental preconceptions regarding the course of the world and human behavior" (Arendt, 1994f [1950], p. 232). In turning away from conventional method,

Arendt was illuminating and diagnosing the historical-philosophical significance of a phenomenon – the Nazi extermination camps – that made orthodox approaches seem obsolete. These "laboratories in the experiment of total domination" (Arendt, 1994f [1950], p. 240) overturned the then dominant social science views about the motives for human conduct and what it means to think about continuity in historical time.

The contention authorizing Hannah Arendt's sweeping conclusion was her claim that totalitarian domination was qualitatively different from all the tyrannies and dictatorships that had come before. In her words,

> It is far from unprecedented to wage an aggressive war; massacres of enemy population or even of what one assumes to be hostile people look like an everyday affair in the bloody record of history; extermination of natives in the process of colonization and the establishment of new settlements has happened in America, Australia, and Africa; slavery is one of the oldest institutions of mankind and forced-labor gangs, employed by the state for the performance of public works, were one of the mainstays of the Roman Empire. Even the claim to world rule, well known from the history of political dreams, is no monopoly of totalitarian governments. All these aspects of totalitarian rule, hideous and criminal as they are, have one thing in common which separates them from the phenomenon with which we are dealing: in distinction from the concentration camps, they have a definite purpose and they benefit the rulers .... The motives are clear and the means to achieve the goal are utilitarian in the accepted sense of the term. (Arendt, 1994f [1950], pp. 233–234)

It was the *anti-utilitarian* character of the Nazi extermination camps – the central institutions of totalitarianism – that fundamentally set them apart from the concentration and labor camps of imperial rule and "explode this whole framework of reference" (Arendt, 1994f [1950], p. 234). Even from the Nazis' own perspective, the vast majority of camp inmates were completely innocent and unthreatening to the regime. The SS men in charge "were completely normal," Arendt claimed: none of those overseeing a system of permanent torture were especially "sadistic or cruel" (Arendt, 1994f [1950], p. 239). Above all, the German state's war effort was never allowed to interfere with efficient camp administration. The Nazi "gas chambers did not benefit anybody" (Arendt, 1994f [1950], p. 236). Yet, they trumped military exigency *even* in the context of total war and in the face of absolute defeat. For Arendt, these facts demonstrated the incommensurability between the concentration camps of imperial rule and the Nazi death chambers. The latter did not "merely" exterminate and degrade particular humans for instrumental ends, though this did indeed occur; they sought to transform human beings as such into mere things (Arendt, 1966 [1951], p. 438). The differences between totalitarian domination and what had come before were so great as to destroy the standards and categories of existing social and historical thought.

To Arendt, conventional historical narrative relied on historical analogies and causal sequence, thereby portraying totalitarianism as the culmination of long-term developmental historical processes. Similarly, the social science of her day largely relied on simplistic ideal-types, utilitarian motives, and/or functionalism. The "modern historical and social sciences," she thus claimed, were beset by a "kind of confusion – where everything distinct disappears and everything that is new and shocking is (not explained but) explained away either through drawing some analogies or reducing it to a previously known chain of causes and influences" (Arendt, 1994e [1953], p. 407). For example, she criticized leading sociologists, such as Jules Monnerot, for reducing totalitarian ideology to a form of political or secular religion (Arendt, 1994h [1953]). Such forms of conventional historical and social science could not adequately comprehend the absolute novelty of totalitarianism. They could not fathom the unprecedented nature of the camps, specifically the attempt to make humans superfluous as human beings, the absolute terror of never-ending experiments in total domination. Arendt located the problem in the hegemony of process-thinking and developmental histories, both of which she argued defined the modern concept of history itself. Before analyzing Arendt's critique of these modes of thought "virtually unknown prior to the modern age" (Arendt, 1958, p. 116), first consider the alternative historical method she adopted in *Origins*. Why spend sixty percent of the book addressing the historical phenomena of racism, anti-Semitism, and imperialism if totalitarianism was not the product of, or continuous with, them? What purpose did that serve? If totalitarianism was not something that could be understood through the setting out of a chain of causes in which totalitarianism was the logical outcome, then how should its history be written?

Part of the difficulty of interpretation is that *The Origins of Totalitarianism*, a title chosen by its American publisher, is not a study of "origins" in this sense, of analyzing racism, anti-Semitism, and imperialism as causal factors in totalitarianism.[1] Anti-Semitism, Arendt explained, could only be said to have "prepared the ground"; it was not the first or earliest manifestation of totalitarian solutions to the Jewish Question somehow already present, for example, at the Dreyfus Affair (1994f [1950], p. 235; 1966 [1951], Chapter 4). This is not possible, she wrote, "because this essence … [of totalitarianism] did not exist before it had come into being" (1994e [1953], p. 405). Instead racism, anti-Semitism, and imperialism were examined as the main "*elements*" that "crystallized" in a particular historical moment to become the phenomenon of totalitarianism itself.

"I therefore talk only of 'elements'," Arendt belatedly explained, "which eventually crystallized into totalitarianism, some of which are traceable to the eighteenth century, some perhaps even further back .... Under no circumstances would I call any of them totalitarian" (Arendt, 1994e [1953], pp. 405–406). Only once racism, imperialism, and anti-Semitism crystallized was it possible, in *retrospect*, to see them as origins of something – totalitarianism – that "illuminates its own past" (Arendt, 1994a [1954], p. 319). Thus, Arendt analyzed these phenomena "in historical terms, tracing these elements back in history as far as I deemed proper and necessary. That is, I did not write a history of totalitarianism but an analysis in terms of history" (Arendt, 1994e [1953], p. 403). To illustrate, Book II of *Origins* – with chapters titled "The political emancipation of the bourgeoisie," "Race thinking before racism," "Race and bureaucracy," "Continental imperialism: The pan-movements," and "The decline of the nation-state and the end of the rights of man" – is clearly not a history of imperialism per se. Rather it examined the "element of expansion insofar as [it was] clearly visible and played a decisive role in the totalitarian phenomenon itself" (Arendt, 1994e [1953], p. 403).

In light of its phenomenally verifiable content, its historical essence, Hannah Arendt claimed totalitarianism was not an event that could be assimilated into the movement of historical processes, as suggested by conventional historical and social science (cf. Aron, 1969 [1965]). Her retrospective narrative involved analyzing those aspects of the complex history of imperialism, racism, and anti-Semitism that combined to become something unprecedented, suggesting their altogether different historical significance from what could have appeared at the time of their emergence. She sought to show how totalitarianism could not be deduced from or caused by its main "elements"; was in no sense the *logical* outcome of what came before; and was not the *inevitable* product of modernity, as if foreordained in the teleological progression of Western history (c.f. Adorno and Horkheimer (1979 [1944]). This is what Arendt meant when she called totalitarianism "an almost complete break in the continuous flow of Western history" (Arendt, 1966 [1951], p. 124). Thus for historical, philosophical, and political reasons, Arendt was deeply reluctant to conceive the central event of the twentieth century as an exemplary instance of some longer term developmental processes or the manifestation of underlying social structures, which is the default position for process-thinking and developmental histories. As historian Richard King (2007, p. 253) has pointed out, the use of the language of "crystallization" to encapsulate the historical coming together of the elements of totalitarianism "was shrewdly chosen, since the process of crystallization can hardly be perceived as taking place *over* time, as opposed to happening, in the shortest historical duration, *within* a moment of time." The language and underlying method that Hannah Arendt developed through the 1940s was her alternative to a chronological historical narrative or process- and development-oriented understandings of totalitarianism. In other words, Arendt's critique and the alternative she would develop in later writing was first and foremost grounded in her own historical and international experiences with and politically charged reflections on totalitarianism.

"THE KEY WORDS OF MODERN HISTORIOGRAPHY"

By the 1950s, and now a citizen of the United States, Hannah Arendt believed that the invention of the atomic bomb had joined totalitarianism as the two most "fundamental experiences of our age" (Arendt, 2005, p. 109; King, 2015). Now moving from the scene of total war in Europe to Cold War America, Arendt's reflections on historical method were still shaped by distinctly international, and now increasingly global, affairs. "The horror that swept over mankind when it learned about the first atomic bomb," she wrote, "was the horror of an energy that came from the universe and is supernatural in the truest sense of the word" (Arendt, 2005, p. 158). Any new political reality of "mankind" after the Holocaust was thus not the product of the "dreams of the humanists," the dangerous fantasy of a world state that was more likely to bring forth a murderous tyranny than world peace (Arendt, 1968h, p. 81). It was occasioned by two facts that emerged from the recent experience of global war, the revolution in communications and the existence of the atom bomb (Arendt, 1968h, p. 87). These technological developments, but especially the nuclear revolution, were at the root of any meaningful existence of "mankind" and, for Arendt, were the influential backdrop for what she saw as an urgent attempt to theorize history and politics anew for a post-totalitarian but now nuclear age.

Based on her readings in the history of science, including works by Copernicus and Galileo, Arendt claimed that the rise of modern science and its commitment to uncovering the laws of scientific and natural processes had a profound effect on philosophies of history (1968d, p. 57; Yaqoob, 2014b). The crucial correspondence between natural science and the "modern concept of history" that emerged with the early modern scientific revolution was their dual emphasis on *development* and *processes*. In Arendt's words,

> Historically, political theorists from the seventeenth century onward were confronted with a hitherto unheard-of process of growing wealth, growing property, growing acquisition. In the attempt to account for this steady growth, their attention was naturally drawn to the phenomenon of a progressing process itself .... From its beginning, this process ... was understood as a natural process ... in the image of the life process itself. (Arendt, 1958, p. 105; also Hyvönen, 2016)

Historical imaginaries dominated by processes not only appeared to be in accord with the laws of science, and the evolution of human life itself, but also compatible with new methods of administering life and prosecuting wars. Capitalist expansion seemed to mirror the natural processes of life in "ever-recurring cycles" (Arendt, 1958, p. 134; Owens, 2015, Chapter 3). With the testing of hydrogen bombs and the spread of thermonuclear weapons it was as though "automatic processes" leading to a nuclear holocaust would "proceed unchecked" (2005, p. 107). The "chain reaction of the atom bomb ..." Arendt wrote, "can easily become the symbol for a conspiracy between man and the elementary forces of nature, which ... may one day take their revenge and destroy all life on the surface of the earth" (1994 [1954], p. 419). On the face of it, capitalism, imperialism, totalitarianism, and nuclear competition all seemed to demonstrate the fundamentally *process*-character of human history. In the modern age, it appeared only as a short step for humans to consider themselves as "part and parcel of the two super-human, all-encompassing processes of nature and history" (1958, p. 307).

Arendt illustrated the flaws of process-oriented historical explanation with Hegelian and Marxist philosophies of history, in which the appearance of events and phenomena primarily served to illustrate a deeper, though hidden, structural cause, development process or law. In Arendt's words,

> Since Hegel watched Napoleon ride into Jena and saw in him not the emperor of France nor the conqueror of Prussia, not the son and not the destroyer or overcomer of the French Revolution, that is, nothing that Napoleon actually was at this moment, but rather "world spirit on horseback" – since that time historians and historiography have believed that they are finished with the investigation and depiction of an event only when they have discovered that which is functionally exponential in it, namely that which itself is hidden imperceptibly behind the visible and the experiential. (Arendt quoted in Hoffmann, 2010, p. 226)

With the arresting image of Napoleon as "world spirit on horseback," time was conceived as a constant flow; historical events and specific individuals were largely meaningful to the extent that they reflected a deeper direction, ultimate end, and reason in history. Though Marx more promisingly sought to ground world historical processes in the actions of the laboring classes he too subsumed the past into a grand teleological narrative of large-scale developmental processes of production. Arendt's critique of historical materialism did not extend to Marxist analyzes of capitalism or imperialism. Probably influenced by her husband Heinrich Blücher, a member of Rosa Luxembourg's Spartacus League, Arendt's analysis of imperial motives centered on outlets for surplus capital and the bourgeois search for profits. Further, in 1949, she complained to her mentor Karl Jaspers that in Cold War America "every little idiot thinks he has the right and duty to look down on Marx now" (Arendt & Jaspers, 1992, p. 137). The problem was that as a grand philosophy of history, Marxism retained a teleological commitment to the direction of history, to historical laws of movement and nature. Real historical persons, phenomena, and events "become almost accidental by-products" or functions of historical processes (Arendt, 1968d, p. 57).

Arendt did not deny the existence of structures or processes. Rather, she argued that historical events were not the mere exterior manifestation of seemingly more fundamental forces. Particular events and specific persons possess an intelligibility and significance on their own; they do not lack meaning outside the "context" of the overarching process, whether natural or man-made, of which modern philosophies of history imagine them to be a part. As already suggested in Arendt's analysis of totalitarianism, transforming a particular phenomenon into a mere example or indicator of deeper processes obscures the meaning and novelty of historical events. This may be legitimate for scientists examining the recurrence of natural processes. "Newness," in contrast, "is the realm of the historian, who – unlike the natural scientist, who is concerned with ever-recurring happenings – deals with events which always occur only once" (Arendt, 1994a [1954], p. 318). Not only did modern, process-oriented philosophies of history explain events away as the completion of natural processes or anonymous structures where "single events and deeds and sufferings have no more meaning here than hammer and nails have with respect to the finished table" (Arendt, 1968d, p. 80). They attempted to overcome the essential frailty, unpredictability, and even futility of political action with the durability of something that is *made* (Arendt, 1958). This was to equate political action with shaping the human condition toward a preconceived end as a carpenter shapes a piece of wood, that is, through violence. Arendt's response to the essential frailty of human affairs was not to assimilate politics into the naturalness of life or the instrumentality and violence of fabrication, both of which defined modern philosophies of history and were so appealing to imperial and totalitarian movements. Rather it was to retrieve a form of historical writing that coincided precisely with the frailty, but also new beginnings, inherent in political action.

HISTORY FOR A "BEING WHOSE ESSENCE IS BEGINNING"

Once again, irreducibly international experiences influenced Arendt's alternative approach to historical-political work. Walter Benjamin's influential essay "Theses on the Philosophy of History," written in early 1940, was among the manuscripts Benjamin entrusted to Arendt and her husband the last time they saw each other before seeking to escape to the United States, from France via Spain and Portugal. Soon after Benjamin took his own life on being told by Spanish authorities that he would be transported back to Vichy France as the border to Portugal from where he wished to sail to the United States was closed. Arendt's biographer recounts how Arendt, Blücher, and other refugees read aloud to each other some of Benjamin's writings, which would later be celebrated as among the most significant in the philosophy of history (Young-Bruehl, 1982/2004, p. 162). Fragments of at least three of Benjamin's "Theses" would have immediately stood out to Arendt: "nothing that has ever happened should be regarded as lost for history .... The true picture of the past flits by," Benjamin says. "The past can be seized only as an image which flashes up at the instant when it can be recognized and is never again seen .... To articulate the past historically does not mean to recognize it 'the way it really was' (Ranke). It means to seize hold of a memory as it flashes up at a moment of danger" (Benjamin, 1969 [1940], pp. 254–255). Hannah Arendt's understanding of fragmentary history as well as her refusal to conceive the past in terms of necessity and progress is deeply indebted to Benjamin. She would later edit and introduce to English readers a volume of his work, titled *Illuminations*, including the "Theses." We can interpret much of Arendt's later postwar writings as the distinctly *political* historical and theoretical rendering of Benjamin's claims.

One of the reasons for the widespread appeal of developmental philosophies of history, Arendt insisted, is that the tradition of Western political thought since Plato failed to properly understand its central object. "Each time the modern age had reason to hope for a new political philosophy," Arendt observed, "it received a philosophy of history instead" (Arendt, 1958, p. 298, no. 62). Any genuinely new political theory required a new philosophy of history, a phenomenology-based analysis of the "anthropological conditions of historical experience" (Hoffmann, 2010, p. 227). We have already seen the influence of a particular form of phenomenology on Arendt's historical writing on totalitarianism. Rejecting all forms of metaphysics, the history of ideas, or abstract analysis of concepts, Arendt's mode of phenomenological analysis was centered on the inherent meaningfulness of the *lived-experience* of events, prioritizing the factual, intersubjective, and experiential character of political being-in-the-world.[2] The interpretive task was one of understanding phenomena and events in their particularity, "separating the phenomenally verifiable content of an event from its genesis" and making distinctions, which is not the same as offering up "definitions" (Arendt, 1994g [1948], p. 166). Arendt most clearly explicated this phenomenology in *The Human Condition* (1958) in which she distinguished between three basic human activities, labor, work, and action. It is worth pausing to note how Arendt's famous distinctions are fundamentally temporal (Ricoeur, 1990).

The endless and repetitive activity of attending to biological life needs through *labor*, Arendt argued, was essentially futile. Though necessary for the survival of the species, the cycle of life on earth produces nothing of permanence. However, the human activity of *work* builds an artificial human-made world on the earth and is thus able to "bestow a measure of permanence and durability upon the futility of mortal life and the fleeting character of human time" (Arendt, 1958, p. 8). The built-environment – works of art, monuments, laws, and institutions – form this more durable world. Finally, there is *action*, the ever-present human capacity to begin something new with plural others, creating a "web of human relationships" in-between people (Arendt, 1958, p. 183). Though "spun of the most ephemeral stuff, of fleeting words and quickly forgotten deeds" (Arendt, 2005, p. 161), action is able to disrupt the continuity of natural processes and undo human-made structures. Yet while action is defined by its frailty and evanescence, since it "goes on directly between men without the intermediary of things or matter …, in so far as it engages in founding and preserving political bodies, [action] creates the condition for remembrance, that is, for history" (1958, pp. 7–9). What Arendt took to be the most political of all human activities, the capacity for action, is defined in terms of *interrupting* natural and historical processes, while also creating the possibility of political memory where "the past lives on in a form of history that goes on speaking and being spoken about" (2005, p. 161). The temporal dimensions of the activities of labor, work, and action underpin individual and collective experiences of time; they are the human conditions of historical experience.

Hence, the first historical counterpart to Hannah Arendt's political theory is the historian's obligation to identify the new, to engage in a form of historical writing that illuminates precisely because it refuses to place everything that happens in some broader "trend" of which the event is a mere example. Thus, the rejection of the modern concept of history is closely related to Arendt's account of political beginning and the human capacity for the new. In a manner not dissimilar to Reinhardt Koselleck's understanding of newness as defining of human history, Arendt turned philosophy's obsession with death on its head to argue that humans "are not born in order to die but in order to begin" (Arendt, 1958, p. 246; 1994a [1954], p. 321; Kang, 2013). A decade later she observed again that "historical processes are created and constantly interrupted by human initiative, by the *initium* man is insofar as he is acting being" (Arendt, 1968e, p. 170). This is why Arendt so often wrote about "historical persons" (Arendt, 1958, p. 184) and engaged in a kind of historical "teaching by example" (Arendt, 1968i, p. 247). This is evident not only in the eleven biographical essays collected in *Men in Dark Times*, which include Rosa Luxembourg, Walter Benjamin, and Karl Jaspers, but also exemplary figures such as Socrates, Robespierre, Rahel Varnhagen, T. E. Lawrence, Benjamin Disraeli, and of course Adolf Eichmann, the Nazi fugitive captured in Argentina by Israeli agents and put on trial in Jerusalem in 1961. Arendt attended the major international event of the trial and her reports for *The New Yorker* were republished as *Eichmann in Jerusalem: a report on the Banality of Evil* (1963). Violating almost all conventions of Holocaust representation and tone, she recounted that Jewish Councils had cooperated with Nazis; criticized Israel for turning the event into a pedagogical occasion such that "history ... stood at the center of the trial" (Arendt, 1963, p. 19); presented Eichmann himself as a nobody, a laughable clown, not the extreme monster many had wanted him to be, that should still hang for his crimes; and intervened in debates on international criminal law, especially crimes against humanity.

More generally, Arendt's historiographical method of using the lives of real people to illuminate particular historical moments was rooted in her political commitment to retain human dignity and capacity for action, judgment, and thought in the face of arguments for historical and/or natural necessities and laws, as Eichmann had pleaded when seeking to justify his utter failure to think for himself. For Arendt, histories were started by real persons precisely because humans are a being whose "essence is beginning" (Arendt, 1994a, p. 321). As she wrote in *Men in Dark Times* of people other than Eichmann, the illumination of the past "may well come less from theories and concepts than from the uncertain, flickering, and often weak light that some men and women, in their lives and their works, will kindle under all circumstances and shed over the time span that was given them on earth" (Arendt, 1968g, p. ix). While Arendt was interested in the history of thought, and contributed enormously to it, she insisted that ideologies and intellectual developments were not central forces in history. "I proceed from facts and events instead of intellectual affinities and influence" (Arendt, 1994e [1953], p. 405). We might also add that she proceeded from real persons. To account for these historical persons and their ideas is obviously not to suggest that individuals shape the direction of history as they wish, nor does she seek to rigidly separate the meaning of their actions and ideas from the present. Events transcend the original intentions of historical actors; they could not have been expected and they could not have been made; "whenever something new occurs," Arendt wrote, "it bursts into the context of predictable processes as something unexpected, unpredictable, and ultimately causally inexplicable" (Arendt, 2005, pp. 111–112). In relating the lives and actions of historical persons and stories of moments of political freedom – political revolutions, wartime resistance, anti-war activism, and civil disobedience – Arendt was breaking the hold of history as continuity, process, and progress. She was also seeking to bring these persons and moments into the present to illuminate something about the contemporary world. Almost all of these stories and moments were essentially international or related to international affairs. Perhaps, this makes sense of Arendt's otherwise strange claim that "Only in foreign affairs, because the relationships between nations still harbor hostilities and sympathies which cannot be reduced to economic factors, seem to be left as a purely political domain" (Arendt, 1968e, p. 155).

Not processes but (international) events themselves become the proper subject matter of historical writing, and these events are no less significant, no less meaningful, when they are removed from the need to situate them in engulfing processes of historical movement or "development": "each event in human history," Arendt claimed, "reveals an unexpected landscape of human deeds, sufferings, and new possibilities which together transcend the sum total of all willed intentions and the significance of all origins. It is the task of the historian to detect this unexpected *new* with all its implications in any given period and to bring out the full power of its significance" (Arendt, 1994a [1954], p. 320). Thus, after the rupture in historical time represented by totalitarian domination, Arendt sought to reclaim moments of human freedom, but also the singularity and fragmentary character of the remembered past. Hence, to conceive a new grounding for politics after totalitarianism and in the face of the threat of nuclear annihilation, Red

Scares, the conformism in mass society, and the dangers to republican government posed by the Vietnam War, it is no surprise that Arendt turned to the question of revolution. In the early 1960s, she was drawn to write *On Revolution* because revolutions "are the only political events which confront us directly and inevitably with the problem of beginning" (Arendt, 1970b [1963]), p. 13). It is also unsurprising that the central purpose of the book, as she saw it, was not to provide the most accurate account of the origins and motives of the French and American Revolutions, far from it. Rather the book was a "political fable," a celebration of the participatory council system and, through the 1960s, was often required reading among American Students for a Democratic Society and the German Socialist Students League (Young-Bruehl, 1982/2004, pp. 403–404). No matter that Arendt conceived the French and American cases as failed revolutions; her purpose was to theorize the capacity for new beginnings and political refounding in her own time and in light of the historical and moral significance of totalitarianism and the challenges posed to revolution by both neocolonialism and the nuclear age.

The need to preserve a relation to the past, to preserve the past itself, was fundamental to humanizing the post-totalitarian world, but this past was necessarily discontinuous. Hence, for Arendt, historical narrative becomes fragmentary history. "What you then are left with," she wrote in her last book, *The Life of the Mind*, "is still the past, but a *fragmented* past, which has lost its certainty of evaluation" (Arendt, 1978 [LM, Vol. 1], p. 212). In previous writing Arendt had illuminated this approach through the conceptual metaphor of the pearl diver who "descends to the bottom of the sea, not to excavate the bottom and bring it to light but to pry loose the rich and the strange, the pearls and the corals in the depths, and carry them to the surface" (Arendt, 1968f, p. 205). "What guides this thinking," she observed, quoting Shakespeare's *The Tempest*, "is the conviction that although the living is subject to the ruin of time, the process of decay is at the same time a process of crystallization, that in the depths of the sea ... some things 'suffer a sea-change' and survive in new crystallized forms and shapes that remain immune to the elements, as though they waited only for the pearl diver who one day will come down to them and bring them up into the world of the living" (Arendt, 1968f, pp. 205–206). The meaning, as distinct from the cause, of an historical event becomes clear once it has been related as part of a story, and this storytelling also shapes history. This emphasis on narrative history does not contradict Arendt's critique of history as continuous and teleological. Rather to make the past comprehensible in this fashion can be to emphasize disjuncture and contingency. For Arendt, it was the poets and historians, not the social scientists, who were responsible for conveying actions deserving of remembrance, actions that become the subject of poetry and history such that they potentially become immortal, that is, inspire and live on in the public, political world. "No philosophy, no analysis, no aphorism, be it ever so profound, can compare in intensity and richness of meaning with a properly narrated story" (Arendt, 1968b, p. 22). Hans J. Morgenthau went so far as to compare Arendt's historical writing to the storytelling of Thucydides (Young-Bruehl, 2006, p. 34). In fact, Arendt had identified a form of writing in Thucydides, and also Homer and Herodotus, in which the meaning of political events is revealed in the reflections of the political actors and the opinion of the judging spectators, the historians.

In posthumously published writings on the political consequences of possible nuclear annihilation, Hannah Arendt turned to "the ur-example" of annihilatory war, the legendary Trojan War recounted in Homer's *The Illiad* (Arendt, 2005, p. 163). How might wars of annihilation be transformed into "political wars," that is, come to an end through an "alliance and a treaty ... according to which yesterday's enemies became tomorrow's allies" (Arendt, 2005, pp. 176–178)? To consider this urgent question, relevant not only to nuclear confrontation but Israel/Palestine, Arendt told a story in which wars "did not end in yet another annihilation of the vanquished, but an alliance and a treaty ... inventing a new outcome for war's conflagration" (Arendt, 2005, p. 176). The ancient Romans, who traced their origins to defeat in the Trojan War, were able to build an empire among the formerly vanquished, establishing new relationships with former foes. To be sure, the turn away from wars of annihilation was not for the sake of ethics, but "for the sake of expanding Rome" (2005, pp. 185–187). Pointing to Rome's peace treaties and alliances was no naïve liberal internationalism, nor any attempt to historically "contextualize" the conditions for averting annihilatory war. Arendt was clear that, for the vanquished, defeat "was synonymous with plunder, murder, and theft" (Arendt, 2005, p. 189). Rather Arendt's reading of Homer for the nuclear age was allegorical and in line with her better known writing on the ancient Greek *polis*, that is, as a monumental form of historical consciousness.[3] This particular response to the dangers posed by nuclear annihilation was an exemplary exercise in pearl diving, of Benjamin's call "to seize hold of a memory as it flashes up at a moment of danger" (1969 [1940], p. 255). Arendt was carrying to the surface a vision of a different kind of politics – and foreign policy – that was itself a "response to an experience of annihilation" (Schell, 2010, p. 257).

CONCLUSION

Hannah Arendt is an historical figure of significance in her own right (Krieger, 1976), the subject of films, documentaries, plays, art exhibitions, and an endless stream of articles and books, almost all commenting on her originality and distance from conventional approaches to historical and social science. This article has examined the neglected international origins and context of Arendt's work, specifically her approach to historical method, a method that crystallized through her political activism and experiences in the 1930s through to her response to the horrors of a different (nuclear) war of annihilation in the 1950s and 1960s. If Hannah Arendt is *the* "political theorist of the post-totalitarian moment," then we cannot fully appreciate her influence and significance without understanding the deeply generative impact of the international on her thought (Benhabib, 1999). Arendt insisted that the event of totalitarianism fundamentally transformed the conditions of historical and political thought, and she directly confronted the consequences of its rupture in the continuity of historical time. Her response to totalitarianism, the danger of nuclear annihilation, and the precariousness of revolutions in a neocolonial age was to innovate forms of historical writing that were compatible with, a counterpart to, human plurality and freedom, and the frailty of, but new beginning intrinsic to, political action. Indeed, the importance of international events and contexts on Arendt's thought corresponds to, and may be partially responsible for, the enormous value she placed on plurality as one of the conditions of human existence. This concept is not limited to Arendt's better-known and celebrated writing on the plurality of persons as the basic condition of politics, that "we are all the same, that is, human, in such a way that nobody is ever the same as anyone else who ever lived, lives, or will live" (Arendt, 1958, p. 8). Arendt's relational and plural understanding of the individual subject is also found in her writing on the value of *international* plurality as the equal plurality of distinct peoples.

To inhabit the world, Hannah Arendt insisted, is also necessarily a form of cohabitation. The fact that there are multiple and plural territorially defined human-made (not naturally defined) entities on the earth gives meaning to the *inter*national, from the Latin "between" and "among," as that which "relates and separates … at the same time." Different polities exist in their unique distinctness, by definition, between and among plural others. They are not simply multiple, "endlessly reproducible repetitions" of themselves (Arendt, 1958, pp. 8, 52). The intrinsic value of a plurality of territorially defined entities clarifies Arendt's rejection of *supra*national solutions to the ever-present danger of totalitarianism, the possibility of atomic war, and the existence of stateless and right-less persons (Arendt, 1972, pp. 230–231).

There was – and should be – "an undetermined infinity of forms of human living-together" within a worldwide federated structure (Arendt, 1966 [1951], p. 443; 1968h, p. 93). Indeed, there were epistemological as well as political and ethical grounds for valuing international plurality and why wars of annihilation, *defined* by their destruction of plurality, were impermissible. Historical representation itself had to be answerable to the human condition of the plurality of peoples. The historical counterpart to Arendt's ontological basis for political action is that "there is nothing in ... the historical-political world that has assumed full reality ... until ... all its sides" have been "revealed" (Arendt, 2005, p. 175). Plurality and reality are inextricably linked; the latter requires the former, is "guaranteed for each by the presence of all" (Arendt, 1958, p. 244). Despite its particular and partial origins in Arendt's own lived experiences, such an historical epistemology is eminently compatible with emerging postcolonial forms of writing international history and theory: skeptical of grand, sweeping generalizations about global processes and developments; wary of easy anachronisms; and more attentive to the lived experiences of a plurality of historical persons and peoples. International history is necessarily fragmentary history.

NOTES

1. The original title first published in Britain by Secker and Warburg in 1951 was *The Burden of Our Time*. The front cover announces the book as, "An historical study of the world-wide crisis of our time, with its evil concept – the deliberate dehumanization of humanity."

2. On the influence of Heidegger on Arendt, but also the significant distance between them, see Villa who brilliantly reads "Arendt as appropriating Heidegger in a highly agonistic manner; as twisting, displacing, and reinterpreting his thought in ways designed to illuminate a range of exceedingly *un*-Heideggerian issues .... Indeed, no small part of Arendt's originality resides in her ability to see the political implications of a body of work in a way that goes against the grain of authorial intent" (Villa, 1996, p. 13).

3. I am grateful to Richard King for suggesting this formulation.

ACKNOWLEDGMENTS

For comments on earlier drafts of this article I would like to thank Beate Jahn, Richard King, Helen Kinsella, Sam Knafo, Daniel Levine, Justin Rosenberg, the editors of the special issue, Tarak Barkawi and George Lawson, and the anonymous reviewers.

REFERENCES

Adorno, T. W., & Horkheimer, M. (1979 [1944]). *Dialectic of enlightenment* (J. Cumming, Trans.). London: Verso.

Arendt, H. (1955). *History of political theory*. Lecture notes. Spring 1955, University of California, Subject file, 1949–1975, HAPLC, 023943. Courses, image 5. Retrieved from https://memory.loc.gov/ammem/arendthtml/arendthome.html. Accessed on June 8, 2016.

Arendt, H. (1958). *The human condition*. Chicago, IL: University of Chicago Press.

Arendt, H. (1963). *Eichmann in Jerusalem: A report on the banality of evil*. New York, NY: Viking.

Arendt, H. (1966 (1951]). *The origins of totalitarianism* (new edition with added prefaces). New York, NY: Harcourt Brace Jovanovich.

Arendt, H. (1968a). Preface: The gap between past and future. *Between past and future: Eight exercises in political thought* (pp. 3–15). New York, NY: Viking.

Arendt, H. (1968b). On humanity in dark times. *Men in dark times* (pp. 3–31). New York, NY: Harcourt, Brace, and World.

Arendt, H. (1968c). Tradition and the modern age. *Between past and future: Eight exercises in political thought* (pp. 17–40). New York: Viking.

Arendt, H. (1968d). The concept of history: Ancient and modern. *Between past and future: Eight exercises in political thought* (pp. 41–90). New York: Viking.

Arendt, H. (1968e). What is freedom? *Between past and future: Eight exercises in political thought* (pp. 143–171). New York: Viking.

Arendt, H. (1968f). Walter Benjamin, 1892–1940. *Men in dark times* (pp. 153–206).

Arendt, H. (1968g). Preface. *Men in dark times* (pp. vii–x). New York: Harcourt, Brace, and World.

Arendt, H. (1968h). Karl Jaspers: Citizen of the world? *Men in dark times* (pp. 81–94). New York: Harcourt, Brace, and World.

Arendt, H. (1968i). Truth and politics. *Between past and future: Eight exercises in political thought* (pp. 227–264). New York: Viking.

Arendt, H. (1970a). Introduction. In J. Glenn Gray (Eds.), *The warrior: Reflections on men in battle* (pp. vii–xiv). London: University of Nebraska Press.

Arendt, H. (1970b [1963]). *On revolution*. New York, NY: Viking.

Arendt, H. (1972). Thoughts on politics and revolution. *Crises of the republic* (pp. 199–233). New York, NY: Harcourt Brace Jovanovich.

Arendt, H. (1974 [1957]). *Rahel Varnhagen: The life of a Jewish woman* (Richard and C. Winston, rev. ed., trans.). New York, NY: Harcourt Brace Jovanovich.

Arendt, H. (1978). *Life of the mind*. New York, NY: Harcourt Brace Jovanovich.

Arendt, H. (1994a). Understanding and politics. In J. Kohn (Ed.), *Essays in understanding, 1930–1954* (pp. 307–327). New York, NY: Harcourt Brace.

Arendt, H. (1994b). Concern with politics in recent European philosophical thought. *Essays in Understanding, 1930–1954* (ed. Jerome Kohn) (pp. 428–447). New York: Harcourt Brace.

Arendt, H. (1994c). The seeds of a fascist international. *Essays in Understanding, 1930–1954* (ed. Jerome Kohn) (pp. 140–150). New York: Harcourt Brace.

Arendt, H. (1994d). Approaches to the "German Problem." *Essays in Understanding, 1930–1954* (ed. Jerome Kohn) (pp. 106–120). New York: Harcourt Brace.

Arendt, H. (1994e). A reply to eric voegelin. *Essays in Understanding, 1930–1954* (ed. Jerome Kohn) (pp. 401–408). New York: Harcourt Brace.

Arendt, H. (1994f). Social science techniques and the study of concentration camps. *Essays in Understanding, 1930–1954* (ed. Jerome Kohn) (pp. 232–247). New York: Harcourt Brace.

Arendt, H. (1994g). What is existential philosophy. *Essays in Understanding, 1930–1954* (ed. Jerome Kohn) (pp. 163–187). New York: Harcourt Brace.
Arendt, H. (1994h). Religion and politics. *Essays in Understanding, 1930–1954* (ed. Jerome Kohn) (pp. 428–447). New York: Harcourt Brace.
Arendt, H. (2005). Introduction into politics. In *The promise of politics* (ed. and introduction by Jerome Kohn) (pp. 93–200). New York, NY: Schocken.
Arendt, H. (2007a). Zionism reconsidered. In J. Kohn & R. H. Feldman (Eds.), *The Jewish writings* (pp. 343–374). New York, NY: Schocken.
Arendt, H. (2007b). To save the Jewish Homeland. *The Jewish writings* (ed. Jerome Kohn and Ron H. Feldman) (pp. 388–401). New York, NY: Schocken.
Arendt, H. (2007c). Achieving agreement between people in the near east – A basis for Jewish politics. *The Jewish writings* (ed. Jerome Kohn and Ron H. Feldman) (pp. 388–401). New York, NY: Schocken.
Arendt, H., & Jaspers, K. (1992). *Correspondence, 1926–1969* (Robert & R. Kimber, trans.). In L. Kohler & H. Saner (Eds.). New York, NY: Harcourt Brace Jovanovich.
Aron, R. (1969 [1965]). *Democracy and totalitarianism: A theory of political regimes* (V. Ionescu, trans.). New York, NY: Praeger.
Ashcroft, C. (2015). Jewishness and the problem of nationalism: a genealogy of Arendt's early political thought. *Modern intellectual history* (pp. 1–29).
Baehr, P. (2002). Identifying the unprecedented: Hannah Arendt, totalitarianism, and the critique of sociology. *American Sociological Review*, *67*(6), 804–831.
Benhabib, S. (1999). The personal is not the political. *Boston Review*, October 1. Retrieved from https://bostonreview.net/books-ideas/seyla-benhabib-personal-not-political. Accessed on June 8, 2016.
Benhabib, S. (2000). *The reluctant modernism of Hannah Arendt*. Oxford: Rowman and Littlefield.
Benjamin, W. (1969 [1940]). Theses on the philosophy of history. In *Illuminations* (edited and with an introduction by Hannah Arendt, H. Kohn, trans.) (pp. 253–264). London: Jonathan Cape.
Canovan, M. (1992). *Hannah Arendt: A reinterpretation of her political thought*. Cambridge: Cambridge University Press.
Curthoys, N. (2010). The pathos and promise of counter-history: Hannah Arendt and Ernst Cassirer's German-Jewish historical consciousness. In A. Schaap, D. Celermajer, & V. Karalis (Eds.), *Power, judgment and political evil: In conversation with Hannah Arendt* (pp.107–132). London: Ashgate.
DuBois, W. E. B. (2015 [1947]). *The world and Africa: An inquiry into the part which Africa has played in the World*. Eastford, CT: Martino Publishing.
Grosse, P. (2006). From colonialism to national socialism to postcolonialism: Hannah Arendt's "Origins of Totalitarianism." *Postcolonial Studies*, *9*, 35–52.
Hayden, P. (2009). *Political evil in a global age: Hannah Arendt and international theory*. London: Routledge.
Hoffmann, S. L. (2010). Koselleck, Arendt, and the anthropology of historical experience. *History and Theory*, *49*(2), 212–236.
Honohan, I. (1990). Arendt and Benjamin on the promise of History: A network of possibilities or one apocalyptic moment? *Clio*, *19*(4), 311–330.
Hull, I. V. (2005). *Absolute destruction: Military culture and the practices of war in imperial Germany*. Ithaca, NY: Cornell University Press.
Hyvönen, A.-E. (2016). Invisible streams: Process-thinking in Arendt. *European Journal of Social Theory*, *19*(4), 538–555.
Kang, T. (2013). Origin and essence: The problem of history in Hannah Arendt. *Journal of the History of Ideas*, *74*(1), 139–160.

Keedus, L. (2015). *The crisis of German historicism: The early political thought of Hannah Arendt and Leo Strauss*. Cambridge: Cambridge University Press.

King, R. H. (2007). Arendt between past and future. In R. H. King & D. Stone (Eds.). *Hannah Arendt and the uses of history: Imperialism, nation, race, and genocide* (pp. 250–261). New York, NY: Berghan Books.

King, R. H., & Stone, D. (Eds.). (2007). *Hannah arendt and the uses of history: Imperialism, nation, race, and genocide*. New York, NY: Berghan Books.

King, R. H. (2015). *Arendt and America*. Chicago, IL: University of Chicago Press.

Krieger, L. (1976). The historical Hannah Arendt. *The Journal of Modern History*, *48*(4), 672–684.

Kühne, T. (2013). Colonialism and the Holocaust: Continuities, causations, and complexities. *Journal of Genocide Research*, *15*(3), 339–362.

Lang, A. F. Jr., & Williams, J. (Eds.). (2005). *Hannah Arendt and international relations: Reading across the lines*. London: Palgrave Press.

Luban, D. (1983). Explaining dark times: Hannah Arendt's theory of theory. *Social Research*, *50*(1), 215–258.

Novák, J. (2010). Understanding and judging history: Hannah Arendt and philosophical hermeneutics. *Meta*, *2*(2), 481–504.

Owens, P. (2007). *Between war and politics: International relations and the thought of Hannah Arendt*. Oxford: Oxford University Press.

Owens, P. (2015). *Economy of force: Counterinsurgency and the historical rise of the social*. Cambridge: Cambridge University Press.

Ricoeur, P. (1990). Action, story and history: On re-reading *The Human Condition*. In G. G. Reuben (Ed.), *The realm of humanitas: Responses to the writings of Hannah Arendt* (pp. 149–162). New York, NY: Peter Lang.

Schell, J. (2010). In search of a miracle: Hannah Arendt and the atomic bomb. In S. Benhabib (Ed.), *Politics in dark times: Encounters with Hannah Arendt* (pp. 247–258). Cambridge: Cambridge University Press.

Selinger, W. (2016). The politics of Arendtian historiography: European federation and the origins of totalitarianism. *Modern Intellectual History*, *13*(2), 417–446.

Sluga, G. (2015). Turning international: *Foundations of modern international thought* and new paradigms for intellectual history. *History of European Ideas*, *41*(1), 103–115.

Villa, D. (1996). *Arendt and Heidegger: The fate of the political*. Princeton, NJ: Princeton University Press.

Villa, D. (1999). *Politics, philosophy, terror: Essays on the thought of Hannah Arendt*. Princeton, NJ: Princeton University Press.

Vollrath, E. (1977). Hannah Arendt and the method of political thinking. *Social Research*, *44*(1), 160–182.

Yaqoob, W. (2014a). Reconciliation and violence: Hannah Arendt on historical understanding. *Modern Intellectual History*, *11*(2), 385–416.

Yaqoob, W. (2014b). The Archimedean point: Science and technology in the thought of Hannah Arendt, 1951–63. *Journal of European Studies*, *44*(3), 199–224.

Young-Bruehl, E. (2004 [1982]). *Hannah Arendt: For the love of the world*. New Haven, CT: Yale University Press.

Young-Bruehl, E. (2006). *Why Arendt matters*. New Haven, CT: Yale University Press.

Zimmerer, J. (2004). Colonialism and the Holocaust: Towards and archaeology of genocide. In A. Dirk Moses (Ed.), *Genocide and settler society: Frontier violence and stolen indigenous children in Australian history* (pp. 49–76). New York, NY: Berghahn.

WHAT KIND OF THEORY IS THE LABOR THEORY OF VALUE? MARX AS GENEALOGIST IN *ZUR KRITIK*

Samuel A. Chambers

ABSTRACT

The labor theory of value (LTV) offers a lucid and forceful example of a "theory" thought to stand outside "history." Considered as an "objective" form of theorizing, the LTV seeks transhistorical truths about the relationship between humans and nature – whereby, as everyone knows, value in the world is produced by the fundamental force of human labor power. Marx is typically taken to have subscribed to some form of the LTV, and thus to have signed on to this form of theorizing. This article refuses to treat Marx as an analytic, ahistorical theorist who would either affirm or deny the LTV. Rather, I read Marx as a genealogist who excavates the story of labor and value within the specific historical context of an emerging capitalist social formation. This genealogical approach to Marx, and particularly to his less-often-discussed, Contribution to the Critique of Political Economy, *shows plainly that Marx never subscribed to the LTV, but more importantly that he*

International Origins of Social and Political Theory
Political Power and Social Theory, Volume 32, 63–98

ISSN: 0198-8719/doi:10.1108/S0198-871920170000032004

eschewed the form of theory that the LTV presumes. Rather than seeking to make transhistorical theoretical claims about the relation between labor and value, Marx meant to demonstrate to his readers something about the way in which a definite and concrete (historically situated) capitalist social formation establishes value. A capitalist social formation establishes its own specific value relations, by first constituting, and then dissimulating, a link between labor and value.

Keywords: Marx; Labor Theory of Value; political economy; capitalism

Like most societies, capitalist social orders tell themselves a number of constitutive stories; for capitalism, the myth of barter and the fictional narrative of a "state of nature" are only the most prominent examples. This article takes the so-called labor theory of value (LTV) as its point of departure. The LTV is like the aforementioned stories to the extent that any history of political economy or economics will contain accounts of the LTV alongside accounts of barter and "natural" exchange. But the LTV is unlike those fictional accounts because it is purported to be not a narrative within history but a theoretical account that stands outside of, and thus explains, history. The LTV is a story that we pretend is not a story. In other words, *it's a theory*.

Using the LTV as a frame enables me to explore an important set of relations between theory and history, both in classical political economy and in the development of capitalist social formations. The LTV offers a lucid and forceful example of a "theory" thought to stand outside "history": the standard approach to the LTV (turned into an acronym so as to make it seem more analytical and less historical) is precisely to consider it as an "objective" form of theorizing that seeks transhistorical truths about the relationship between humans and nature – whereby, as everyone knows, value in the world is produced by the fundamental force of human labor power. It is in just this sense that Marx has typically been taken – both within those histories of political economy and within contemporary texts that refer to Marx – to have subscribed to the LTV. Not only that, the common assumption is that "Marx was the greatest champion of the labor theory of value," as Steve Keen puts it in a representative quote (Keen, 1993, p. 1). Claims such as these carry two concomitant presumptions: first, that the LTV is precisely an ahistorical theory, and second, that Marx himself was just such a theorist – that his goal as a theorist was to come up with transcendental or ahistorical explanations, to give an ontological account of the universal truth of labor as the ground for his critique of capitalism.

This background leads me to broach the primary questions of this article: what kind of theory is the LTV, and what kind of theorist was Marx? I follow a still-nascent yet already-rich tradition of reading Marx not as an "adherent" to the LTV; quite the contrary, the value-form reading of Marx shows decisively that Marx never subscribed to the LTV in the sense of an abstract and ahistorical set of theoretical claims about the universal power of labor to bestow value on its objects (Heinrich, 2012). Rather, as a thinker, Marx's primary concern was to grasp how the very idea that labor produces value could emerge within a society in the first place. What sort of society establishes a configuration of production and exchange such that labor becomes, within that social order, the source of value? This question bears only the faintest resemblance to the question posed by the LTV, which asks for the abstract and ahistorical source of value and finds it in the universal power of laboring.

To see that Marx asks profoundly different questions about labor and value makes it possible to glimpse the possibility of a wholly different account of history, and to see Marx as doing a completely distinct kind of theory. I argue that vis-à-vis what we now call the LTV,[1] Marx is doing here something quite similar to what he does with Robinsonades – the popular eighteenth- and nineteenth-century literary genre centering on the island castaway, à la Robinson Crusoe. Marx engages with this literary genre as a way to develop his own unique critique of both liberal political theory and bourgeois political economy. Unlike recent challenges to "contract theories," Marx does not complain that the state of nature is hypothetical or unrealistic, or that the conditions it imposes are problematic. Marx turns all of that inside out and asks first, where does the idea of a state of nature come from? For Marx, such a "theory" is just another version of a Robinsonade. In other words, classical political economy gets its founding ideas from a popular literary genre; they are telling Robinson Crusoe stories. And Marx takes his genealogy one step further by giving it a materialist twist: how, he asks, did we get the idea of a Robinsonade in the first place? Such stories are part and parcel of a larger social formation, one in which the bonds of feudal society have been broken, in which bourgeois revolutions have created conditions of equalization and individuation – conditions that themselves give rise to the very idea of what Marx incisively yet cuttingly calls, "the individuated individual." We don't get the state of nature without Robinson Crusoe, and we don't get Robinson Crusoe without contract wage labor and all the rest (Marx, 1996, pp. 128–129).

With the case of the so-called LTV, this context clarifies the key point that rather than seeking to make transhistorical theoretical claims about the relation between labor and value, Marx meant to demonstrate to his readers something about the way in which a definite and concrete (historically situated) capitalist social formation establishes value. However, this type of analysis is totally eclipsed if not erased by the LTV as an abstract analytical theory that must either be true or false. Only if we reject the very idea of the LTV, if we resist and overturn the relation between theory and history that it presupposes, only then can we analyze the relation between labor and value within the historical development of capitalism. Only after jettisoning the framework of the LTV as an analytic theory might we be able to see what Marx himself tries to show, that *a capitalist social formation establishes its own specific value relations, by first constituting, and then dissimulating, a link between labor and value.*

Any abstract, generalizing theory – any theory with a capital T that seeks to stand outside of history – will prove utterly incapable of grasping these value relations, of seeing how a historical social formation can itself produce theoretical forms. To track this process (in order to grasp these relations) depends upon first refusing to play the role of "theorist" or grand philosopher, whose task would be to prove or disprove ahistorical theoretical claims. In other words, theorist A can propose that abstract human labor is the essential origin of value in commodities, while theorist B can reject this claim as logically untenable and propose an alternative. Yet both, claim and counterclaim, uphold the generic idea of "objective theorizing," abstracted from historical events and agents. Thus in dismissing the LTV, for example, modern marginalist theory simultaneously reifies the idea of theory as ahistorical.[2] This explains why in this article I refuse to read Marx as either an economic theorist or as a philosopher of human nature.

Instead, I read Marx as a genealogist who excavates the story of labor and value within the specific historical context of an emerging capitalist social formation. Marx always follows – *avant la lettre*, of course – some of the primary precepts of genealogy by consistently "refus[ing] to extend his faith in metaphysics," and this allows him with respect to value and labor to consistently eschew "the search for 'origins'" (Foucault, 1984, pp. 77–78; Nietzsche, 1967). Marx traces the line of descent of value, thereby showing that it has no single source – and certainly not one that would lie outside history. In reading the classical political economists genealogically, Marx concomitantly develops his own understanding of the relation between value and labor, a relation always produced *socially* and *temporally*. Marx neither signed on to the LTV nor offered a theoretical refutation of it; instead, he attempted to make sense of the relation between labor and value as itself a historical production. Marx was not answering the philosophical question "what is the source of value?" – with "labor" as his philosophical answer. Rather, he was answering the historical question, "how is value established under the concrete circumstances and specific historical practices of a capitalist social formation?" Here, Marx answers not as a "theorist" but as a genealogist. In emphasizing the distinctiveness of both Marx's approach to, and his conclusions about, theory and history, I am also indicating the limited nature of a now-standard framing of Marx on value. Here I refer to the trope frequently invoked in the secondary literature which proposes two options: either Marx had a classical "labor theory of value" or he had a "value theory of labor." I am suggesting that, thought in these stark analytic terms, i.e. "theory of X," Marx, like a good genealogist, *had no theory at all.*[3] He had a subtle and sophisticated understanding of the historical development of the logic of capital as part of a broader social formation. To read Marx's genealogy of value and labor within a bourgeois order is to rethink the importance of capital in establishing value relations, and along the way to reconceive the relationship of theory to history.

CAPITALISM AND VALUE

The question of value within a capitalist regime is neither a random nor ancillary idea, because the relationship between capital and value is not at all arbitrary, since as I already suggested above, *one of the things capitalism does is to establish relations of value*. Of course, today our intuitive understanding of value within capitalism depends on the fundamental idea that "the market" itself produces value. Competition, the hallmark of the capitalist economy, is understood to create conditions in which all objects within the economy attain their true value. And market value is objective in two senses. First, I personally cannot decide the value of a loaf of bread. When I go to the store, the value of the bread is fixed, given – written legibly on the price tag. Second, according to pure microeconomic theory, the grocer does not establish the value of the bread either: Sell too dearly and no one will buy, so the grocer will go out of business; sell too cheaply and costs will not be covered, so again the grocer will go out of business. Only the "clearing" of markets, the equilibration of supply and demand, can determine the price of a commodity. Under capitalism, objective valuation is an achievement of the system itself.

Capitalist value thus appears not to need metaphysical moorings. Commodities and money are valuable because the market says so: If Apple stock is trading at $110/share, then it clearly must be *worth* $110 a share, since there is no other value given for it, and because no individual can alter that price. Only the aggregation of all buyers and sellers of Apple stock, working through the magic of the market, can collectively (but non-intentionally) produce an outcome that changes the value of the stock. This is the power of the "invisible hand" metaphor: The hand writes the value of commodities directly onto them (through price), but the hand is *invisible* since it is the hand of the market itself.

But what would it even mean to think of value within a capitalist society in any other way? How could value *not* be understood as market price? Situations such as these, those in which it seems hard to think past or outside of our intuitive understandings, call for the work of genealogy. Genealogy moves backward in time, not to find the original source or putative truth of our present (not to locate an *Ursprung*), but instead to reveal a fractured line of descent (*Herkunft*), to expose the past as different and strange, and thereby ultimately to render the present contingent – to make it anything but inevitable (Chambers, 2001; Foucault, 1984; cf. Cook, 1990).

In order to ask the question of capitalist value from a perspective other than our own, we can effectively turn to the work of the classical political economists. They saw value under capitalism quite distinctly, because they approached capitalism differently. Where we take capitalism to be a given, a naturalized system that admits of no alternative, the classical political economists, even in their most ardent defense of capitalism, understand capitalism as something *new*, something particular and special. They see what we have a hard time seeing today: That capitalism is one among many different ways of ordering a society, and that capitalism's radical reorganization of the previous social order (feudalism) led to a revolutionary reconstruction of value systems.

The classical political economists came at the question of value in a manner that will surely strike us as odd, but the most important point is not their strangeness to us, but our strangeness to them. In requiring us to turn our attention to the past, the purpose of genealogy is not merely to make that past seem alien and unfamiliar, but rather to help us (or force us, as the case may be) to look *through* that past perspective, back toward the future – that is, our present – and to render it curious, even alien. In this way genealogy can go beyond rendering the past foreign (a feat easily achieved anyway, as evidenced by most "period piece" movies) to producing a certain alterity of our own present. This, I think, is what Foucault meant by doing a "history of the present" (Chambers, 2009; Halperin, 2002; Sedgwick, 1990).

The classical political economists did not speak with a unified voice, yet they would all tend to see our sense of capitalist value as failing to answer the fundamental question of where value comes from. For them, our answer – the market – would amount to no answer at all; it would appear as nothing other than bald-faced question begging. Doubtless the classical economists grasped the power of markets, appreciated the mechanisms of supply and demand, and understood that markets both establish the equivalence of commodities and operate by way of monetary prices. They could easily perceive, just as plainly as we do, that markets establish value. However, *for them such a phenomenon was itself in need of explanation.* Again, this is certainly because for the political economists the mechanisms by which markets establish value were anything but given or natural; they were a radically new, *historical* development established by massive technological, social, and political change. The system by which the logic of capital established value did not have the imprimatur of objective truth for the classical political economists, and therefore they set out to give it the metaphysical moorings that it lacked. Where, they queried, does the value of commodities come from? How, they asked, could we trace market value to a more fundamental, underlying value?

Today, we see no need to ask such questions; the mainstream profession of economics has not asked them for over a century. Nonetheless, the classical political economists shared with us the fundamental sense that a society's value system needed to be based on genuine, stable foundations. But here lies the key twist: For the classical political economists, the market itself could not serve as that foundation (as it does for us today). The reason is simple: For them the market did not yet have the metaphysical reality that it attained in the 20th century.[4] Therefore, for thinkers from the 17th through the 19th centuries, the question of the value of commodities needed to be answered by finding some element of *intrinsic* worth that could explain the value of commodities as they operated under (according to) the logic of capital.

Political economy as a field was forged in the fierce debates over the question of value, with most centering on "labor" as a potential answer.

Entire schools of thought and diverse political projects were born in the process of trying to understand what labor is and how it might be that labor could constitute the essence of value within a capitalist social order. In this context I now turn to Marx.

MARX AS GENEALOGIST

Marx matters for me here, first of all, because of his genealogical work. Marx followed the descent of classical political economy, showing how the answer to the value question changed, shifted, was reworked, faced challenges, and was reformulated over the course of almost 200 years of political economy. I want to call attention to the *genealogical work* that Marx does in relation to classical political economy and to use a certain reading of him *as* a genealogist to draw out the stakes of his self-titled *critique* of the political economists. In short, treating Marx as if he were a genealogist reveals a great deal that is otherwise occluded in other approaches to Marx, and in certain contexts we see clearly that he operates as a genealogist – that is, according to the precepts and methods of genealogy as later outlined by Nietzsche, Foucault, and their recent readers. But my point is not to "make" Marx into a genealogist, or to contend that all of his writings should be read this way. Marx wore many hats when he wrote: historian, journalist, polemicist, pamphleteer, and economic pedagogue; it would be at best naive to think all those roles could be contained under the heading of genealogy. Moreover, there can be no doubt that Marx's presentation of his critique of political economy in *Capital* looks far less genealogical than that in the earlier writings on which I focus. I intend not to deny that difference, but to highlight it, and along the way to show that we learn a great deal from the genealogical Marx of the 1850s that might otherwise be missed in the much more famous (and less genealogical) published writings of the 1860s.[5]

My broadest contention is that it would prove impossible to make sense out of, much less evaluate or judge, any answer that Marx himself might have given to the question of value, without first laying out his detailed and precise description and criticism of those answers that had recently preceded him in political economy. This claim would hold even if one's primary aim was to uncover Marx's own answer: Marx says over and over again – he repeats it throughout his writings over a long span of time – that his account of capitalism emerges out of his engagement with political economy. But in some ways this is to understate the point. We might do better to put it this way: Marx's delineation of the logic of capital *is his critique of political economy*. Here I paraphrase Marx, who, in a famous quote from a letter, once described his work-in-progress on capital by referring to it as "the system of bourgeois political economy critically presented," and in case that were not clear enough, Marx continued "it is the *Darstellung* of the system and, at the same time, through the *Darstellung*, its *Kritik*" (Marx and Engels, 1963; quoted in Carver, 1975, pp. 28–29). I leave the German in the quotes to emphasize the way in which for Marx the "presentation" is intimately bound up with "critique." And I might go one step further to suggest that the *Darstellung* here is not simply a direct "presentation" or "description" of the precepts of classical political economy, but also a "representation," a "production," perhaps even a "performance," of Marx's own thought.

I am of course not the first to make the case that Marx cannot be understood outside of the context of his critical engagement with classical political economy; the claim is commonplace, and few readers of Marx would deny the obvious facts – that he read the classical political economists closely and carefully and that he developed his own understanding of capitalism through, and in distinction to, their works. Nonetheless, aside from a general gesture in the direction of Smith and Ricardo, it is surprising how rarely the fact of Marx's engagement with political economy actually shapes or influences the interpretation of Marx on offer. In other words, showing that we have taken seriously the idea that the *Darstellung* of political economy is also the *Kritik* of the logic of capital requires a concrete payoff in the form of the reading of Marx. What do we see differently in Marx? Where are we encouraged to look in his corpus? How ought we to approach it?

To produce that payoff, I focus on a text in which Marx does much more than mention political economy generically, a text where Marx provides his own focused genealogy of classical political economy. This is Marx's published work of 1859, *Zur Kritik der Politischen Ökonomie*, appearing half a century later in English as *A Contribution to the Critique of Political Economy* (1904).[6] This book has been doubly eclipsed: first by *Capital* and then by the so-called *Grundrisse* (both of which in a way "contain" *Zur Kritik* in their own titles[7]). The latter text is often *presumed to be* more saturated by Hegelian philosophy than it is engaged with classical political economy,[8] while the former work removes, or confines to the footnotes,[9] most of the direct evidence of that very engagement. *Zur Kritik* hits the sweet spot: It retains a sharp focus on, and for the most part only on, the work of classical political economy. At the same time, *Zur Kritik* offers ample confirmation that Marx's further development of his own understanding of the logic of capital did not entail starting over from scratch or otherwise abandoning the general approach whereby Marx advanced his understanding of capital *through* an engagement with the work of classical political economy. The best evidence here is surely the extent to which the opening chapter of *Capital, Vol. I* closely tracks the first chapter of *Zur Kritik* (Rubin, 2008 [1928]).

Here, I narrow my focus even more tightly, to look at an entire section of *Zur Kritik* that has no presence at all in *Capital. Zur Kritik* begins almost exactly as *Capital* does: In both books, chapter one is titled "The commodity," and the opening sentence of the latter book is only a slight extension of the exact same sentence in the former book. Many have analyzed the subtle historical and textual details of the evolution of Marx's thought over the course of the various versions of this chapter, but the most glaring difference between *Zur Kritik* and *Capital* appears at the end of the chapter: where *Capital* moves straight to chapter two, *Zur Kritik* contains an unexpected *supplément* in the form of a section titled "Historisches zur Analyse der Ware."

English translations of *Zur Kritik* have not known quite what to do with this section. In the original German, the section appears as an organic part of the chapter, marked off with the lettered heading "A," but otherwise integrated into chapter one. And a section titled "Historical analysis of the commodity" (a literal translation, but also a straightforwardly obvious one to choose) seems a fitting continuation of a chapter on "the commodity." Indeed, as I will argue, it offers just the needed, clarifying genealogical context for Marx's critical presentation of the commodity in the earlier parts of the chapter. On my reading of Marx – not just in this text, but as a whole – the *historical analysis of commodities is essential to any contemporary understanding of commodities within a capitalist social order.* Commodities are not timeless objects, nor are they the primary building blocks of a capitalist system; commodities are historical productions of capitalism, at the very same time as they provide the conditions of possibility for capitalism itself. The *Darstellung* of the history of commodities is therefore the *Kritik* of the capitalist logic that circulates commodities.

But this is not at all how the English translations present this section. Most acutely, both translations change the title of the section in a way that marks it as supplemental, perhaps even unnecessary. The more recent, 1970, translation by Ryazanskaya (2009) – widely available through the marxist.org website – comes closest to the German with its "Historical notes on the analysis of commodities." It thus does far better than Stone's original translation (1904), which strangely renders the section title, "Notes on the history of the theory of commodities" – somehow suggesting that Marx meant "theory" (*Theorie*) when he clearly wrote "analysis" (*Analyse*). In any case, the appearance of a "historical notes" heading at the end of chapter one signals decidedly to the reader that the section is ancillary, appendix-like. The heading says that what follows are merely historical footnotes to the primary work done in the main body of the chapter. Indeed, the online version of the Ryazanskaya's translation actually places the entire section *after the endnotes* from chapter one.[10] Such a staging surely tempts the reader to approach the section like so many of Marx's "notebooks" from the same period. Those notebooks included outlines and sketches of engagements with other authors that Marx himself eventually discarded in favor of his final, published formulation. The problem with this framing is obvious, however, since unlike the so-called *1844 Manuscripts*, or the *Grundrisse*, or *The German Ideology*, all texts that were published after (often long after) Marx's death, and that in most cases were editorial constructions, not "books Marx wrote" – in contrast to all of that, *Marx himself published Zur Kritik* in his own lifetime (Carver & Blank, 2014a, p. 80; Marx & Engels, 1987, 1970). We thus have every reason to believe that this section at the end of chapter one contains material that Marx thought was essential to the argument, not preparatory or auxiliary. In the terms I have been developing here, this would mean that Marx saw the genealogy of political economy's treatment of the commodity as central to his own conceptual articulation of the commodity within a capitalist social formation. Hence, I will now trace the historico-analytic map that Marx draws, thereby starting with his genealogy, rather than with his more abstract and decontextualized presentation of "the commodity" as it appears not only at the beginning of *Zur Kritik* but also in the various editions of *Capital*.

THE GENEALOGY OF CAPITALIST VALUE

Marx's main goal in this portion of the chapter seems to be less to sort through the political economists' broad understandings of the commodity, and instead to home in on their specific sense of the relation between three terms/objects within capitalism: value, the commodity, and labor. For Marx, there is something of a progress narrative to be told in charting the history of political economy from the late 17th to the mid-19th century. As each theorist builds from the work of his predecessors and quarrels with his contemporaries, so he comes closer to getting something *right* about this relationship, to grasping the very nature of value under capitalism. Thus, Marx's genealogy can itself be boiled down to a series of theses defended by the various political economists, each of which asserts the relationship between value and commodities in terms of labor.

Marx starts with Petty,[11] who, writing a century before Smith, first lays claim to the central importance of "division of labor" as productive of material wealth. In Marx's eyes Petty's work is important, and genuinely deserves the title of "political economy ... as a separate science," because Petty, unlike Hobbes, sees that within an emerging bourgeois social formation, value can be produced in a way that is not determined by "natural factors" (Marx, 2009 [1859], p. 22).[12] For Marx this means that commodity value has a "*social aspect*." The importance of this "social aspect" absolutely cannot be underestimated. In specifying this dimension, Marx indicates to his readers that we must trace the value of a commodity not to something physically inherent or naturally integral to the object itself, but rather to something about the larger social order that would produce, distribute, exchange, and consume such commodities (Marx, 2009, p. 115, emphasis added; cf. Murray, 1999, 2000).[13] Petty, however, makes a mistake common to his day, and in a distinct way, even to our own: "he accepts exchange-value as it *appears* in the exchange of commodities" (Marx, 2009, p. 22). Much like we do today, Petty sees market value as the truth of value, but more to the point, in Petty's own time period, to assume the truth of market value was to mistakenly take gold itself for value. Of course, as I underlined above, all of the political economists share the goal of going outside of market exchange itself in order to locate the *source* of market (i.e., commodity) value. In Petty's case that means finding value literally in gold. And here Petty can only resort, according to Marx, to locating the value of gold (and thus of all commodities) within "the particular kind of concrete labor by which gold" is mined from the earth (Marx, 2009, p. 22). In other words, for Petty the source of market value is exchange, which depends upon gold, and the source of gold's value is the labor of mining. Marx does not even bother to say to the reader explicitly how nonsensical he finds such a conclusion; general value under capitalism cannot be traced to any one, specific type of concrete labor (there is no magical property of mining for gold).

Boisguillebert sees the other side of the coin (no pun intended), as he recognizes that exchange-value cannot be traced to any concrete labor practices, but must instead be understood in terms of an abstract labor time. This is, indeed, a great advance in grasping value under capitalism, but as Marx reads him, Boisguillebert remains hopelessly confused because he cannot clearly perceive the difference between, on the one hand, the production of commodities for exchange (the production of use-values for exchange, use-values understood in terms of their exchange-value, i.e., capitalist production), and, on the other, the direct production of a use-value as a "material substance of wealth" (Marx, 2009, p. 22). Marx portrays Boisguillebert as trapped in the Old World, wishing to affirm bourgeois labor (the labor that produces commodities as exchange-values) while railing against bourgeois forms of wealth (particularly money).

The breakthrough in grasping bourgeois relations could only come from a (naive) New World man. Marx credits Benjamin Franklin with nothing less than "formulat[ing] the basic law of modern political economy ... he declares it necessary to seek another measure of value than the precious metals, and that this measure is labor" (Marx, 2009, p. 23). Franklin is the first, says Marx, to free himself from the temptation to think of value in terms of gold and silver, and this enables him to establish not a natural or universal law (not even a law of capitalism) but a *law of political economy*: Franklin was the very first to "deliberately and clearly (*so clearly as to almost be trite*) reduce exchange-value to labor time" (Marx, 2009, p. 23, emphasis added).

What does it mean to call this a "reduction" (a "trite" one at that) and what sort of force could effect this reduction – Franklin, capital, Marx? To arrive at an answer, Marx must first bring into view what Franklin misses. Marx treats Franklin as an "idiot savant," who was never taken seriously as a political economist and did not influence the field directly. Franklin thus fails to perceive the potential breakthrough offered by his insight into capitalist exchange. Nevertheless, Franklin sees that capitalist exchange is effectively the exchange of quantities of labor for other quantities of labor, and therefore the only *possible* measure of value within capitalism is labor time. The question Franklin thereby brings to the fore (without himself realizing it) is the key question for Marx: *What type of labor is exchanged in capitalism* – and relatedly, how does a bourgeois social order make such exchange possible in the first place?

Franklin cannot answer this question, first, because he has no sense whatsoever of production – "the transformation of actual products into exchange-values is taken for granted" – and he therefore, second, cannot grasp the transformation, the *revolution* in production wrought by capitalism. (More than any other thinker of this time period, Marx stresses the fact that what really changes under capitalism is not the general idea of market exchange, but the fundamental nature of production.) More importantly, Franklin's blindness to the transformative effects of a bourgeois social order also prevents him from coming to a deeper understanding of labor. Like Smith, as we shall see, Franklin is tempted by the notion that labor is, or partakes of, some essence; this would make "labor-time" the source of value because of the nature of labor itself. Marx will slyly suggest something radically different: that "labor itself" should really always be understood as "labor under capitalism" or labor within a particular historical conjuncture. In other words, there is no such thing as labor *itself*, but only labor as it operates within a particular social order.

Marx articulates this claim – subtly at first, and then more forcefully – by referring to a particular type of object, an object produced by a capitalist social formation (Chambers, 2014, pp. 2–8). We can pick out this profound point in Marx's reading of Franklin by taking care to note the conceptual and terminological work that Marx does here, yet to bring the claims out clearly we will need to work our way past what the English translations might unintentionally obscure. In his most forceful concluding remarks, Marx tells his reader that Franklin "fails to see the intrinsic connection between money," on the one hand, and "*Tauschwert setzende Arbeit*," on the other (Marx, 2009, p. 23). What is "*Tauschwert setzende Arbeit*" and how is it intrinsically connected to money? The phrase is hard to render in smooth English because in it labor (*Arbeit*) is modified by both the noun "exchange-value" (*Tauschwert*) and the present participle "positing" (*setzende*). A literal translation would thus be "exchange-value-setting-labor" or "exchange-value-positing-labor."

I will return to the question of translation shortly, but first I want to clarify that throughout *Zur Kritik* Marx repeatedly refers to *Tauschwert setzende Arbeit* as the unique historical production of a bourgeois society. Only under capitalism does this particular element, *Tauschwert setzende Arbeit*, make its first appearance. As I read Marx, he wishes to underscore the novelty of this production and to emphasize its historical specificity. Therefore, rather than saying that labor (a transhistorical force) takes on new features or gains new capacities, Marx argues instead that through complex historical development a completely new type of object emerges, and that object is *Tauschwert setzende Arbeit*. The phrase appears over and over again throughout the entirety of the book; one could even argue that *the conceptual innovation* of *Zur Kritik* lies here, with Marx's discovery of *Tauschwert setzende Arbeit* as the unique object produced by a capitalist social order.

With this in mind, one can consider the translation. The multiple hyphens of the literal translation, exchange-value-setting-labor, is ungainly, and so one can easily understand why the English translators looked for alternatives that would scan better. Ryazanskaya chooses "labor which posits exchange-value" and Stone picks "labor which produces exchange-value." In an overall functional sense, neither translation is wrong: both translations have Marx, in his discussion of Franklin, comparing two objects – money on the one hand, and a unique type of labor on the other. That is, in English "labor which posits" or "labor which sets" exchange-value is still itself a grammatical object. Nonetheless, the English translations have made a subtle change that matters: in order to create a smoother-reading English prose, these translations sacrifice a crucial element of Marx's conceptualization and they make it easier to miss or to misread one of the central points of his account. The translations have substituted for the German participle *setzende* the English phrase "which sets" (or "which posits"). That is, rather than go directly to an English participle, "setting," the translations give a relative pronoun, "which," followed by a present tense verb, "sets." All of this matters because it places an active verb (*sets* or *posits*) in the center of the phrase, giving the false appearance of labor functioning as an active force,[14] rather than portraying it as a particular kind of object produced by a bourgeois society.

Readers of the English translation can thus easily lose a sense of the very specific, highly particular *type of object* Marx is delineating here: exchange-value-positing-labor, or exchange-value-producing-labor. The difference is not merely semantic. Rather than identifying particular capacities that a generic labor has (to do certain things or achieve particular ends), and rather than describing a distinct aspect or property of labor itself, Marx is pointing to the *unique type* of labor under capitalism. In this sense the awkwardly hyphenated term proves to be utterly appropriate, since the hyphens (in English) call attention to the distinct, peculiar nature of this object, an object only possible under the definite conditions created within a capitalist social formation.

This conclusion needs to be underscored: Capitalist labor proves to be a strange sort of labor. It is for just this reason that there can be an intrinsic connection – the connection Franklin thoroughly misses – between money and the type of labor we see in capitalism, exchange-value-positing-labor. That is to say, *there is no inherent link between money and labor itself*, and so Franklin's inability to see the specific peculiarity of labor within capitalism is of a piece with his incapacity to grasp the link between money and exchange-value-setting-labor.

Many writers after Franklin never even attempt to grasp this link because they explain value within emerging bourgeois society by looking for the concrete elementary particle (or practice) that would be the generative source of such value. For the physiocrats the answer is land itself; for the 18th-century economist James Steuart it is, for example, "the silver in the silver filigree, its '*intrinsic worth*'" (Marx, 2009, p. 24, quoting Steuart, 1807 [1767], p. 361). We might understand these blunt, empiricist answers – "empiricist" because they seek the intrinsic value of commodities in some concrete substance – as products of the period of transition; these thinkers hold on to feudal understandings of wealth while trying to make sense of the newly emerging sense of value under capitalism.

Despite his confusions, Steuart, Marx tells us, also sees through the fog to reach some striking insights. Steuart benefits from being able to witness the *emergence* of a capitalist social order, allowing him to observe the "*difference* between bourgeois and feudal labor" (Marx, 2009, p. 24, emphasis added). Marx thereby derives a powerful insight from Steuart: "the commodity as the elementary and primary unit of wealth, and alienation as the predominant form of appropriation are characteristic only of the bourgeois period of production, so exchange-value-positing-labor is specifically bourgeois" (Marx, 2009, p. 24, translation modified). Marx again returns to the phrase *Tauschwert setzende Arbeit*, but here he goes further to underscore the point that exchange-value-positing-labor belongs in particular to a capitalist social order. It is *specifically bourgeois*. At this stage in his genealogy Marx grows more emphatic; the idea of labor creating, producing, or positing exchange-value is not a metaphysical truth – it is not something intrinsic to labor itself (cf. Mandel, 1990 [1976], loc822). Exchange-value-setting-labor is bourgeois labor – labor as it manifests in a social order structured by the logic of capital. Ryazanskaya's translation helps here, as he renders "*spezifisch bürgerlich*" as "a specifically bourgeois feature." This language has Marx (rightly, I contend) suggesting to his readers that the very capacity for labor to produce exchange-value depends upon the structural dimensions of a social order centered on, and driven by, the logic of capital. In brief: Only under capitalism can labor create exchange-value, because only capitalism creates the object Marx calls *exchange-value-positing-labor*.

This crucial historical contextualization effected by Marx's reading of Steuart simultaneously provides him with the background against which he will address the work of the most famous (to us) and most important (for him) political economists, Smith and Ricardo. Hence Smith's answer to the question of how to understand the value of commodities appears squarely within the context of Steuart's establishment of the fact that exchange-value-producing-labor is not an ontological fact but a definite historical construction of specific capitalist practices. And Smith's significance to political economy's development cannot be dissociated from his own conceptual slippages. Ironically, Smith's impact on the history of thought on capitalism (and value) is bound up with the fact that his own text lacks a clear thesis on value and commodities for the precise reason that it offers not one, but two, conflicting theses. Smith's major contribution to our understanding of capitalism, as Marx tells the story in numerous places, comes from his formalization of the inchoate understanding articulated by Franklin. Smith gives his readers, and future political economists, the concept of "labor in general" – an intellectual production that Marx elsewhere unequivocally names "an immense step forward" (Marx, 1996, p. 149; see Chambers, 2014, pp. 98–105). Going back to Petty, Marx makes it clear that "labor in general" should be understood as "the entire *social aspect* of labor as it appears," particularly within the very division of labor that Smith unceasingly celebrates (Marx, 2009, p. 24, emphasis added).

This means that *as Marx reads him,* Smith's "labor in general" is absolutely not "labor itself." Paradoxically, as Marx explains elsewhere, "labor in general" is a particular historical form of labor (Marx, 1996, p. 151; Chambers, 2014, p. 103). Labor in general [*Arbeit überhaupt*] is exchange-value-positing-labor (Marx, 2009, p. 7). This labor can be grasped as "general" in contradistinction to concrete labor practices, which are specific, but it is decisively not transhistorical – not a philosophical essence, not a Platonic *eidos*. Labor in general is not "labor itself" in a transcendental sense because labor in general only emerges within a capitalist social formation, only first appears as a particular, historical type of labor, exchange-value-producing-labor.

Smith, however, sees almost none of the above points. For him, having established the facticity of "labor in general" as if it were a metaphysical truth (rather than a historical one) Smith then equivocates, or confuses himself (the text is not determinative here). Working in both cases with the idea of labor in general, Smith makes two competing claims. On the one hand, he contends that the value of commodities is determined by the labor (*sans phrase*) contained within them, that is, required for their production: "what everything really costs to the man who wants to acquire it, is the toil and trouble of acquiring it" (Smith, 1999 [1776], p. 31). On the other hand, he asserts that the value of commodities can be understood in terms of the labor that they themselves can buy or control – that is, by the amount of labor one can exchange them for: "The value of any commodity, therefore, to the person who possesses it … is equal to the quantity of labour which it enables him to purchase or command" (Smith, 1999, p. 31).

Yet, Smith himself does not propose these as two *alternatives*. Rather – and as Marx sees it, much to his detriment – Smith seems to think that the two accounts are compatible (perhaps even that they are the same). Indeed, the two quotes I have given above to illustrate each of Smith's two respective articulations of the value of commodities appear back-to-back in Smith's own text. He presents them not as two distinct theses, but as different formulations of the same claim. Nonetheless, the two positions are neither the same nor equivalent. In his own exegesis of Smith here, Marx moves quite quickly (not giving the quotes I provide, above). More to the point, Marx does not even bother to detail what he surely thinks is obvious (and which he remarks on in greater detail in different contexts):[15] The amount of labor time necessary to produce a commodity does not equal the value of that commodity when translated into a certain number of wage hours. For example, if it takes four labor hours to produce commodity A, and the going wage rate is $5/hour, there is simply no reason to assume that the value/price of A will be $20. In fact, as other political economists (including, but by no means solely Marx) show, there is every reason to believe that the price of the commodity will exceed $20. Furthermore, were that price not to exceed $20, that fact would itself be taken as evidence of a firm on its way out of business – or perhaps as a sign of a temporarily dysfunctional market (one in which supply has by no means "equilibrated" demand).

Marx condenses his entire presentation of Smith into a succinct formulation of the Smithian contradiction (between the two theses on the value of commodities in terms of labor), and then Marx suggests that the explanation for Smith's own confusion can be linked to Smith's failure to understand the "social aspect" of production under capitalism. Here is the key quote from Marx (2009, p. 25):

> Adam Smith constantly confuses the determination of the value of commodities by the labour-time contained in them with the determination of their value by the value of labour; … he mistakes the objective equalisation of unequal quantities of labour forcibly brought about by the social process for the subjective equality of the labours of individuals.

In the first sentence Marx is merely pointing to the contradiction in Smith's two claims that I have unpacked in greater detail above. To be sure, this argument comes directly from Ricardo, who builds his project of political economy on a patient and detailed delineation of the Smithian inconsistency; much of Ricardo's greatest contribution to the field of political economy emerges out of his explanation for why one of Smith's theses is valid, the other invalid (Ricardo, 1996 [1821], pp. 9–10). Marx does more than claim that Smith is in contradiction with himself; having read Ricardo, Marx takes that point as obvious to any student of political economy. Marx goes further, in that he explains what leads Smith into this impasse: Smith's confusion of the value of commodities with the value of labor *depends upon a logically prior confusion* of (A) the objective process by which a capitalist social formation "forcibly" renders "unequal quantities" of labor somehow *equal* to one another and (B) the idea that distinct, concrete labors of individuals could somehow be the same, be "equal."

Any effort to grasp Marx's own understanding of value in relation to labor and capital depends on discerning how and why Marx sees (A) as not simply valid but essential to capitalism and (B) as not simply wrong but deeply confused and mystifying with respect to our conceptual comprehension of a capitalist order. To elucidate Marx's position, we need first to make some sense of his frustrating use of, and repetition of the word "equal." For Marx, we might say that capitalism is that social order that accomplishes the "equalisation" of distinct, "unequal" quantities of labor. "Equalization" here refers to the process by which commodities can be equated to one another because they can be exchanged. Under capitalism, and only under capitalism, three pairs of socks can be "equal to" two cans of soup. "Unequal quantities," therefore, simply means different quantities, but the point – and the otherwise awkward way of putting the point; that is, the reason Marx says "unequal" rather than different – is a deeper one. We know that $3 \neq 2$, and yet we also know that, within the terms of a capitalist market, 3 pairs of socks = 2 cans of soup can be an utterly valid equation. This is just the sense in which Marx declares that the "objective equalisation of unequal quantities" is the profound result of capitalism. As the quote from above indicates, the process is both *objective* and *social,* and it depends on *force*. This already demonstrates that there is nothing in the nature of commodities themselves that would inherently or inexorably lead to this process. And this is just why Marx, at the same time as he affirms part of Smith's analysis – part (A) – remains adamant, contra Smith, that the labor of the shoemaker and the labor of the carpenter are not the same. In the sense that they produce utterly different use-values, they could never be equal, since making a shoe and building a house are not the same activities (and neither are needing shoes and needing shelter the same needs).

Why does Smith make such an obvious, rudimentary mistake? This question seems crucially important, yet Ricardo never poses it. Neither does Marx, despite the fact that Marx's own analysis makes an answer to the question possible. Of course, there could be numerous hypothetical explanations, but I want to work though the most viable candidate for a response by building from my reading of Marx. From that perspective, Smith contradicts himself due to his own failure to conceptualize labor in general as the particular type of labor (exchange-value-positing-labor) that it is and must be. In other words, Smith often implies that labor in general simply is labor itself (a generic and transhistorical force); if this were so, then the general labor required to produce a commodity and the general labor such a commodity commands would necessarily be equal. The equation would be validated not by the economic arithmetic but by metaphysical definitions. Marx contributes to the explanation as follows: "[Smith] tries to accomplish the transition from concrete labour to exchange-value-positing-labor, i.e., the basic form of bourgeois labour, by means of the division of labour" (Marx, 2009, p. 25, translation modified). Smith repeatedly calls on the division of labor as a sort of *magical force*. These are my words, but I do not use them casually or hyperbolically. Smith's own text gives the reader this sense of the inherent, overwhelming power of the division of labor. Here, Marx is suggesting that Smith desires a division of labor that serves as a fundamental force, to effect the transition from distinct concrete labors (the shoemaker and the carpenter) to labor *sans phrase*, which as Marx has shown is precisely exchange-value-setting-labor. But because Smith cannot see that labor in general is not labor itself, that *Arbeit überhaupt* can never be anything other than *Tauschwert setzende Arbeit*, he thus goes on to ascribe the same sort of transhistorical force to the division of labor that he thinks resides within labor in general.

Despite its central importance to his overall account, Marx's critical reply to Smith may appear elliptical to some readers. My conceptual and exegetical work above throws Marx's criticism into sharper relief: "But though it is correct to say that individual exchange presupposes division of labour, it is wrong to maintain that division of labour presupposes individual exchange" (Marx, 2009, p. 25). Marx contends that in order to have capitalist exchange of commodities, one must already have a developed division of labor; one cannot conceive of producing objects for their "inherent" exchange-value – making them only in order to sell them – without assuming a division of labor, and this is because exchange-value is never "inherent" but always *social*. However, the reverse is not at all true. Logically, one could easily imagine a social order with a highly advanced division of labor in which goods are produced (even traded) directly for their use-values (or perhaps on some other basis entirely). Each labor, divided though they may be, would be a concrete labor, not labor in general. The labor of workers would be specific to their trade because exchange-value-positing-labor would not exist. (Marx's text also offers the historical example of the Peruvians as a society with a highly developed division of labor, but no capitalist circulation of commodities.) In other words, one can only have exchange-value-positing-labor against a background of a given division of labor. The division of labor neither gives rise to a type of labor which *produces* exchange-value nor does it constitute the object, exchange-value-setting-labor. Smith's mistake is that he thinks the "labor in general" developed by bourgeois society is nothing other than a "labor itself" as it has appeared throughout time and across all space.

As Marx reads him, Ricardo overcomes Smith's error, yet then manages to repeat it in even more egregious form. Ricardo exceeds Smith in his clear articulation of the historical preconditions required for the emergence of exchange-value-positing-labor. Explicating Ricardo, Marx writes: "the full development of the law of value [*Gesetz des Wertes*] presupposes a society in which large-scale industrial production and free competition obtain, in other words modern bourgeois society" (Marx, 2009, p. 25). Despite this apparent insight, Ricardo spends much of his time projecting all of the features of "modern bourgeois" society back onto historical or mythical times and places. And Marx cannot help but mock Ricardo for the profound depth of anachronistic thinking, for taking "primitive" fishers and hunters as modern "owners of commodities," such that they "calculate the value of their implements in accordance with the annuity tables used on the London Stock Exchange in 1817" (Marx, 2009, p. 25).

Thus we might say, in the language I have been developing here, that Ricardo's analysis contains the evidence needed to demonstrate the distinction – the very difference Smith continuously elides – between, on the one hand, labor in general as the form of appearance of exchange-value-positing-labor and, on the other, the transhistorical "labor itself" *hypostatized* by Smith. Yet, Ricardo himself fails to grasp the implications of that evidence and thereby winds up with even worse hypostatizations than Smith before him.

THE "FORM OF VALUE" UNDER CAPITALISM

Where does Marx's genealogical reading of the political economists take us with respect to the general question of the relation between labor and value under capitalism? Overall, Marx wishes to affirm the idea that a bourgeois social formation produces a new, unique type of labor: exchange-value-positing-labor. More importantly, the type of labor that can itself "produce" or "set" exchange-value is absolutely not any sort of particular, concrete form of labor; neither sewing clothes, nor mining gold ore, nor any other specific form of labor can be understood as exchange-value-positing-labor. Only labor in general (*Arbeit überhaupt*) is exchange-value-setting-labor (*Tauschwert setzende Arbeit*). Perhaps most significantly, "labor in general" is itself a highly developed form of labor, one that emerges exclusively under a capitalist social order – only where there develops a certain "indifference" to the type of labor done since all labor is labor for the production of commodities (exchange-values) and all labor is wage labor (Marx, 1996, p. 150; see Murray, 1999, p. 45). But this set of facts entails something crucially important for Marx: Labor in general, a monumental developmental achievement of capitalism, is not, and can never be conflated with "labor itself." Smith's error, repeated by Ricardo, is the failure to see the difference between, on the one hand, a generalized abstract labor that takes shape *within* capitalism and, on the other, a generic idea of a transhistorical labor – an idea of labor as an essential metaphysical force for all time and place.

At the end of the genealogical journey, we can productively turn our attention to the so-called LTV. The LTV is a textbook answer to the question, as I summarized it at the very beginning, "where does value come from?" According to the LTV, value comes from labor, which has an intrinsic, essential – indeed, universal – power to bestow value on the objects it produces. The innate source of the value *in* commodities is thus the labor required to create those commodities in the first place; value in society can be traced directly to labor as its source. The LTV provides a straightforward, concise, and sharp account of value in relation to capitalist commodities, and it generalizes this account to an understanding of value across all time and place. Moreover, from Marx's genealogical reading of the political economists, we can witness numerous ways in which those thinkers might be seen to articulate, support, or subscribe to the LTV. Smith, in particular, sees "labor itself" as the source of value, and thereby offers a general, metaphysical account of value – both under capitalism and elsewhere.

Marx's genealogy of the political economists therefore makes it starkly, unquestionably clear that he himself does not endorse, support, or in any way subscribe to *this classical version of LTV*.[16] At its core, the LTV rests on an idea of "labor itself," the very concept that Marx takes Smith (and Ricardo) to task for endorsing. Marx's insistence on the contrast between "labor in general" and "labor itself," his account of exchange-value-setting-labor as the *historical achievement* of capitalism, and his refusal of the idea that different concrete labors (e.g., weaving and painting) could be "equalized" – all of this amounts to a thoroughgoing rejection of the LTV. Indeed, Marx's genealogical account of classical political economy gives us the perspective needed to see the LTV as a rather strange idea – to understand its theoretical status. For Marx, labor has no intrinsic, metaphysical powers that would allow it to "create value." The classical political economists saw labor as the source of value, in the sense of an *Ursprung*, a metaphysical origin. Marx saw it differently, because his genealogy refused the idea of an *Ursprung* to begin with; he rejected the idea of what I would call an "elementary particle" – something that could stand outside the social formation and explain its development.[17] These central and significant differences make Marx's critique a wholesale displacement of the paradigm of classical political economy, a whole new way to understand value in a social order itself – not some minor quibbling over the particular way the political economists saw it. The creation of value under capitalism is always, for Marx, a systemic effect of a capitalist social order.

But the question of how to understand value under capitalism cannot be reduced to an either/or choice vis-à-vis the LTV. And, indeed, there are good reasons why Marx has so often, and so consistently been *misread* as somehow articulating his own version of the LTV. To see why, I want to look more closely at Marx's understanding of "the law of value" that he points to in his reading of Ricardo, and to analyze how this relates to his larger understanding of the "form of value" under capitalism. To put it succinctly: *Marx is mistaken for an LTV theorist precisely because his goal is not merely to refute the LTV, but to show how something like the LTV could emerge within capitalism in the first place.*[18] To unpack this formulation requires stepping back from the particulars of Marx's reading of the classical political economists to take a wider view of his understanding of value and the value-form (*Wertform*).

The histories of various schools of interpretation of Marx, not to mention Marxism, prove multiply fractured and highly complex. I will not provide a contextualist reconstruction of all those histories. However, I think it safe to say that today we can trace the tradition of value-form reading of Marx, or "value-form theory" (VFT), to the early work and lasting influence of Hans-Georg Backhaus, a student of Adorno whose 1965 seminar work is now seen as the source-point for what would later become VFT, also known as *neue Marx-Lektüre* (NML).[19] Since the development of the NML, many well-known and well-respected figures have continued to read and to criticize Marx as either subscribing to the LTV, endorsing his own version of it, or otherwise seeing value as an "objective" or "physiological" property of commodities (Carver, 1998; Keen, 1993; Wolff, 1981). But the conclusions I have drawn above – that Marx absolutely departs from an LTV, that his task is not to modify that theory but to explain its very emergence – would come as no surprise whatsoever to value-form theorists. Indeed, the central point of departure for a VFT reading of Marx lies in rethinking the very question of value and capitalism by analyzing the *form that value takes* under capitalism. The primary question is not so much what is the source of value, but "why value?" in the first place: "what are the conditions of possibility of the existence of value, which is an 'objective social dimension', according to which commodities are exchanged?" (Bellofiore & Redolfi Riva, 2015, p. 24). Marx does not try to show *that* labor is the source of value, but rather to ask *why* that should be so within a capitalist social formation. Patrick Murray helpfully formulates the point by referring to "Marx's idea that value comes not from labour but from a *historically specific form* of labour" (Murray, 1999, p. 34). In some ways this formulation seems like nothing more than a matter of emphasis, reflected in Murray's own use of italics, but the implications prove profound.

Backhaus's early article, "On the Dialectics of the Value-Form," makes a forceful case for the subtlety of Marx's account of value in terms of the value-form. Moreover, Backhaus strongly suggests that part of the difficulty in grasping Marx's conception of the value-form – the aspect of his argument that Marx himself always maintained was the most difficult to understand (Marx, 1990 [1887], loc1589) – was that Marx, in effect, "dumbed down" his presentation as he repeatedly revised it.[20] Indirectly, then, Backhaus points readers of Marx back to the text that I have taken as my central focus here: According to Backhaus, *Zur Kritik* contains the first developed presentation of Marx's value-form analysis, and, I would add, perhaps the one that most maintains the dynamic, dialectical element that is essential to understanding Marx's sense of the historical development of a capitalist social formation.[21] Backhaus cites *Zur Kritik* extensively in order to advance his own account of the value-form,[22] and I have tried to show in my reading that the focus on *Zur Kritik* is no accident since it is there that Marx emerges most clearly as a genealogist.

LABOR, VALUE, AND STORIES CAPITALISM TELLS

The value-form approach dovetails with my genealogical reading since both allow us to see Marx as *diagnosing* the LTV, not arguing for, or even against it. Marx's central claim is that value under capitalism appears only in social form. This argument does not merely depart from the LTV; it turns it inside out. Moreover, the unravelling is not a mere debunking, since the uptake of my reading of Marx here does not lie only in a refutation of the LTV as an analytic, abstract theory; it comes in the form of a genealogical account of its emergence and functioning. Along with many other political economists, Ricardo and Smith both endorse the general idea that labor is the source of a commodity's value; labor is the answer to where value comes from. For them, we might say, the LTV functioned much like the myth of barter: as a foundation narrative for understanding the basic laws of capitalism. But Ricardo and Smith, as Marx says repeatedly, mistake the *social forms* of value under capitalism for *natural forms*; hence, they claim that labor's capacity to produce value is an inherent force of labor itself. It is this core idea that Marx refutes most powerfully. Crucially, however, he refutes it not analytically, not by opposing this theory with another that mirrors it. Marx's refutation is more radical because it takes the form of a genealogical unravelling of the LTV – a taking-apart that shows how it was put together. For Marx there is no such thing as "labor itself"; not even "labor in general" can be mistaken for labor itself.[23] Marx has no LTV because he has no "theory of value" (nor a "theory of labor") in the sense of an objective theory that would trace value to its ahistorical source (cf. Postone, 1993).

To see Marx as a genealogist is to see why the marginalist critique of the LTV is not a critique of Marx. Neoclassical economics, of course, does away with the LTV. Rather than entrenching the LTV as a founding tale (a good myth), it discards it as an outdated and entirely false theory (a bad myth). Thorstein Veblen coined the term "neo-classical school" in order, first, to *minimize* the gap between contemporary competing schools – Marshall's marginalism on the one hand, and the "Austrian school" on the other – as "scarcely distinguishable," and second to *maximize* the gap between these schools and both "the historical and Marxist schools." This second gap, Veblen emphasizes, "is wider, so much so, indeed, as to bar out a consideration of the postulates of the latter under the same head of inquiry with the former" (Veblen, 1900, p. 261). Veblen here makes two important moves at once: He lumps Marx in with the classical political economists, right before tossing the entire lot aside as simply incomparable with the work being done in early 20th-century economics. Marx thus becomes a supporter of the LTV just as the LTV is turned into an already refuted theory.

However, if Marx is not a theorist of labor or value, but a genealogist of the form of value as it emerges within particular social orders, then he clearly can neither affirm nor simply reject the LTV. To read Marx genealogically is therefore to make sense out of what some have seen as Marx's *peculiar* emphasis on both "the social" and the word "social." I previously noted that Marx begins his genealogy by underlining as most important in Petty's work this notion of the "social aspect" of the commodity. These lines themselves are only echoes of Marx's frequent repetition of this theme in the main pages of the chapter. Marx underscores "the specific way in which exchange-value-setting-labor, that is commodity-producing labor, is *social labor*" (Marx, 2009, pp. 7–8, my translation; see Bonefield, 1992). It should be obvious, however, that if we trace the "source" of value to social labor, then that so-called source is not an intrinsic feature of labor itself but instead must be understood as a specific dimension of the social order. In this context, Rubin makes a crucial comment: *not* "every distribution of social labor ... give[s] the product of labor the form of value" (Rubin, 2008, p. 72). The product of labor takes on the value-form – often itself a "deranged" form (Backhaus, 1992) – only in the unique structure of a capitalist society in which labor is "regulated" through the force of market circulation. Other societies can produce use-values, but value in the sense of the value-form only appears when commodities are "produced specifically for sale" such that they then take on the value-form when they appear as exchange-value. Only a capitalist commodity economy allows for the product of labor to be/become value. And only through his genealogical work can Marx show that labor does not create value in the metaphysical manner postulated by the LTV, yet a capitalist order does entail that labor take the form of value.

This account makes it possible to come to terms with the long history of otherwise brilliant, rigorous, and incisive readers of Marx who have found his account of value utterly lacking, from Eugen von Böhm-Bawerk to Ernst Mandel, from Robert Paul Wolff to Terrell Carver. To give the most concise formulation of the point, these readers mistake Marx's genealogy of the value-form for an ahistorical theory of value. For example, both Böhm-Bawerk, writing at the end of the 19th century, and Carver, writing at the end of the 20th, find hollow and dissatisfying (Carver calls it "circular") the idea that abstract labor somehow serves as the "common substance" that equalizes both the exchange of commodities and the various concrete forms of labor that produces those commodities (Böhm-Bawerk, 1966[1949], p. 68; Carver, 1998, p. 17). Yet, the genealogical reading of *Zur Kritik* makes it quite clear that Marx himself would find such an argument wanting: Abstract labor cannot "produce value"; exchange-value-setting-labor produces value, with the latter understood as a highly developed social form existing only under the historical conditions of capitalism.

Therefore, in response to the critique of Marx for adhering to an "old-fashioned" Aristotelian natural philosophy in which value is understood as the property of a material body, one must first simply clarify by saying that Marx never espouses such a position. And one can go on to stress that Marx himself was very much concerned to understand how such a position came to be within a capitalist social formation. Hence, the concept Marx calls "abstract labor" is not a philosophical concept, but a historical concept, a concrete abstraction. As Rubin argues, "abstract labor" has nothing to do with either physiological or psychological equality, but with "*a social equalization of different forms of labor*," which only comes about within a social formation structured by the logic of capital (Rubin, 2008, p. 75). What "kind of labor creates value"? Exchange-value-positing-labor, itself the achievement of the development of a capitalist social order. The answer to the question of what is the "common substance" that equalizes commodities under capitalism is not, therefore, to be provided *analytically by Marx*. To read him this way is to miss the point of his entire approach. The answer to that question is provided *dialectically by the historical development of a capitalist social formation*. "What renders commodities equal?" is not a philosophical question, but a historical one. And therefore the answer cannot simply be "labor." That would amount to an analytic answer that posits "labor itself" as having the "property" of "producing value." The answer must be a historical, genealogical one: Under capitalism, labor creates value, but only the abstract labor (labor in general) as a developed social form achieved by capitalist historical development; exchange-value-positing-labor is precisely "the kind of labor that creates value."

When it comes to the question of value (in relation to labor) under capitalism, Marx's task is therefore not to "find the right answer," but to analyze, to deconstruct and reconstruct, the very answer that the historical development of capitalist social formations has already provided in definite form. This is genealogical work. Rubin brings out this decisive notion by arguing that to understand capitalism we have to deal directly with "the entire *mechanism which connects value and labor*" (Rubin, 2008, p. 78). In other words, value is not traced to labor by way of metaphysics but through the system of capitalist production, distribution, exchange, and consumption – that is, through political economy itself. Like all "laws" of political economy, the so-called LTV is therefore not Marx's "theory," and in a way, it is not even Smith and Ricardo's theory; it is capitalism's theory.[24]

To read Marx as a genealogist of political economy is to track the production of the LTV as an abstract, ahistorical theory. Yet, in tracing its emergence, we simultaneously *reconnect the LTV to the history it pretends to transcend.* In other words, the work of genealogy can map the logic of ostensibly "objective" theory while at the same time making palpably clear that theory is not, in fact, either objective or ahistorical. Classical political economy's construction of a "theory of value" rooted in the ahistorical qualities of human labor depends directly upon precise historical conditions, namely the emergence of a bourgeois social formation in which value comes more and more to be determined by market-based exchanges of commodities, themselves produced specifically for those markets (for exchange). However, the "theory" within the texts of classical political economy consistently elides or ignores such history, instead taking the relations of value established by a capitalist social formation and projecting them back across time so as to pretend that they are universal, ahistorical. This genealogical reading illuminates myriad dimensions of the LTV, since we come to see it: as theory, as object of critique, and as a strange and peculiar tale unique to a capitalist social order. Above all, the turn to reading Marx as genealogist serves to demonstrate the deep and rich mutual imbrication of theory and history; theory emerges from a social order even as it tries to grasp the relations that constitute that order – relations that are themselves both historical and theoretical.[25]

NOTES

1. The phrase "labor theory of value" post-dates classical political economy, and I am suggesting here that idea of the LTV as an analytic theory that stands outside history also becomes consolidated much later – even if it does so by retroactively pulling together concepts and ideas that are indeed present in the texts of classical authors.

2. I distinguish my work here from a very different project of historical contextualism, one that might seek to chart the emergence within neoclassical economics of the idea (attributed to classical political economy) of the LTV as an abstract and substantialist theory of human labor power. In other words, I suspect that one could chart, through close readings of the marginalists, the time and manner by which the LTV shifts from being an older, yet still viable, explanation of capitalism, to being nothing more than 18th- and 19th-century "metaphysical nonsense" – but such is not my task here.

3. To read Marx as a genealogist is therefore also to set aside the problem of trying to get Marx's theory "correct" or make it "consistent." These latter tasks, it seems to me fair to say, adequately capture the project of those committed to so-called temporal single-sector interpretation (TSSI) of Marx. Kliman has described his own recent synthetic contribution to the TSSI as "the most accessible full-length treatment of the controversy over Marx's *value theory* to date"

(Kliman, 2007, p. xv, emphasis added). I have italicized Kliman's reference to "value theory" to highlight the fact that for the TSSI group, Marx's "value theory" is precisely an analytical "theory of X" in the way I have described above. This fact partially explains why Kliman could write such a line in the preface to a book that does not even cite *any* of the value-form theorists. (Of course the value-form reading of Marx has its roots in Germany and thus in German-language texts, and TSSI is mainly an English-language theoretical development, but Kliman also fails to mention major English-language interpreters of Marx on value such as Postone or Harvey.) None of this is meant as a substantive critique of TSSI, but merely as one explanation (along with the usual space and time constraints) of why I do not address it here. Indeed, it seems to me that there are some unexplored overlaps between TSSI and VFT, but there is undoubtedly also a major and perhaps incommensurable difference in approach.

4. As Tripp Rebrovick shows, the market had a reality and a certain force for the classical political economists, yet it was not a substantive, circumscribed domain, and it did not have metaphysical depth; relatedly, the "economy" as a domain of existence in the way we understand it today had not yet come into being (Rebrovick, 2016).

5. The above calls for two ancillary elaborations. First, some writers would explain Marx's move from the 1850s to the 1860s in terms of a shift from his "transitional works" to his "mature works" (Althusser, 1969), while others would explain all of Marx's developments as a march toward "science" (Engels, along with countless 20th-century Marxists). I accept that Marx changed his presentation, sometimes quite significantly, but I completely reject the idea that he did so in order to make that presentation more "scientific." Quite to the contrary, the evidence from Marx's letters and other writings indicates that above all else, Marx desired to make the presentation in *Capital Vol. I*, as *clear as possible* for the widest possible audience, and not at all to make it "more scientific." Marx's attempt to make himself understood as broadly as possible marks his work from early to late; see, for example, the clarifications of Marx's presentation of early drafts of *Capital* in his talk "Value, Price and Profit" (1995a). Ultimately, of course, Marx thought that the best way to present his discoveries about capitalism was *not* through genealogy; hence my clarification in the text above to the effect that reading Marx as a genealogist should not at all be confused with the notion that Marx himself meant to be a genealogist. None of this changes the basic fact that the emphasis on science surely comes after Marx, and while not all of the blame can be laid at Engels's feet, a great deal of it surely can (Carver, 2003, chapter 6; cf. Arthur, 2005). Second, a delimited reading of Marx as a genealogist opens up a number of avenues for fruitful comparison and contrast with much more famous genealogical thinkers – namely, Nietzsche and Foucault. In order to make the case that one *can* read Marx this way, I point to some of the comparisons, below, but I would not want to diminish the differences. In particular, both Nietzsche and Foucault point to something like an "art of the self," a creative and transformative *ethos*, that plays no real part in Marx's thought. Thanks to Bill Connolly and Patrick Giamario for help on this last point.

6. Marx also gives a genealogical-like presentation in *Theories of Surplus Value* (1969 [1863]), where he again works through the classical political economists one by one.

As I see it, the 1859 text holds an advantage because there we witness Marx engaging these thinkers while still discovering his own position, and so, in short, he offers a much more genuine *reading* in this earlier text. The later work places the political economists into little boxes that Marx has already worked out; it reads more like a post hoc summary. In contrast, *Zur Kritik* stages a genuine *encounter* between Marx and the thought of the political economists, allowing the reader of this earlier text to better capture Marx's thinking as it happens. In this context, see Carver and Blank (2014a, 2014b) on the process of producing the so-called *German Ideology*.

7. That is, in literal terms, "the critique of political economy" – to which *Zur Kritik* is a contribution – is the subtitle of *Capital Vol. I*, and the very thing that the *Grundrisse* outlines or sketches. The former text would seem to be the definitive, published presentation of Marx's critique of political economy, while the latter – in its size and scope and serious entwinement with Hegelian thought – would seem to be the widest and deepest presentation. *Capital* thus swallows up *Zur Kritik* in its subtitle, while the *Grundrisse* displaces *Zur Kritik* in its reification of the untranslated German word for "outlines." For more historical and conceptual discussion on treating the *Grundrisse* as a book of Marx's, if not *the* book of Marx's, in its own right see Chambers (2014) and Rozdolski (1977).

8. I reject the common presumption of a binary between Marx's interest in Hegel (understood as Hegelian *philosophy*) and his interest in political economy. As Carver forcefully argues, "Marx's detailed interest in Hegel was precisely in his [Hegel's] 'political economy'"; moreover, "'Hegelian philosophy' isn't intellectual or politically 'other' to Marx's detailed engagement with political economists, who aren't themselves absent in Hegel's work" (Carver, personal communication, 2016). My point in the text above is therefore not to reify such a binary, but merely to invoke its very real existence in the secondary literature on Marx, as a partial explanation for why the interpretive attention paid to the *Grundrisse* has sometimes come at the expense of careful analysis of Marx's own readings of the classical economists.

9. The distance between Marx's presentation of value and the commodity in *Zur Kritik* and that in *Capital* can be significantly reduced if one pays careful attention to the footnotes to Chapter 1 of *Capital*. There Marx preserves the running commentary on the classical political economists, and he emphasizes over and over the importance of the value-form. Indeed, and as I will discuss in much greater detail below, the standard reading of Marx as signing on to a (version of) the LTV depends upon ignoring the footnotes, since this is the place where Marx quite clearly delineates the insufficiency of such a theory. It is worth noting that these are some of the longest, most substantive footnotes in Marx's entire oeuvre.

10. The online German version of the text integrates the "Historical Analysis" section into the main body of the chapter and places all endnotes together. The paperback version of the Stone translation uses running footnotes.

11. Readers of Marx all know that he read and referenced Smith and Ricardo, but Marx's engagement with the field of political economy stretched back well beyond his 19th-century contemporaries. He opens this section by pointing out that the research outcomes of Marx's present could be traced to the work of Petty and Boisguillebert in the 17th century.

12. For the English translation, all my citations are to the online version of the Ryazanskaya translation of *Zur Kritik*. Retrieved from https://www.marxists.org/

archive/marx/works/1859/critique-pol-economy. This version has no obvious page numbers (or paragraph or section numbers); however, to help orient the reader, I will give page numbers of a standard printout of the website. In instances where I have modified the translation myself I have drawn from the online presentation of the German edition of *Zur Kritik* (Marx & Engels, 1971).

13. In the first chapter of *Zur Kritik*, Marx places enormous emphasis on *social labor*. And in exactly this context, Marx makes it clear that the "reduction" of value to abstract labor is not a philosophical reduction (or a philosophical abstraction) carried out by Marx, or any other thinker, it is a real reduction (and a real abstraction): "This reduction *appears* to be an abstraction, but it is an abstraction *which is made every day in the social process of production*" (Marx, 2009, p. 8, emphasis added).

14. This is not to deny that the English participle ("setting" or "positing," in this case) also takes on the verb form, but as a contemporary grammar guide explains, a participle is a verb form functioning as an adjective. Moreover, the "-ing" form of the participle also operates, in the case of gerunds, as a noun, and it operates as a verb only in the progressive tense – a tense that is much less direct and active than the present tense that appears in the English translation (CCCF, 2004). To boil this down: "setting-labor" *sounds like* some very odd or downright bizarre object, while "labor which sets" sounds like a description of labor doing something. The former sense, I argue, is exactly what Marx had in mind, while the latter is not even close.

15. The Smithian contradiction (resolved but not overcome by Ricardo) centers Marx's analysis in the "Value, Price and Profit" lecture, where it serves to construct the paradox that Marx's concept of "labor-power" sets out to resolve – or better, make manifest (Marx, 1995a [1898], p. 13).

16. This is not, of course, to say that Marx does not develop his own account of how value is established within a capitalist social formation *in relation to labor*. Thus, we might well claim that Marx has a theory of value that is related to labor, and some might want to go further to describe this as *Marx's own version* of the LTV. Logically, such a move is surely tenable, but for at least two reasons I choose not to make it. First, there is a long history of referring to Marx's version of the LTV as precisely the same as the classical LTV, so the reference to "Marx's LTV" would easily be mistaken for the very theory *and type of theorizing* that Marx himself rejected. Second, the phrase "labor theory of value" connotes something quite different than genealogy and is therefore misleading from the outset; LTV suggests the sort of metaphysical account whereby essential properties of things produce specific effects. Marx is producing a historical account, a genealogy of value under the specific and concrete terms of a capitalist social formation, and in this sense he has no general "theory," whether it be the LTV or anything else.

17. It is often thought that Marx identifies just such an elementary particle in his frequent references to "labor-power," and it would be easy enough to take "labor-power" as a physical force in nature, one that creates value. But especially in his later works, when Marx refers to "labor-power" he is not referring to the general "power of labor." For Marx, "labor-power" is an absolutely specialized term (arguably the most important such term in all of *Capital*), since it names/describes the unique historico-political creation of the one commodity that is essential to capitalism. "Labor-power," says Marx, is not a force, but a thing. It is a commodity –

and not just any commodity, but a unique commodity. Capitalists can use their access to large-scale means of production to produce commodities for exchange and sell them. During the transition to capitalism, small-crafts producers, calling on access to small-scale means of production, can also create commodities and sell them. But after the transition to developed capitalism, we witness the emergence, and the *production*, of an entire class of people with no capital, and no access to means of production. This class has no objective commodities to sell. Their only choice, then, is to work for a wage, an act that Marx redescribes – under the specific terms of capitalism in which everything is subject to market exchange – as a worker selling his "labor-power." Labor-power is the only commodity you have when you have no commodities at all. But this makes labor-power a specific product of capitalist historical development. It could not be further from a transhistorical force (cf. Rubin, 2008, p. 24).

18. Of course Marx is also mistaken for an LTV theorist because of the history of Marxism as a political movement on behalf of the working class, and because working class radical politics derived so much leverage and inspiration from a Ricardian LTV. Paul Mason nicely details the historical turn here: "after Ricardo, the labour-theory [of value] became the signature idea of industrial capitalism," being used to "justify profits" and "attack the landed aristocracy." But it soon thereafter "proved subversive. It created an argument for who gets what, which the factory owners immediately started to lose. Amid the candlelight of the pubs where the early trade unions met, David Ricardo suddenly had a whole new set of followers" (Mason, 2015, p. 148). Yet, we cannot hesitate to add: it is precisely what Mason calls the "doctrine of 'Ricardian socialism'" that Marx himself is at such pains to refute in his frequent attacks on socialist utopianism (Marx, 1995b, 1996).

19. The phrase *neue Marx-Lektüre* was first used by Backhaus himself in the preface to a collection of his essays (Backhaus, 1997; see Heinrich, 2012, p. 229). While, to repeat, there are no self-identified or consciously practicing schools here, we can say that NML and VFT are roughly "the same" because the "New Reading of Marx" hinges on reemphasizing Marx's understanding of the form of value. Often the general gloss for NML is that it departs from scientific or deterministic accounts of Marx in order to return to his critique of political economy and connect that project to his larger critique (or understanding) of society. To show how Marx does this, thinkers within the NML tradition attend closely to Marx's understanding of the value-form. Hence, in many ways NML names the broad approach to Marx, and VFT names the substantive pivot point. Both VFT and NML can be distinguished from, but also overlap with, *Wertkritik*, an approach developing somewhat later than (we now date) VFT, associated closely with the writings of Robert Kurz, focusing more on questions of reification or crisis, and more tightly linked to early forms of Frankfurt School Critical Theory. Backhaus's original seminar paper was translated and introduced more than a decade later by *Thesis Eleven* (Backhaus, 1980; Eldred & Hanlon, 1981). For a very recent and helpful overview of NML, see Bellofiore and Redolfi Riva (2015). For a recent text introducing *Wertkritik* to an English-speaking audience, see Larsen, 2014. My own work in the text below, concerning the emergence of VFT, focuses on Backhaus, but it needs to be said that he never worked in isolation: His original work was done under the supervision of Adorno, and a great deal of his output was completed in collaboration with Helmut Reichelt. I spend

some time on a description of VFT and its history in order to situate my reading of Marx, but I want to emphasize that this is a massive and growing literature, and here I only barely scratch its surface. For just a few examples of writings that I have found particularly influential, see Bidet (2007), Elson (1979), Campbell (1997), and Mosely and Campbell (1997). In this context let me also mention other political theorists who have recently written about VFT (Roberts, 2017; Vatter, 2014, Chapter 2).

20. "Dumbed down" are my words, not Backhaus's, but they effectively capture a line of argument that Backhaus has consistently advanced over the years, starting with his original rhetorical question "has Marx gone so far in his popularisation" of the opening sections of *Capital,* Vol. I, that the value-form can no longer be grasped? (Backhaus, 1980, p. 100; Reichelt, 1995, cited in Bonefield, 1998).

21. This move may not be as radical as it seems, since Marx himself points the way to it in his preface to the first German edition of *Capital.* There Marx both emphasizes the importance of the value-form – saying "the human mind has sought in vain for more than 2,000 years to get to the bottom of it" – and admits that the presentation of the value-form in *Capital* is a "popularized" version of the fuller account in *Zur Kritik* (Marx, 1990, loc1589).

22. I have tried to summarize briefly the overall VFT approach, in order to demonstrate that my own engagement with Marx follows a long tradition of reading Marx. My claims about the relationship between value and labor under capitalism are not necessarily all that new, even if they do fly in the face of still-canonized understandings of Marx as a critic of alienation and a celebrant of labor as the essential creator/producer of value. (Here I might productively contrast my approach with that of Moishe Postone (1993), whose analysis overlaps with mine, and with VFT, in numerous places and manners, but whose major work on Marx spends a large proportion of its time working out a "traditional Marxism," in contrast to which Postone's reading will appear radically new.) I should also make clear that the broader value-form reading of Marx applies not just to the texts that center my analysis here (mainly *Zur Kritik*). One can take the entire argument and work it back straight through *Capital* itself, as many VFT thinkers have done. Marx does not change his mind; he changes his formulation and presentation in a way that makes it easier to misread him on value. Backhaus points in just this direction, and other VFT and NML thinkers have done the work to demonstrate it. In this context, see also the crucial and lifelong work of Harvey (1982, 2005, 2010).

23. The semantic differences between these two terms are, of course, quite subtle. I have tried to mark clearly the conceptual difference in my account of Marx, without introducing new terminology. Murray goes the latter route, introducing the difference between "abstract labor" and "practically abstract labor" in an effort to make Marx's value-form approach sharper and more rhetorically forceful (Murray, 1999).

24. Rubin himself holds on to the nomenclature by which Marx himself "has" a labor theory of value. But as should be plainly evident, Rubin's reading of Marx on value thoroughly resignifies the meaning of such a claim. Indeed, for Rubin, what we would call "Marx's LTV" is not even really about labor or value; it concerns the fetishism of both, achieved as an actual fact by capitalism. "The labor theory of value did not discover the material condensation of labor (as a factor of production) in things which are the products of labor; this takes place in all

economic formations and is the technical basis of value but not its cause. The labor theory of value discovered the fetish, the reified expression of social labor in the value of things. Labor is 'crystallized' or formed in value in the sense that it acquires the social 'form of value'" (Rubin, 2008, p. 76).

25. Thanks to Tarak Barkawi for some of the language in these closing lines. Thanks also to George Lawson and to all the participants in the International Origins of Social and Political Theory workshop, held at the LSE in March 2016. This article also benefited from feedback at the Political and Moral Thought Seminar at Johns Hopkins in November 2016. Final and special thanks for crucial, timely help goes to Zachary Reyna and Rebecca Brown.

REFERENCES

Althusser, L. (1969). *For Marx*. New York, NY: Pantheon Books.

Arthur, C. (2005). *The Myth Of 'Simple Commodity Production'*. Retrieved from https://chrisarthur.net/the-myth-of-simple-commodity-production/

Backhaus, H. (1997). *Dialektik der wertform: Untersuchungen zur marxschen ökonomiekritik*. Freiburg i. Br.

Backhaus, H. (1980). On the dialectics of the value-form. *Thesis Eleven*, *1*(1), 99–120.

Backhaus, H. (1992). Between philosophy and science: Marxian social economy as critical theory. In *Open Marxism* (Bonefield, ed., Vol. 1), London: Pluto Press.

Bellofiore, R., & Redolfi Riva, T. (2015). The 'Neue Marx-lektüre': Putting the critique of political economy back into the critique of society. *Radical Philosophy: A Journal of Socialist and Feminist Philosophy*, *189*, 24–36.

Bidet, J. (2007). *Exploring Marx's capital philosophical, economic and political dimensions* (D. Fernbach, trans.). Leiden: Brill.

Bonefield, W. (1992). *Open marxism* (Vol. 1), London: Pluto Press.

Bonefield, W. (1998). Review of Hans-Georg Backhaus *Dialektik Der Wertform*. *Capital and Class*, *66*, 1–4.

Böhm-Bawerk, E. (1966). *Karl Marx and the close of his system*. New York, NY: A.M. Kelley.

Campbell, M. (1997). Marx's theory of money: A defense. In F. Moseley & M. Campbell (Eds.), *New investigations of Marx's method* (pp. 89–120). Atlantic Highlands, NJ: Humanities Press International.

Carver, T. (1975). *Texts on method*. New York, NY: Barnes & Noble.

Carver, T. (1998). *The postmodern Marx*. Manchester: Manchester University Press.

Carver, T. (2003). *Engels*. Oxford: Oxford University Press.

Carver, T. (2016, March). Email to author.

Carver, T., & Blank, D. (2014a). *A political history of the editions of Marx and Engels's "German Ideology manuscripts."* New York, NY: Palgrave Macmillan.

Carver, T., & Blank, D. (2014b). *Marx and Engels's "German Ideology" manuscripts: Presentation and analysis of the "Feuerbach chapter."* New York: Palgrave Macmillan.

CCCF. *Guide to grammar and writing*. Retrieved from http://grammar.ccc.commnet.edu/grammar/. Accessed November 30, 2016.

Chambers, S. A. (2001). Foucault's evasive maneuvers: Nietzsche, interpretation, critique. *Angelaki*, *6*(3), 101–123.

Chambers, S. A. (2009). *The queer politics of television*. London: IB Tauris.
Chambers, S. A. (2014). *Bearing society in mind: Theories and politics of the social formation*. London: Rowman & Littlefield International.
Cook, D. (1990). Nietzsche and Foucault on ursprung and genealogy. *Clio*, *19*, 299–309.
Eldred, M., & Hanlon, M. (1981). Reconstructing value-form analysis. *Capital and Class*, *1*, 24–60.
Elson, D. (1979). *Value: The representation of labour in capitalism*. London: CSE Books.
Foucault, M. (1984). *The Foucault reader*. New York, NY: Penguin Books.
Halperin, D. M. (2002). *How to do the history of homosexuality*. Chicago, IL: University of Chicago Press.
Harvey, D. (1982). *The limits to capital*. Chicago, IL: University of Chicago Press.
Harvey, D. (2005). *A brief history of neoliberalism*. Oxford: Oxford University Press.
Harvey, D. (2010). *The enigma of capital and the crises of capitalism*. Oxford: Oxford University Press.
Heinrich, M. (2012). *An introduction to the three volumes of Karl Marx's Capital* (A. Locascio, Trans.). New York, NY: Monthly Review Press.
Keen, S. (1993). Use-value, exchange value and the demise of Marx's labor theory of value. *Journal of the History of Economic Thought*, *15*(1), 107–121.
Kliman, A. (2007). *Reclaiming Marx's capital: A refutation of the myth of inconsistency*. Lanham, MD: Lexington Books.
Larsen, N. (2014). *Marxism and the critique of value*. Chicago, IL: MCM Publishers.
Mandel, E. (1990). *"Introduction"* to Capital. New York, NY: International Publishers.
Marx, K. (1969). *Theories of surplus value*. London: Lawrence & Wishart.
Marx, K. (1990). *Capital: A critique of political economy* (Vol. 1) (B. Fowkes, Trans.). New York, NY: Penguin.
Marx, K. (1995a). *Value, price and profit*. New York, NY: International Co. Inc.
Marx, K. (1995b). *The poverty of philosophy*. Amherst, NY: Prometheus Books.
Marx, K. (1996). *Marx: Later political writings*. T. Carver (Ed.). Cambridge: Cambridge University Press.
Marx, K. (2009). *A contribution to the critique of political economy* (S. W. Ryazanskaya, Trans.). Moscow: Progress Publishers.
Marx, K., & Engels, F. (1963). *Werke* (Vol. 29), Berlin: Dietz Verlag.
Marx, K., & Engels, F. (1970). *The German ideology*. New York, NY: International Publishers.
Marx, K., & Engels, F. (1971). *Werke* (Vol. 13), Berlin: Dietz Verlag.
Marx, K., & Engels, F. (1987). *Economic and philosophic manuscripts of 1844*. Buffalo, NY: Prometheus Books.
Mason, P. (2015). *Postcapitalism: A guide to our future*. New York, NY: Farrar, Straus and Giroux.
Moseley, F., & Campbell, M. (1997). *New investigations of Marx's method*. Atlantic Highlands, NJ: Humanities Press.
Murray, P. (1999). Marx's "Truly social" labour theory of value: Part I, abstract labour in Marxian value theory. *Historical Materialism*, *6*(1), 27–66.
Murray, P. (2000). Marx's 'Truly social' labour theory of value: Part II, how is labour that is under the sway of capital actually abstract? *Historical Materialism*, *7*(1), 99–136.
Nietzsche, F. W. (1967). *On the genealogy of morals* (W. Kaufmann, Trans.). New York, NY: Vintage Books.

Postone, M. (1993). *Time, labor, and social domination: A reinterpretation of Marx's critical theory*. Cambridge: Cambridge University press.
Rebrovick, T. (2016). *Routine maintenance: Forming, reforming, and transforming social formations*. Doctoral dissertation. Johns Hopkins University.
Reichelt, H. (1995). Why did Marx conceal his dialectical method? In W. Bonefield, R. Gunn, J. Holloway, & K. Psychopedis (Eds.), *Open marxism* (Vol. 3), London: Pluto Press.
Ricardo, D. (1996). *Principles of political economy and taxation*. Amherst, NY: Prometheus Books.
Roberts, W. (2017). *Marx's inferno: The political theory of capital*. Princeton, NY: Princeton University Press.
Rozdolski, R. (1977). *The making of Marx's 'capital'*. London: Pluto Press.
Rubin, I. I. (2008). *Essays on Marx's theory of value*. Detroit, MI: Black & Red.
Sedgwick, E. K. (1990). *Epistemology of the closet*. Berkeley, CA: University of California Press.
Smith, A. (1999). *The wealth of nations*. London: Penguin.
Steuart, J. (1807). *An inquiry into the principles of political economy*. Retrieved from marxists.org. Accessed on December 15, 2015.
Vatter, M. (2014). *The republic of the living: Biopolitics and the critique of civil society*. New York, NY: Fordham University Press.
Veblen, T. (1900). The preconceptions of economic science. *Quarterly Journal of Economics*, *14*(2), 240–269.
Wolff, R. P. (1981). A critique and reinterpretation of Marx's labor theory of value. *Philosophy and Public Affairs*, *10*, 89–120.

"THESE DAYS OF *SHOAH*": HISTORY, HABITUS, AND REALPOLITIK IN JEWISH PALESTINE, 1942–1943

Daniel J. Levine

ABSTRACT

This article explores the role of history and historical memory in the formation of early Zionist/Israeli national security doctrine. To that end, it makes three moves. First, it explores a series of public addresses made by Zalman Rubashov (Shazar) in 1942–1943. A key public intellectual in the Jewish community of preindependent Palestine (the Yishuv*), Rubashov means to help his listeners make sense of, and respond collectively to, the unfolding destruction of European Jewry. Second, it draws cautious parallels between those public intellectual pronouncements and the postwar work of Friedrich Meinecke, a prominent German historian and public intellectual and a sometime teacher of Rubashov. In both cases, I suggest, history does more than make sense of a moment of political transition: It seeks to reframe the self-understandings of citizens and their collective political relations. Third, drawing on a recent memoir by Noam Chayut, a prominent Israeli antioccupation activist, I explore how*

International Origins of Social and Political Theory
Political Power and Social Theory, Volume 32, 99–125

ISSN: 0198-8719/doi:10.1108/S0198-871920170000032005

those self-understandings can be lost when the historical claims upon which they are predicated lose their sense of immediacy, naturalness, or coherence.

Keywords: Friedrich Meinecke; Noam Chayut; international relations; historicism; *Shoah*; political realism; Zalman Rubashov (Shazar)

INTRODUCTION

The burden of building a bridge to his people remains with the historian.
Yerushalmi (1996, p. 100)

Drawing on a particular moment in the public discourse of pre-1948 Jewish Palestine, this article explores the process by which historical events are distilled and operationalized into prudent political counsel: used, that is, to guide the everyday work of individuals, to identify the larger aims and interests of the institutions and political movements in which they take part, and to give the former normative and existential meaning within the context of the latter. The moment in question is late 1942–early 1943, as the Hebrew-speaking community of Palestine (the *Yishuv*) learns of the systematic destruction of Polish Jewry. The medium for the provision of such counsel is *Ma'arakhot* ("military campaigns"), a semiunderground strategic studies journal published by the Haganah, the largest of the Zionist paramilitary groups then operating in Palestine. The work of distillation and operationalization is done by Zalman Rubashov (Shazar), a prominent Zionist public intellectual, activist, and sometime historian. The bulk of the article will focus on two public addresses – "On the Dusk of Our National Mourning," and "On Israel's Military Character" – as reproduced within the journal's pages.

A few preliminaries may help frame that discussion. *Ma'arakhot* had by then been in print for some four years. What would come to be known as the *Thawara al-Kubra* – the Great Revolt of 1936–1939 – had forced both Britain and the Zionist movement to reckon publicly with the reality of Palestinian collective identity and political aspirations. To suppress that revolt, British counterinsurgency forces would, at their height, include two full army divisions (some 25,000 servicemen) as well as expanded police and Jewish supernumerary forces. Some 5,000 Palestinian Arabs (and by most accounts, several hundred Jews) would be killed in clashes with British and Zionist forces and in intracommunal violence as well (Hughes, 2009, p. 314; see also Kimmerling & Migdal, 2003, Chapter 4; Matthews, 2006, Chapter 8; Norris, 2008; Swedenburg, 1993). With tensions mounting in Europe, and with its official policy of developing Palestine jointly for Jews and Arabs now plainly in tatters, Britain would, in May 1939, declare its intention to quit the country in 10 years.

Ma'arakhot's first issue appeared some four months later. Without the British to enforce the terms of the Balfour Declaration, the *Yishuv* would now be solely responsible for its own collective, national defense. For that, in turn, the Haganah's operational capabilities would need to be dramatically expanded. It is in this context, as well as the prospect of a second world war, that the journal was first conceived. It was to be that forum in which the Haganah's expansion might be "hashed out": conceptually, doctrinally, and operationally. "[T]he dangers of war from without and of insurrection from within have turned the attention of many in the *Yishuv* and in the Zionist movement to military and defensive considerations," the editors of *Ma'arakhot* noted in the first issue. "We must now channel that attention to productive ends" (*Ma'arakhot*, 1939, p. 1; see also Bauer, 1970; Livne, 1960; Luttwak & Horowitz, 1975, pp. 1–25; Pa'il, 1979; Schiff, 1985, pp. 1–20; Sheffy, 1991; Tamari, 2011; Van Creveld, 1998, pp. 31–62).

So understood, the journal functioned in a manner akin to what Ansorge and Barkawi have called a *utile form*: a medium "with a standardized layout" designed to make specialized social-scientific and technical knowledge "available to, and useful for, civil and military bureaucracies" (Ansorge & Barkawi, 2014, pp. 4–5). To that end, it served as a discursive space in which the language of grand strategy and combat doctrine, long a staple of the command and staff colleges of the great powers, could be translated into a specifically "Hebrew" milieu: "[T]he main, first, and essentially only source," as one longtime editor would later note, "for the development of military thought and operational, strategic, and tactical concepts" outside of routine training and everyday operations (Rivlin, 1960, p. 4; see also Pa'il, 1979, pp. 57–58; Slutsky, 1976, pp. 47–48).[1] With Israel's independence in 1948, *Ma'arakhot* would become an official organ of the Israel Defense Forces, as it remains to this day.

It is thus telling that Rubashov's speeches are reproduced on *Ma'arakhot*'s pages; the editors evidently saw them as aligning with their "utile" aims. Taken together, his speeches took issue with an ostensibly dominant stream of "whiggish" liberal-national Jewish historiography and with the political and affective sensibilities and self-understandings that followed from it (Butterfield, 1931; Guilhot, 2015). On that account, the emancipation and civic rehabilitation of European Jews – their entry into politics and cultural life, and the exceptional nature of their contributions to that life – promised to undo centuries of Jewish aloneness and precarity. Modernity and progress had "normalized" the Jews, or was in the process of doing so.

Not surprisingly, Rubashov's speeches dispute this "normalizing" account. Liberal ideals, scientific progress, and the rationalization and demystification of society did not undo the basic realities of power politics, nor the abiding, ineluctable nature of Jewish alterity and existential aloneness. To believe otherwise was to fall into a "utopianism" akin to the one decried by the likes of Carr (1964) and Morgenthau (1946): early Anglo-American practitioners and expositors of political realism and/or *realpolitik*. But where the latter wrote from a presumptively global (and perhaps self-consciously world-historical) perspective, Rubashov is writing from the cramped quarters of a small nation "with an exceptional sense of collective fragility"; a people that "dwells alone, not to be reckoned among the nations" (Abulof, 2015, p. 6; Numbers 23:9).

So understood, anti-Semitism (or perhaps more properly, anti-Judaism) was folded into the broader pessimism that is foundational to political realism: one of the malign "forces inherent within human nature" with which political actors must come to terms, and which foil any promise of politics' subsumption to reason, science, or universal ethics (Gismondi, 2004; Morgenthau, 1967, p. 3; Nirenberg, 2013). This line of thinking, moreover, produced a sense of public vocation in mid-century Zionist political-historical thinking that was essentially similar to the one classical realists saw themselves fulfilling in Anglo-American ones: to guide citizens and policymakers toward prudent, meaningful political action.[2]

Rubashov's critiques in these speeches are thus Janus-faced. He exhorts Jews to understand their place in history and to cultivate the moral – and specifically the martial – virtues needed to survive within it. Yet, he also asks why these virtues seem so foreign to Jews in the first place. Conditions in the Jewish diaspora, he argues, did, in fact, suborn their own moments of valor and courage – the same sensibilities that could nourish the "Hebrew fighters" of his own day. It is only that earlier generations of Jewish historians consciously sought to downplay those moments, with an eye to peacefully assimilating into the emergent national families of Europe. What Jewish "whigs" and utopians had taken away, Zionist historicists must now restore.[3] This, then, is history not merely as the systematic recollection of past events. Rather, it constitutes an attempt to offer context and existential meaning in the midst of what Jahn (this volume) has characterized as the "fragmentation of modern knowledge" and of political experience.

If there is a distant ideal at work here, perhaps it is the historicism, and the public intellectualism, of Friedrich Meinecke, Rubashov's sometime mentor: the political historian whose work sought to trace out the emergence of a particular kind of German subjectivity in the early 20th century and then to dismantle it after the second world war. That connection certainly does not erase the horror of Jewish suffering at German hands. Neither does it make simple moral equivalences nor place determinist causal "arrows" between that horror and the ethnic cleansing of Palestine. But neither does it relegate these events to comfortably isolated moral-political universes (viz., Shaw & Bartov, 2010). The mutual imbrication of history and theory that emerges from this comparison raises questions that are as much ethical as epistemological. The present article aims more to sharpen those questions than to answer them.

The remainder of this article seeks to develop this connection though comparative readings of the public intellectualism of both Rubashov and Meinecke. In each case, the public historian effects a presentist critique of history: Jews and Germans have inherited a public understanding of their collective pasts that is at odds with the strategic imperatives of the present. The aim of the historian must therefore be to reimagine the past: to construct an historical narrative that provides a coherent framework for understanding and acting in the present. Or, as the epigraph to this article puts it, "to build a bridge" between peoples and their pasts.

Three sections follow. The next section undertakes a close reading of Rubashov's addresses, as described above. Two key moves comprise this reading: First, Rubashov connects the destruction of Polish Jewry to earlier episodes of anti-Jewish violence: the past is made prologue; second, Rubashov uses this narrative of unending violence to sketch out a vision for a sovereign Jewish citizen soldier. If Jews do not typically think of themselves as a martial people, Rubashov notes, it is only because they misremember their past – because Jewish historians have bequeathed them a quietist habitus, better suited to assimilation than self-determination. Reframing that inheritance is thus a matter of prime strategic and political importance.

The third section develops a parallel – if much briefer – analysis of the postwar work of Friedrich Meinecke. The German people, nourished on a martial heritage and on dreams of global power, must be taught new ways of being. To be sure, the German past furnishes resources that could be put to this end; it is only that German historians – Meinecke places himself chief among them – must renegotiate their understanding of power and its relationship to the state. German history, it seems, is not quite "whiggish" *enough*: alongside Rankean power politics, historians must cultivate a renewed appreciation for the cultural historian, Jakob Burckhardt. Nothing less than a reimagination of "our own German way of being men" is needed, Meinecke asserts; it, too, is a matter of prime strategic importance.

A brief, but hopefully suggestive, conclusion follows. Drawing on a recent memoir by a prominent Israeli antioccupation activist, I consider the lived moment of "losing" one's history and consider its meaning for the mutual imbrication of history and theory.

Two brief provisos. First, we are dealing here with what Habermas (1988, p. 48) has called "the public use of history": less with scientific or academic questions about rules of argument or the critical analysis of documents than with the use of the past to create cultural memory – and strategic-doctrinal consensus – in the present. Second, and related: What matters less than the factual *basis* of claims made by particular historians is what White (1975) has called their *figurative content*: their ability to artfully and compellingly summon up a world that coheres morally, ontologically, and aesthetically.[4] Factual and procedural-methodological disagreements are of course possible; but they are also, at least partly, beside the point. It is the world that these historical narratives summon up and make meaningful that is at issue here, as distinct from their correspondence to specific things, or the rules by which they are adduced from source texts. To be sure – here following Funkenstein (1992) – the two are not entirely distinct from one another, but neither are they definitively linked.

"THESE DAYS OF *SHOAH*": THE PAST AS PROLOGUE

In its November–January (1942–1943) and May–July (1943) issues, the editors of *Ma'arakhot* reprinted two public speeches given by Zalman Rubashov: "On the Dusk of Our National Mourning" and "On Israel's Military Character." As noted above, Rubashov was by then a well-known Zionist public intellectual. He had studied history and philosophy first at the Jewish Academy in St. Petersburg and then later in Freiburg and Berlin under Heinrich Rickert, Friedrich Meinecke, Ernst Fabricius, and George Simmel. His movement activities had brought him in close touch with Zionist leaders in both Central Europe and Palestine: Ber Borochov, Yitzhak Ben-Zvi, Berl Katznelson, and the poet Rachel Bluwstein. In 1944, he became the editor of *Davar*, the highly influential newspaper of the General Federation of Hebrew Workers (the *Histadrut*) and of its *Am Oved* literary series. After independence (and after Hebraizing his last name to Shazar), Rubashov would become Israel's first Minister of Education. In 1963, he was elected as its third president (Tidhar, 1949; Tsoref, 5768 [2007/2008], pp. xi–xiv, 14; Wikipedia, 2016).

Deeply schooled in central European intellectual traditions but with close ties to traditional and Hasidic Judaism, Rubashov was a public intellectual of a very particular kind. Voluble, impossibly productive, peripatetic, politically radical but socially traditional, he was part of that small group of labor-Zionist elites who understood themselves to have brought the *Yishuv* (and later, the Israeli state) into being by sheer collective will and persistence (Elon, 2001; Etzioni-Halevy, 1997; Horowitz & Lissak, 1978; Medding, 1972).

From a different point of view, perhaps Rubashov was the sort of scholar-activist whom Theodor Herzl had in mind when he wrote of those "mediocre intellects which we produce so superabundantly in our middle classes"; "semi-civilized" *ostjuden* whose liberal educations did not erase (indeed, somehow magnified) their stubbornly Jewish *habitus* (Herzl, 1995, p. 131). "The fact of having been born a Jew" might still be a kind of misfortune, but its upshot was less the pariah's endless "struggle against [one] self" than a new kind of worldly activism.[5] Viewed from still a third perspective, he recalls those historicists for whom worldly forces had replaced divine providence or natural law and for whom mastery of those forces had become essential, given "the unraveling of that common network of belief and praxis" that had rooted many traditional communities in time and place.[6]

The timing of these speeches also bears noting. The first can be dated precisely, as it has been widely reprinted. Delivered before the General Council of the *Histadrut* on December 2, 1942, it follows the end of three days of public mourning for the fate of Polish Jewry: the first sustained, public response by the *Yishuv* to the policy of Nazi extermination (Rubashov, 5703 ([1942/1943]); Tsoref, 5768 [2007/2008], p. 254; on the broader context, see Bauer, 1970, p. 243; Friling, 2005, pp. 66–75; Porat, 1990, Chapter 4). The second speech is harder to date. *Ma'arakhot*'s editors inform the reader that it was given "before a gathering of Hebrew [i.e., Zionist] military men," while references within the text seem to suggest that it was delivered at about the same time as the first: late 1942/early 1943 (Rubashov, 1942/1943b, p. 5). It may have been delivered as part of a training course or as a cultural "enrichment" activity for one of the Haganah's various covert or overt formations.

Perhaps what is most striking about these addresses is that Rubashov is already using the term *shoah* to describe the events that prompt them:

> We have been blaming [others] quite a lot of late [for the fate of Polish Jewry]. Our three days of public outcry ... have turned into three days of accusations, lodged at the feet of the wide world ... Now, at the end of these three days ... I find that I have no wish to confine my accusations to others .... In these days of *shoah*, I wish now to speak of *our* moral failings; our threefold [sources of] shame, which sear at the soul. (Rubashov, 1942/1943a, p. 4)

Rubashov's *shoah* is not exactly our own. The term does not yet have the definite article (and in English, the capital "S") that marks its contemporary usage: "the name given to the mass murder of the Jewish people in Europe during the Second World War" (Even-Shoshan, 2003). Nor indeed had that cluster of events entirely come to pass. It is rather, as the historian Dina Porat explains, that the term's Biblical usage – and sometimes, its contemporary one – denotes a catastrophe that sits just beyond the human power of imagination: "a sudden destruction or ruin, a sudden or unexpected blow" (Lentin, 2000, pp. 125–131; Ofer, 1996; Porat, 1990, p. 44; Shaw & Bartov, 2010, p. 247). "And what will ye do in the day of visitation," asks Isaiah (10:3), "and in the *shoah* which shall come from afar"? The term would grow in capaciousness as the events in question reset the limits of extremity and imagination (Ihrig, 2016, p. 5; Porat, 1990, p. 44). That *shoah* became *The Shoah*, in part, because we know what happened after. Further, because that event, or at any rate those pieces of it through which it is represented, shared, and jointly understood, has, for good or ill, since been "transformed into a generalized symbol of human suffering and moral evil" in a way that Rubashov did not foresee (Alexander, 2009, p. 3; Rothberg, 2009).

Nor is Rubashov invoking more recent critical discourses regarding the "unmasterability" of the *Shoah*, "the limits of representation" that attend its consideration, or the notion of a "grey zone" that resists the penetrating stare of comparative analysis or ethical judgment (viz., Adorno, 1973; Agamben, 2002; Baumann, 1989; Friedlander, 1992; Maier, 1988). Rather the opposite. "Thirty generations separate us from the Crusades," he notes, evoking the 11th- and 12th-century massacres carried out against the Jews of Speyer, Worms, Mainz, and Cologne. "No aspect of culture and economics, of the state or of science" in our day resembles theirs. And yet, "one need only glance" at historical sources "to be shocked" by the similarities "between that *shoah* and the *shoah* of our own day" (Rubashov, 1942/1943b, p. 10).

> The same enmity whipping up the masses. The same systematic cultivation of a crisis. The same solution, physical extermination. [...] Read the *Hebräische Berichte* of 1096 on the massacres in Speyer and in Worms, in Mainz and Cologne, in Trier and in Prague, and it is as though you were reading about Hitler's emissaries in 1942 and their councils of extermination [*vaadot ha-hashmadah*] ... it is as though the acts of the fathers had been as a portent to their children and ... grandchildren.[7]

In relaying Rubashov's interpretive framework, I do not ask that the reader approve of it or share it. Only that she see his "shock of recognition" – the realization that "our *shoah* and theirs" are of a piece – as kindred to the kind of unmediated access to the past to which political historians from Morgenthau to Machiavelli have long made appeal: when they "look over [the] shoulder" of a long-departed policymaker, or assert the constancy of human nature and the utility of historical study since "heaven, the sun, the elements, and men" remain essentially as they were "in ancient times" (Hom, 2016; Hutchings, 2008, pp. 49–52; Kaplan, 1964, p. 314; Machiavelli, 1940, pp. 104–105; Morgenthau, 1967, p. 5).

That holds, even if we would *also* hold that such "shocks" are less a reflection of having captured the essence of a thing than of the scholar's subjective desire to effect such capture. Rubashov's concern was not to do justice to an aporia, but to nurture purposeful, effective, prudent political action. The murder of millions – relatives, friends, fellow Jews, and (on the understanding of many Zionists) fellow nationals – in the face of global indifference was undoubtedly harrowing.[8] But it was *also* a hard political fact, from which correct lessons had to be drawn. Hence, his call for a public reckoning – the "threefold moral failings" – in the twilight of the *Yishuv*'s period of collective mourning.

What, then, were these failings? Rubashov names three. The first is that Jews in the *Yishuv* allowed themselves to be surprised. "Did they" – Rubashov here means non-Jews, and in particular anti-Semites – "not warn us, time and again?" (Rubashov, 1942/1943a, p. 4). For years, we have talked about the "destruction" of the Jews of Germany and Poland.[9] *How could we not know "what awaited us among the gentiles"* – we, the movement "that claims responsibility for our people's future, studies its fate, lives amidst its pathologies, and is privy to its secret woes"? (Rubashov, 1942/1943a, p. 4). To be sure Rubashov himself had, as early as 1939, expressed the fear that "there would be no one left for whom to upbuild this land [i.e, Palestine]" (Tsoref, 5768 [2007/2008], p. 240). But that was in the context of a war whose effect on civilians – and on Jewish civilians in particular – was expected to be severe, perhaps in the vein of the Russian civil war, as this would have been known and reported at the time (Ansky, 2002; Babel, 2002). Awful enough in its own terms, such violence is not yet a coordinated policy of universal extermination. *That* is the epistemic barrier that Rubashov is chastising "us" for failing to have crossed.[10]

Our second failing "has no solution, and brooks no clarification": it must be directed to "this entire generation and the one preceding it" (Rubashov, 1942/1943a, p. 5). How is it, he asks, that we lacked the strength "to bring ourselves out of the spiritual aloneness in which we find ourselves?"

> For did we not cease, some generations ago, to be an isolated people, closed up within the walls of our ghetto? Are not things now entirely otherwise? Never before has our nation been so bound up in the life, and in the midst, of other nations [*bikerev goyim*] as in these our [most recent] generations. [...] For some 150 years we sought to speak their languages, to live ... among them. We dreamt with them, we fought with them, and we drew strength from the same spiritual wells as they did. Which of our secrets did we withhold from their view, which of their secrets did we not strive to uncover? (Rubashov, 1942/1943a, p. 5)

The third failing follows from the previous two. Even in the midst of a catastrophe that reveals the limits of our own moral and political imagining, even in the midst of a persistent, unbridgeable gap between Jews and gentiles, the Jews of the *Yishuv* continue to be divided along petty rivalries and factionalisms. Has the coming of this catastrophe finally united us? "Does ... the *Yishuv* now wear a new sense of true responsibility, a different sense of seriousness as to its obligations, a spirit which we did not know before the coming of this *shoah*?" (Rubashov, 1942/1943a, p. 6).

Put differently, Rubashov's threefold moral self-critique means to stress a particular historical sensibility: that Jews are well and truly alone in history. Did "we" still cling to the idea that anti-Semitism might be a side effect of overrapid industrialization and social instability? Did we still think scientific study of the "Jewish Question" might disenchant or dispel it? (Rubashov, 1942/1943a, p. 4). Did we still think Jewish aloneness could be pierced by a true meeting of hearts, by the creation of new national "families," or by the norms of liberal, inclusive, public spheres? Did we think the Jewish people could create a state without first becoming a nation – without, that is, setting aside fractional and ideological divisions, in favor of a shared general will or national interest? If so, then we were mistaken. An older, earlier logic governs our external relations. If we are to survive, we must master that logic, as other nations have learned to do. That means remaking ourselves in its image.

If all of this seems like esoteric fodder for a journal devoted to tactical and strategic studies – other articles in the May–July issue of *Ma'arakhot* included translated articles by Cyril Falls and Basil Liddell-Hart, reports on recent allied engagements at Dieppe and Habbaniya, and on military and institutional developments in Transjordan – recall here the discussion of "utile forms" made in the introduction. By asserting a visceral anti-Judaism, Rubashov's exhortations mean to nurture a particular cluster of strategic and affective sensibilities: diaspora Jews were to be remade "from victims into warriors" – into free, self-determinate political subjects and determined soldiers (Rubashov, 5703 [1942/1943]). That work, the editors of *Ma'arakhot* had maintained since their first issue, was not "merely technical"; it involved matters that were "spiritual and organizational as well" (Ma'arakhot, 1939, p. 1). For them as for Rubashov, "self-defense [*haganah*] is not merely a matter of expertise, or of forces, or of equipment ... or of rules to be mastered." Rather, "it is first and foremost a quality, a spiritual disposition, a virtue [*segulah*]." With proper cultivation – but only with such cultivation – "it can even become, sometimes and to some degree, the virtue of a generation" (Rubashov, 1942/1943b, p. 5).

HISTORICAL REINTERPRETATION AS STRATEGIC IMPERATIVE

The need for such cultivation had become acute. As briefly noted above, the question of Jewish self-defense had been a matter of growing concern within the *Yishuv* since at least the Palestinian revolt of 1936–1939. The coming of the war sharpened these concerns considerably. The noose seemed to be tightening. In the early years of the war, Haifa and Tel Aviv were bombed by the Italian air force; the British Navy struggled to retain control of the Mediterranean; and German Arabic language radio propaganda – including addresses by Amin el-Husseini [Husayni], a leading figure in the Palestinian national movement – seemed ubiquitous. An attempted pro-German coup in Iraq in 1941 had resulted in the *Farhud* – two days of anti-Jewish pogroms in Baghdad – in which nationalists from Husseini's circle were also implicated.[11] Fear of German invasion, whether via Greece (where Britain had also suffered reversals), Vichy-held Syria, the Caucasus, or North Africa, rose steadily until the Second Battle of El Alamein, in late 1942. In the months prior to that battle – a period that the journalist Haviv Canaan (1973/1974) would later call the "two hundred days of dread" – British and Zionist forces collaborated on a series of emergency plans that included the evacuation of British (but not Zionist) civil and military forces from Palestine, and the possibility of a final, Masada-like standoff between the *Yishuv* and the Wehrmacht.[12] Rubashov himself, though by then in his 50s, had been mobilized into a special training program in partisan warfare set up by the *Haganah* for "intellectuals and free professionals" (Tsoref, 5768 [2007/2008], p. 252).

Given the magnitude of the task at hand, Rubashov notes, it is natural that we may have doubts about our potential to become a nation fully possessed of the martial virtues. True, he notes, Biblical verses and classical sources from the time of the Roman revolts affirm the warlike abilities of our ancient ancestors – the tribe of Dan was "a serpent in the path … who bites at horses' heels," the Tribe of Gad "dwells as does a lionness" (Rubashov, 1942/1943b, p. 5; Genesis 49:17; Deuteronomy 33:20). The unforgiving topography and geography of the Land of Israel, he continues, fairly demands this: "to strike roots here," between "the sea, the [powers of] the east, and the desert" from which new foes constantly emerged, the ancient Israelites must have been fierce and valorous (Rubashov, 1942/1943b, p. 6).

Nor was that prowess lost even in the days of diaspora, when "Israel was as scattered sheep, whom the lions had driven away" (Jeremiah 50:17). For in those days we see a remarkable power for self-sacrifice – not always military to be sure, Rubashov notes, but no less lacking in courage for that: "The lion of Judah did not cease its roaring" (Rubashov, 1942/1943b, p. 8). A "chain of valor" linked every part of Jewish history.

> When you deepen your examination [of Jewish history], when each of us strings together link after link in this chain [of valor], we will see clearly, not only spiritual valor of the sort needed for a nation of exile … but also the sort of revealed valor that comes to light in times of great transformation. The examples of this, it seems to me, are numerous. (Rubashov, 1942/1943b, p. 8)

If so, Rubashov asks, why are our doubts so great? The answer, he suggests, lies within our own historical tradition: *We have blinded ourselves to our own true abilities.*

> The science of Hebrew history, the examination of facts, of books – is not only the fruit of a popular spirit, the spirit of a certain people which produced certain documents, but it is also the fruit of the spirit of a generation of … historiographers, who must consciously seek them, examine them, and impart them to a generation [of readers]. Hebrew historiography from 1821 to the present, *this particular* Hebrew historiography, did not seek out those documents. When it found them, it didn't examine them closely. The ear was sealed off from hearing the echoes of valor, preserved still within the documents and books, in the testimonies of Jews and non-Jews alike.

> The ear was sealed because the heart and mind were directed elsewhere. (Rubashov, 1942/1943b, p. 7)

Why was this? The answer lies in the political commitments of the historians themselves. Those scholars, well-meaning though they might have been, were blinded by false hopes: the initial flush of Jewish emancipation and the promise of assimilation had made too great an impression upon them.

> The historians from the generation of emancipation ... (and up to now it is only they who have written histories of the Jews) – their hearts were not at all attuned to this rich web [*masekhet*] of Jewish valor. The matter was placed in abeyance [*nidunah li-hatimah*]. For it was clear [to them]: henceforth, we will not try our hands at these sorts of adventures with the neighbouring peoples. The covenant that was struck, or that would be struck, or that [they] aspired to strike between Israel and the other nations was of a different sort; self-defence, it was to be hoped, would no longer be needed. If so, then better not to devote attention to it. *What the heart does not desire, the eye does not see.* (Rubashov, 1942/1943b, p. 7, emphasis added)

What is needed Rubashov asserts, "is a new generation," possessed of its own experiences: "A generation of struggle has different desires"; its historians will find different meanings from their sources (Rubashov, 1942/1943b, p. 7).

MEINECKE'S "GERMAN CATASTROPHE": FROM RANKE TO BURCKHARDT

In 1948, the German Academy of Sciences in Berlin published an address given earlier that same year. Entitled "Ranke and Burckhardt," the speaker was the aged professor of history, Friedrich Meinecke. Meinecke was then 86, "the Dean of German historians" and "the first to draw courageous conclusions from the ... catastrophe of 1945" (Kohn, 1954, p. 141). Meinecke had, of course, long been one of Germany's preeminent historians. In addition to some 20 books – with six translated into English – he had authored dozens of academic articles and addresses, and essays in the popular press (Sterling, 1954, pp. 310–311). From 1894 until 1935, he edited the *Historische Zeitschrift* and headed the *Historische Reichskommission* until it was disbanded under National Socialism (Clark, 2006, pp. 15, 26–27; Craig, 1978, p. 660–661; Knudsen, 1994, p. 59; Stieg, 1986, Chapter 2; Wolfson, 1956, pp. 515–516).

Meinecke had also been a prominent Weimar public intellectual, who had tangled openly – if selectively – with the new regime (Clark, 2006, pp. 24–26;

Pois, 1973, pp. 121–123). A self-proclaimed *vernunftsrepublikaner* – one whose heart "remained with the monarchy," even if he felt obliged to serve the republic – he had, together with Max Weber and Ernst Troeltsch, been an active intellectual force in the liberal-nationalist German Democratic Party and a critic of fascism (Pois, 1976, p. 35 and *passim*). It was in this context that Meinecke had been removed from the *Zeitschrift* and the *Reichskommission*. He spent the war years in relative obscurity: "forbidden to teach and cut off from public life in general" (Stark, infra Meinecke, 1957 [1924], p. xxxvi; see also Olick, 2005, Chapters 7 and 8).

Meinecke's distance from the regime is nevertheless difficult to assess. In practical terms, Knudsen observes, he was never – even after his public dismissals – denied publication; indeed, he was granted (and accepted) some fairly significant academic honors (Knudsen, 1994, p. 65). Nor can one fail to detect uncomfortable turns in his thinking. During the first world war, he had written dismissively of "the Slavic peoples," with their "primitive national spirit" and "semi-barbarian ethics," and had given his assent to plans for mass expulsion and "Germanization" along the Polish border (Meinecke, 1915, p. 25; Wehler, 1985, p. 112). In *The German Catastrophe* (1946), he saw it fit to criticize the Jews of inter-war Germany: "inclined to enjoy indiscreetly [their] favorable economic situation," he suggested, they had exercised a "negative and disintegrating influence" on German liberalism (Iggers, 1983, p. 228; Meinecke, 1950, p. 15; Pois, 1973, pp. 122–123; 1976, pp. 79–87).

Whatever one makes of these views, Meinecke's postwar role as a leading voice of reflection and reform is hard to dispute. It is here – at the inflection point between Meinecke's pre- and postwar attempts to fashion, and then refashion, German history – that the parallels with Rubashov appear. The "German catastrophe" had foreclosed old hopes and imposed new limitations on German political freedom. "The desire to become a world power has proven to be a false idol for us," Meinecke noted in 1946. "Our geopolitical and geophysical situation alone forbids it" (Meinecke, 1950, p. 109).

If Germany was to forgo its global ambitions, however, then *Germanness* itself needed to be re-conceived. German historians, he noted in 1948, must be part of this work:

> We Germans live today amid the ruins of state and nation; all that is involved in our culture is gravely threatened. Everywhere new paths must be searched out; everywhere these paths are in darkness. [...] One thing, however, has remained to us, our own German way of being men. It presents to us unanticipated problems of the most somber hue. The inner difficulties of establishing a scholarly foundation for the solution of

these problems is no easier. But, at the same time, the task of finding such a foundation becomes more urgent. For that purpose we must rediscover ourselves by throwing light upon the historical transformations of our own character and the interweaving of our guilt and our fate. (Meinecke, 1954, p. 156)

Meinecke's call to "rediscover ourselves" was *not* a call to reconsider what history was or did. Just as Rubashov was not anticipating poststructural critiques regarding the *Shoah* and the limits they posed to the possibility of historical representation, Meinecke was not anticipating the *historikerstreit* (Eley, 1988; Knowlton & Cates, 1994; Sternhell, 2010, pp. 422–443). History was not to be critiqued so much as retooled: put to different ends.

In the historian's mind, historical observation and the experience of living in his own time and sharing in its destiny form an indivisible inner unity. The things we have lived through in the last fourteen years thrust us before quite novel aspects and problems in our own historical past. There is much we must relearn. (Meinecke, 1954, p. 144)

That "relearning" centered on the misplaced optimism of Leopold von Ranke. For Ranke – and for Meinecke too, in his early writings – the creation of a robust Prussian (and later German) military had, in turn, created a new kind of moral-political individual: a citizen soldier, who freely and willingly accepted his duty to king and empire.[13] There was, of course, the fear that the one might outstrip the other: that the desire for political freedom might overwhelm one's sense of duty. If that happened, there would be no way for the rational calculation of state interest to temper the fervent revolutionary demand for national liberation unlocked by the Napoleonic wars. In that event, what Meinecke would later call "mass machiavellism" might well take over the state; as indeed, he argued in 1946, had happened with the rise of National Socialism (Meinecke, 1950, pp. 51–56). Ranke, Meinecke noted in 1948, had always dismissed this possibility: The monarchy, on his account, would never lose the power to hold such forces in check. The majority of German historians – including, he admitted, himself – had accepted that judgment too readily.[14]

Older, sadder, and wiser, Meinecke now realizes that he and Ranke may have been wrong. "Mass machiavellism," combined with the coarsening effects of industrial society and what would elsewhere be called the "culture industry" had produced a wave of chauvinist resentment against liberal principles and ideals, that, in turn, had overwhelmed the delicate balance between liberalism and nationalism. As Meinecke had noted as early as 1924:

[T]oday the idea of *raison d'état* (like many other ideas of western culture) is in the middle of a severe crisis. The natural basis of the elemental passions which it possesses and which cannot ... be subdued by its utilitarian middle ground makes a more terrible

> impression today than ever before; and the civilizing achievements of the modern world tend rather to exaggerate than to restrict it. All the ways in which the modern State has become enriched by successive influxes of liberal, democratic, national and social forces and ideas (which hitherto we have tended to regard as pure enrichment and increase) have now shown their other face, and have brought *raison d'état* into contact with forces which it is no longer capable of controlling. (Meinecke, 1957 [1924], p. 423)

That crisis, combined with a "global geopolitical and geophysical situation" that left no path for Germany to become a great power, had led Meinecke to reorient German history (Meinecke, 1950, p. 109). Where once "Ranke had been my guiding star," he noted, historians would now do well to consider "whether in the end, [Jakob] Burckhardt will not have greater importance … for us" (Meinecke, 1954, pp. 145, 156).

Why Burckhardt? For all the reasons that Rubashov would reject an earlier generation of Jewish historians – but in reverse. Since the state *cannot* be counted upon to channel the nationalistic impulses of its citizens toward a higher notion of interest, then those impulses must themselves be critiqued, unmade, or rethought. Rubashov – and Meinecke *junior* – had sought to emancipate their peoples from a "paralyzing schism between the self and the world," by releasing "intangible and inexhaustible qualities" that are to be found when "culture and intellect freely join … the state" (Meinecke, 1977, p. 3).

By contrast, Meinecke *senior* sought to "merge … political history in cultural history" (Meinecke, 1954, p. 151). German particularism was to be expressed not through conquest, but through the cultivation of German culture – Meinecke envisioned "Goethe communities" forming across the country to express pleasure in the uniqueness *and* the universality of German *belles lettres* – and through "manfully" allying with larger powers in the context of the postwar order (Meinecke, 1950, pp. 110, 119–120). If that happened, some variant mode of "our own German way of being men" might emerge. As with Rubashov, however, he is not writing history so much as calling for new history to be written: "[t]oday I can look no farther than to the threshold of this problem" (Meinecke, 1954, p. 156).

CONCLUDING THOUGHTS: HISTORY BETWEEN THEORY AND PRACTICE

> I don't know why, of all people, it was you who stole my Holocaust. After all, there was also the shackled kid in the Jeep and the girl whose family home we had broken into late at night to remove her mother and aunt. And there were plenty of children,

> hundreds of them, screaming and crying as we rummaged through their rooms and their things. (Chayut, 2013, pp. 59–60).

In 2010, the Israeli antioccupation activist Noam Chayut published *Ganevet ha-Shoah Sheli* [*The Girl Who Stole My Holocaust*] with Am Oved – the same literary series that Rubashov had edited some six decades earlier.[15] Part autobiographical memoir, part *bildungsroman*, part redemption narrative, the book retraces Chayut's life before and after a particular moment in his military service: a moment, we are asked to believe, in which his moral-political-historical universe comes apart. The moment is narrated thus: Chayut, an officer in an elite infantry-reconnaissance unit, encounters a group of Palestinian children playing in a village. He's a handsome young man, deeply patriotic, but with a broad, unguarded humanism.[16] Someone who expects to win the respect and affection of others easily. He smiles at the children, "a sweet but serious smile," one he had cultivated as a youth movement counselor, a student leader, an overseas "youth ambassador" (Chayut, 2013, pp. 58–59; Eastwood, 2016). The children are not charmed. All of them flee, save one:

> You did not smile back at me .... No, you froze on the spot, grew very pale and looked terrified. You neither screamed nor ran off. You only stood there, facing me with a horrified face and your black eyes staring .... Then you shook yourself out of your frozen stance, turned silently – a scrawny girl in light-colored clothes – and ran off, not looking back. (Chayut, 2013, pp. 58–59)

It takes a while, but Chayut gradually realizes that he has lost something in this encounter. "For that girl," he realizes, "I embodied absolute evil." Raised with a stark remembrance of fascism – both from public commemoration and from family – Chayut resists facile comparisons between the Israeli occupation and the *Shoah*. Nevertheless, he finds, "the absolute evil that had governed me until then began to disintegrate. And ever since, I have been without my Holocaust" (Chayut, 2013, p. 63).

That loss brings other losses. Other convictions also start coming undone. Social relationships begin to falter; old friendships, many of them forged while in uniform, fade away. A love affair ends badly. He goes on extended trips overseas, returns, and then embarks on a lengthy "purification" journey, hiking the length of the land. He passes through checkpoints normally reserved for Palestinians and is scolded by both the military personnel who do not know how to process him and by the "locals" (i.e., Palestinians) whose movement is delayed. His wanderings end only when he is hospitalized with an injury while in India. No longer able to outrun his thoughts, he begins to write and to reflect. *The Girl Who Stole My Holocaust*, we are informed, is the fruit of that effort.

A full rereading of Chayut's story – both its political/practical "upshot" and a critique of the various narrative techniques through which it is related – exceeds present purposes.[17] Viewed through the lens that Rubashov and Meinecke provide, the key point is this: Once Chayut no longer "owns" his *Shoah* – once his military service no longer seems to him as a link in Rubashov's chain of "revealed valor" – his hard-won habitus as a morally upstanding citizen-soldier begins to come apart. His only choices are to become a moral automaton – to give in to the fast tempo of operations and give up or suppress his powers of reflection – or to stop. He tries the former before settling on the latter.

Chayut, to be clear, has lost none of the technical skill or practical expertise that made him an effective soldier. His training and discipline continue to stand him in good stead in other contexts, where his new inner convictions are better served. Only the moral-historical link – the link which placed that training at the service of the state – is severed. It was to the purpose of forming such links that addresses like Rubashov's were reprinted in *Ma'arakhot*. No less than Germany, Israel has been through its own *historikerstreit* since the late 1980s, in which the politics of memory, and of the *Shoah*, figure prominently (Ben-Josef Hirsch, 2007; Isacoff, 2006; Morris, 2007; Pappé, 2009; Segev, 1993; Zertal, 2006). Chayut is of course not a historian. But this is precisely the point: his disenchantment demonstrates precisely how ostensibly recondite arguments about historiography and collective memory "cash out" into political practice. History, theory, and praxis remain linked as ever they were – even if this particular configuration of them no longer quite fits together.

Nor does that link disappear when one changes sides. Against Rubashov's Zionism, consider Edward Said's call for dual Palestinian-Israeli histories to be written jointly and contrapuntally. Drawing on the political realism of Raymond Williams, Said imagines "an emergent composite identity based on ... shared or common history, irreconcilabilities, antinomies, and all" (Said, 2001, p. 218). This, he asserts, would produce "an overlapping and necessarily unresolved consciousness of Palestine/Israel *through* its history, not *despite* it" (*ibid.*, emphasis added). Said is *not* calling for a "relentless critique of all existing history" – that would leave Israelis and Palestinians nowhere. It is rather the same wager that we saw with Rubashov and Meinecke: that a remembered past – in his case, a diasporic, "emergent composite" one – is needed to create a shared political habitus in the present day.[18] Here, as before, the call for such history precedes its actual creation. A few such histories have since been written (Adwan, Bar-On & Naveh, 2012; Yazbak & Weiss, 2011).

One is of course free to accept or reject any of these agendas, or their associated epistemological or observational claims: Said and Chayut no less than Rubashov and Meinecke. Chayut's story is uncomfortable in the ways it seems to translate agency (but no real voice) to his "holocaust thief," and for the unsettling gender politics bound up in his "sweet but serious smile" (Boyarin, 1997, pp. 271, 313; Weiss, 2002, pp. 42–57; Zertal, 1998, pp. 263–274). For its part, Said's diasporic binationalism would almost certainly make new kinds of ethical and political relations possible, as Judith Butler (2012, p. 30) has evocatively noted.[19] And yet, Massad (2013, p. 68) points out, it is no less indebted to its own kind of foundationalism.[20] In saying this, I do not mean to adjudicate in favor of one or the other, only to show that the two claims are essentially similar in their indebtedness to a particular mode of historical appropriation. That holds, even if their substance, and their practical political "upshots," are entirely orthogonal.

What holds constant across them is simply the conviction that history *matters*; further, it matters for each in essentially the same way. It delineates the ontological ground of political understanding and practice; it bears the "chips of messianic time" that, on Walter Benjamin's well-known account, shoot through any attempt to narrate "the time of the now": for "no fact that is a cause is for that very reason historical" (Benjamin, 1968, p. 263; Hutchings, 2008, pp. 62–64; Raz-Krakotzkin, 2013). For this reason, too, one cannot properly speak of history or theory as isolates; theory is always *in* history and predicated upon it. If that is so, the appropriate questions are less about epistemology than ethics: what modes of critical self-reflection are necessary, and sufficient, for the student of international politics who wishes to be something other than a partisan actor within history?

NOTES

1. The public role of *Ma'arakhot* is harder to assess. Like the Haganah itself, it occupied an ambiguously covert/overt space. Officially, the journal was a "legal" publication: It appeared under license, could be sold openly, and was submitted to the censor. As such, it had a more moderate, "official" tone than did the Haganah's underground publications. That said, the same section of the Haganah published overt publications and covert ones – the former provided institutional cover for the latter – and they shared a common circle of editors, publishers, and contributors. Moreover, the government censor in Tel Aviv was a Haganah commander, and oversight of the Hebrew language press seems to have been laxer than that of the

Arabic language press. Censorship may, indeed, have been viewed strategically: a means to offer the authorities a version of Labor Zionist strategic sensibilities that would be broadly conversant with what were presumed to be British interests. That said, *Ma'arakhot*'s authors and editors clearly sometimes felt constrained. Articles were occasionally penned under assumed names, and some local events (such as training exercises) were masked through reference to overseas locations. To understand such references fully, one would have to be "in the know" (Rivlin, 1960; compare with Hughes, 2009, p. 336; see also Haganah Archive Box 73, file 150).

2. On Anglo-American realism, see Tjalve and Williams (2015). On Israel, see Harkabi (1982). For critical engagements with each see, respectively, Levine (2016) and (2014).

3. To be sure, Rubashov is not actually writing this history; he is calling for others to do so. That work will get done in the immediate wake of the 1948 war, when considerable efforts will be put to creating new archives (such as the Haganah archives in Tel Aviv), and in producing books (and scholars) to draw upon them. On this point, see Dinur (1954). Rubashov's narrative, in other words, *predates* the archive from which it would ostensibly be drawn.

4. "When ... we move a great historical work out of the sphere of 'science' in order to enshrine it in the sphere of 'literature' as a 'classic', what we are paying tribute to, ultimately, is the historian's command of a power that is plastic and figurative .... Robert Frost once said that when a poet grows old, he dies into philosophy. When a great work of historiography or philosophy of history has become outdated, it is reborn into art" (White, 1975, p. 67).

5. Arendt (2000, p. 92). One could think of these intellectuals as analogous to Grovogui's (2006, pp. 10–12, 57–61) *evolués*: the "culturally and intellectual hybrid" elites that emerged from the French colonial milieu.

6. Yerushalmi (1996, p. 94). So understood, Zionism responds, as do many modern political movements, to "the evaporation of eternity as the divine measure against which human time is understood," and at the same time, to a loss of faith "that the past, present, and future join harmoniously in the self's experience and in the human world as a whole" (Chowers, 2013, p. 19). On historicism in this context, see *inter alia*, Beiser (2012, pp. 2, 3, 19–23), Wright (2003), Raz-Krakotzkin (2007), Myers (2003), and Rossi (1975).

7. *Ibid.* The reference is to Neubauer and Stern (1997 [1896]).

8. Soon after Israeli independence, Benzion Dinur (Dinaburg), another prominent historian-turned-public official, would favor granting retroactive Israeli citizenship to Jews murdered in the *Shoah* (Myers, 1995, p. 179).

9. Rubashov speaks consistently in the first person plural in these speeches; spoken Hebrew constituted a culturally intimate milieu. On this point, see Subotic and Zarakol (2013).

10. "But nowhere in all this was it ever apparent that anyone in the *Yishuv* understood *Shoah* in the sense of total annihilation, or that anyone envisioned a Europe left almost without Jews as a result of the Nazi murder machinery" (Ofer, 1996, p. 571).

11. The question of Husseini's collaboration with wartime Germany has long been deeply politicized (Pappé, 2011; Sells, 2015; Wien, 2010). I have no wish to add to this; my claim here speaks only to what Zionist leaders (and Haganah

commanders in particular) believed in 1942–1943, insofar as this can be discerned. In that vein, Palestinian antipathy to both British rule and Zionism was keenly felt. Haganah commanders noted with concern the role that *agents provocateurs* and fifth columnists had played in the German occupation of Norway and the Low Countries; Palestine seemed ripe for similar tactics. On this point, read Ben-Yisrael's (1940) essay in *Ma'arakhot* against Brenner (1981), Gelber (1990), and Dagan (1994). *Ma'arakhot* also featured discussions of German propaganda and intelligence networks in the Middle East; see 7 (May 1941), 52–53 and 28 (July 1945), 67–72. For contemporary discussions of these issues, see *inter alia*, Achcar (2009), Herf (2010), and Motadel (2014).

12. Just how fully formed these "plans" actually were is a matter of some dispute (Gelber, 1990; Segev, 1993, pp. 67–72). That said, even before the extent of German eliminationism was generally understood, the assumption of most within the *Yishuv* seems to have been that a German occupation would enjoy substantial Palestinian collaboration; and that as such, it would lead to the eventual destruction of the *Yishuv*. These were, after all, the same Palestinians whose own uprising had been "unrelentingly put down" by the British army only a few years earlier, with the Haganah's active assistance (Slutsky, 1976, pp. 106, 300–302, 344; Hughes, 2016).

13. "The Fredrician soldier had had been a means to an end, little more than a machine. Now the ideal of German neo-humanism, man as an end in himself, had to be realized for the common soldier .... If he could imagine the harsh duties of his calling not solely as external restraints but as innate personal obligations toward the fatherland, then he changed into the moral individual idealized by neo-humanism" (Meinecke, 1977, pp. 99; 1915, pp. 47–52).

14. "To [Ranke] the most important thing in that movement seemed the conflict between the two principles of monarchy and popular sovereignty. Though his heart beat for the old monarchy, he was led by his historical insight to what we may call historical dialectic. This was the process by which antagonistic elements may make each other productive and stronger, maintaining each other's vitality and leading to new syntheses" (Meinecke, 1954, p. 144).

15. All citations here are from the Verso translation, published in 2013.

16. At one point, a Palestinian student about his own age asks him in at a checkpoint search "how [he] could be so mean." Chayut's inner response: "Mean? Me?? No, I am not mean. I have a sense of belonging to the State. I have loyalty, sometimes compassion, lots of fear and a lot of love and longing for a better future. I feel optimism and hope for real peace, that we shall know how to divide the country and its treasures among all humans living here." And yet, he slowly recognizes, that narrative itself, the sense of enlightenment and self-regard it imparts, is what made it possible for him to continue to participate in the occupation *even as* he professed to despise it (Chayut, 2013, p. 62).

17. On these points, see also Löwenheim (2015).

18. For a fuller discussion of these themes, see Levine (2015).

19. "As I read Said's words ... I found myself grateful for the understanding of Jewishness that I would not quite have arrived at without him."

20. "Said's analysis urges us not to remember or forget Orientalism, the Muslim, the Arab, and ultimately the Palestinian without remembering the forgetting of European Jewish history and the history of European anti-Semitism in the context

of European colonialism, which made and makes all these historical transformations possible and mobilizes the very discourses that produce them as facts."

ACKNOWLEDGMENTS

Ali Fuat Birol, David Blaney, Chris Brown, Sam Chambers, Christine Field, Beate Jahn, Oliver Kessler, Helen Kinsella, Ned Lebow, Utz McKnight, Daniel Bertrand Monk, Nawal Mustafa, Patricia Owens, Mira Sucharov, Lauren Wilcox, and the anonymous reader offered helpful comments. Andy Hom, Sammy Barkin, Yehonatan Abrahamson, and Yoav Galai pressed me on key points; I regret that I have not been able to address them all. To Tarak Barkawi and George Lawson, especial thanks. The usual provisos apply.

REFERENCES

Abulof, U. (2015). *The morality and mortality of nations*. Cambridge: Cambridge University Press.

Achcar, G. (2009). *The Arabs and the Holocaust*. New York, NY: Picador.

Adorno, T. (1973). *Negative dialectics*. New York, NY: Continuum.

Adwan, S., Bar-On, D., & Naveh, E. (2012). *Side by side: Parallel histories of Israel-Palestine*. New York, NY: The New Press.

Agamben, G. (2002). *Remnants of Auschwitz*. New York, NY: Zone.

Alexander, J. C. (2009). *Remembering the Holocaust: A debate*. Oxford: Oxford University Press.

Ansky, S. (2002).*The enemy at his pleasure: A journey through the Jewish pale of settlement during World War I*. New York, NY: Metropolitan Books.

Ansorge, J. T., & Barkawi, T. (2014). Utile forms: Power and knowledge in small war. *Review of International Studies*, *40*, 3–24.

Arendt, H. (2000). *Rahel Vernhagen, The life of a Jewess*. Baltimore, MD: Johns Hopkins University Press.

Babel, I. (2002). *Red cavalry*. New York, NY: Norton.

Bauer, Y. (1970). *From diplomacy to resistance: Jewish Palestine, 1939–1945*. Philadelphia, PA: Jewish Publication Society.

Baumann, Z. (1989). *Modernity and the Holocaust*. Ithaca, NY: Cornell University Press.

Beiser, F. (2012). *The German historicist tradition*. Oxford: Oxford University Press.

Ben-Josef Hirsch, M. (2007). From taboo to the negotiable: The Israeli new historians and the changing representation of the Palestinian refugee problem. *Perspectives on Politics*, *5*(2), 241–258.

Benjamin, W. (1968). *Illuminations*. New York, NY: Schocken.

Ben-Yisrael, A. (1940). Military observations on the invasion of Holland. *Ma'arakhot*, *2–3*, 44–50.

Boyarin, D. (1997). *Unheroic conduct: The rise of heterosexuality and the invention of the Jewish Man*. Berkeley, CA: University of California Press.

Brenner, U. (1981). *Nokhah Iyyum ha-Plishah ha-Germanit li-Eretz Yisrael, 1940-2*. Ramat Efal: Yad Tabenkin.

Butler, J. (2012). *Parting ways*. New York, NY: Columbia University Press.

Butterfield, H. (1931). *The whig interpretation of history*. London: G. Bell.

Canaan, H. (1973/1974). *Matayim Yemei Haradah*. Tel Aviv: Mol-Art.

Carr, E. H. (1964). *The twenty years crisis*. New York, NY: Harper and Row.

Chayut, N. (2013). *The girl who stole my Holocaust*. London: Verso.

Chowers, E. (2013). *The political theory of Zionism*. Cambridge: Cambridge University Press.

Clark, M. (2006). *Beyond catastrophe: German intellectuals and cultural renewal after World War II* (pp. 1945–1955). Lanham, MD: Lexington Press.

Craig, G. (1978). *Germany, 1866-1945*. Oxford: Oxford University Press.

Dagan, S. (1994). *Tokhnit ha-Tsafon: Tobruk, Haifa, Musa Dagh*. Tel Aviv: Ministry of Defence Press.

Dinur, B. (1954). On *The history of the Haganah* and its programme. *Sefer Toldot ha-Haganah: Me-Hitgonenut le-Haganah* (Vol. 1, Parts 1, 3–8). Tel Aviv: Am Oved.

Eastwood, J. (2016). 'Meaningful service': Pedagogy at Israeli pre-military academies and the ethics of Militarism. *European Journal of International Relations*, 1–25. doi:10.1177/1354066115594855

Eley, G. (1988). Nazism, politics and the image of the past: Thoughts on the West German Historikerstreit, 1986–1987. *Past & Present*, *121*(November), 171–208.

Elon, A. (2001). *The Israelis: Founders and sons*. London: Faber & Faber.

Etzioni-Halevy, E. (1997). *Makom bi-Tzameret*. Tel Aviv: Cherikover.

Even-Shoshan, A. (2003). Shoah. *Milon Even-Shoshan [The Even-Shoshan dictionary of the Hebrew language]* (Vol. 6, p. 1849). Israel: ha-Milon he-Hadash Ltd.

Friedlander, S. (1992). *Probing the limits of representation*. Cambridge, MA: Harvard University Press.

Friling, T. (2005). *Arrows in the dark: David Ben-Gurion, the Yishuv leadership, and rescue attempts during the holocaust* (Vol. 1). Madison, WI: University of Wisconsin Press.

Funkenstein, A. (1992). History, counterhistory, and narrative. In S. Friedlander (Ed.), *Probing the limits of representation* (pp. 66–81). Cambridge, MA: Harvard University Press.

Gelber, Y. (1990). *Masadah: ha-Haganah al Eretz-Yisrael bi-Milhemet ha-Olam ha-Shniyyah*. Ramat Gan, Israel: Bar-Ilan University Press.

Gismondi, M. (2004). Tragedy, realism and postmodernity: *Kulturpessimus* in the theories of Max Weber, EH Carr, Hans Morgenthau, and Henry Kissinger. *Diplomacy and Statecraft*, *15*(3), 435–464.

Grovogui, S. (2006). *Beyond eurocentrism and anarchy*. London: Palgrave.

Guilhot, N. (2015). Portrait of the realist as a historian: On anti-whiggism in the history of international relations. *European Journal of International Relations*, *21*(1), 3–26.

Habermas, J. (1988). Concerning the public use of history. *New German Critique*, *44*, 40–50.

Harkabi, Y. (1982). *The Bar Kokhba Syndrome: Risk and realism in international politics*. Chappaqua, NY: Rossell.

Herf, J. (2010). *Nazi propaganda for the Arab world*. New Haven, CT: Yale University Press.

Herzl, T. (1995). A Jewish state. In O. Dahbour & M. Ishay (Eds.), *The nationalism reader* (pp. 125–131). Atlantic Highlands, NJ: Humanities Press.

Hom, A. R. (2016). Angst springs eternal: Dangerous times and the dangers of timing the 'Arab Spring'. *Security Dialogue*, *47*(2), 165–183.

Horowitz, D., & Lissak, M. (1978). *The origins of the Israeli polity*. Chicago, IL: University of Chicago Press.

Hughes, M. (2009). The banality of brutality: British armed forces and the repression of the Arab Revolt in Palestine, 1936–39. *English Historical Review*, *CXXIV*, *507*, 313–354.

Hughes, M. (2016). Palestinian collaboration with the British: The peace bands and the Arab revolt of 1936–39. *Journal of Contemporary History*, *51*(2), 291–315.

Hutchings, K. (2008). *Time and world politics*. Manchester: Manchester University Press.

Iggers, G. (1983). *The German conception of history*. Middletown, CT: Wesleyan University Press.

Ihrig, S. (2016). *Justifying genocide: Germany and the armenians from bismarck to hitler*. Cambridge: Harvard University Press.

Isacoff, J. (2006). *Writing the Arab-Israeli conflict*. Lanham, MD: Lexington Books.

Kaplan, M. (1964). *The conduct of inquiry*. New York, NY: Chandler Publishing.

Kimmerling, B., & Migdal, J. (2003). *The Palestinian people: A history*. Cambridge, MA: Harvard University Press.

Knowlton, J., & Cates, T. (1993). *Forever in the Shadow of Hitler? Original Documents in the Historikerstreit, the Controversy Concerning the Singularity of the Holocaust*. Atlantic Highlands, NJ: Humanities Press.

Knudsen, J. (1994). Friedrich Meinecke, 1862–1954. In H. Lehmann & J. van Horn Melton (Eds.), *Paths of continuity: Central European historiography from the 1930s to the 1950s* (pp. 49–72). Cambridge: Cambridge University Press.

Kohn, H. (1954). *German history: Some new German views*. Boston, MA: Beacon.

Lentin, R. (2000). *Israel and the daughters of the Shoah*. New York, NY: Bergahn Books.

Levine, D. J. (2014). The apocalyptic sting and the rise of Israeli unrealism: Toward a negative-dialectical critique. *Globalizations*, *11*(5), 643–659.

Levine, D. J. (2015). Between late style and sustainable critique: Said, Adorno, and the Israel-Palestine conflict. In J. Amoreux & B. J. Steele (Eds.), *Reflexivity in international relations* (pp. 102–122). London: Routledge.

Levine, D. J. (2016). *After tragedy: Melodrama and the rhetoric of realism*. Working Paper.

Livne (Levinstein), E. (1960, November 9). *Personal testimony*, RG 30.00019 (old identifier: 3886). Haganah Archive, Tel Aviv. [Hebrew].

Löwenheim, O. (2015). Back to Hebron's tegart fort: An autoethnography of shame, love, loss, and the de-securitization of the self. *Journal of Narrative Politics*, *1*(2), 133–149.

Luttwak, E., & Horowitz, D. (1975). *The Israeli army*. New York: Harper & Row.

Ma'arakhot [Unsigned Editorial]. (1939, September). Divrei Petichah. *bi-Yemei Ma'arakhot: Me'asef li-She'elot Mediniyot, Kalkaliyot ve-Estrategiyot*, pp. 1–2.

Machiavelli, N. (1940). *The prince and the discourses*. New York, NY: Modern Library.

Maier, C. (1988). *The unmasterable past*. Cambridge, MA: Harvard University Press.

Massad, J. A. (2013). Forget semitism! In E. Weber (Ed.), *Living together: Jacques Derrida's communities of violence and peace* (pp. 59–79). New York, NY: Fordham University Press.

Matthews, W. (2006). *Confronting an empire, constructing a nation*. London: I.B. Tauris. mat.

Medding, P. (1972). *Mapai in Israel: Political organization and government in a new society*. Cambridge: Cambridge University Press.

Meinecke, F. (1915). *The warfare of a nation*. Worcester, MA: Davis Press.

Meinecke, F. (1950). *The German catastrophe*. Boston, MA: Beacon.

Meinecke, F. (1954). Ranke and Burckhardt. In H., Kohn (Ed.), *German history: Some new German views* (pp. 141–156). Boston, MA: Beacon Press.

Meinecke, F. (1957 [1924]). *Machiavellism: The doctrine of raison d'état and its place in modern history*. Introduction by W. Stark. New Haven, CT: Yale University Press.

Meinecke, F. (1977). *The age of German liberation*. Berkeley, CA: University of California Press.

Morgenthau, H. J. (1946). *Scientific man and power politics*. Chicago, IL: University of Chicago Press.

Morgenthau, H. J. (1967). *Politics among nations*. New York, NY: Knopf.

Morris, M. (2007). *Making Israel*. Ann Arbor, MI: University of Michigan Press.

Motadel, D. (2014). *Islam and Nazi Germany's war*. Cambridge, MA: Harvard University Press.

Myers, D. N. (1995). *Reinventing the Jewish past: European Jewish intellectuals and the Zionist return to history*. Oxford: Oxford University Press.

Myers, D. N. (2003). *Resisting history: Historicism and its discontents in German-Jewish thought*. Princeton: Princeton University Press.

Neubauer, A., & Stern, M. (1896). *Hebräische Berichte über die Judenverfolgung während der Kreuzzüge*. Berlin: Verlag von Leonhard Simion. Reprinted New York, NY: Georg Olms Verlag, 1997.

Nirenberg, D. (2013). *Anti-Judaism*. New York, NY: Norton.

Norris, J. (2008). Repression and rebellion: Britain's response to the Arab revolt in Palestine of 1936–39. *Journal of Imperial and Commonwealth History*, *36*(1), 25–45.

Ofer, D. (1996). Linguistic conceptualization of the Holocaust in Palestine and Israel, 1942–53. *Journal of Contemporary History*, *31*(3), 567–595.

Olick, J. (2005). *In the house of the Hangman*. Chicago, IL: University of Chicago Press.

Pa'il, M (1979). *Min ha-Haganah li-Tsva ha-Haganah*. Tel Aviv: Zmora, Beitan & Modan.

Pappé, I. (2009). The vicissitudes of the 1948 historiography of Israel. *Journal of Palestine Studies*, *39*(1), 6–23.

Pappé, I. (2011). *The rise and fall of a Palestinian dynasty: The Husaynis, 1700–1948*. Berkeley, CA: University of California Press.

Pois, R. (1973). *Friedrich Meinecke and German politics*. Berkeley, CA: University of California Press.

Pois, R. (1976). Bourgeois democrats of Weimar Germany. *Transactions of the American Philosophical Society*, *66*(4), 1–117.

Porat, D. (1990). *The blue and the yellow stars: The Zionist leadership in Palestine and the Holocaust*. Cambridge, MA: Harvard University Press.

Raz-Krakotzkin, A. (2007). Jewish memory between exile and history. *Jewish Quarterly Review*, *97*(4), 530–543.

Raz-Krakotzkin, A. (2013). "On the right side of the barricades": Walter Benjamin, Gershom Scholem, and Zionism. *Comparative Literature*, *65*(3), 363–381.

Rivlin, G. (1960, March 6). *Personal testimony*, RG 44.00036 (old identifier: 4105). Haganah Archive, Tel Aviv. [Hebrew].

Rossi, P. (1975). The ideological valences of twentieth-century historicism. *History and Theory*, *14*(4), 15–29.

Rothberg, M. (2009). *Multidimensional memory: Remembering the holocaust in the age of decolonization*. Stanford, CA: Stanford University Press.

Rubashov, Z. (1942/1943a). bi-Shalhei Evleinu ha-Le'umi [On the Dusk of our National Mourning]. *Ma'arakhot*, 4(1) (November–January), 4–7.

Rubashov, Z. (1942/1943b). le-Sgulot ha-Haganah be-Yisra'el [On Israel's Military Character]. *Ma'arakhot*, 4(2–3) (May–December), 5–15.

Rubashov, Z. (5703 [1942/1943]). *me-Kurban le-Lohem*. Tel Aviv: Workers' Party of Eretz-Israel Press.

Said, E. W. (2001). Afterword. In E. L. Rogan & A. Shlaim (Eds.), *The war for Palestine: Rewriting the history of 1948* (pp. 248–261). Cambridge: Cambridge University Press.

Schiff, Z. (1985). *A history of the Israeli army*. New York, NY: Macmillan.

Segev, T. (1993). *The seventh million: Israel and the Holocaust*. New York, NY: Hill and Wang.

Sells, M. A. (2015). Holocaust abuse: The Case of Hajj Muhammad Amin al-Husayni. *Journal of Religious Ethics*, *43*(4), 723–759.

Shaw, M., & Bartov, O. (2010). The question of genocide in Palestine, 1948: An exchange. *Journal of Genocide Research*, *12*(3-4), 243–259.

Sheffy, Y. (1991). *Sikat Mem-Mem*. Tel Aviv: Ministry of Defense Press.

Slutsky, Y. (1976). Sefer Toldot ha-Haganah. *me-Ma'avak li-Milhamah* (Vol. 3, Part 1). Tel Aviv: Am Oved..

Sterling, R. (1954). *Ethics in a world of power*. New Haven: Yale University Press.

Sternhell, Z. (2010). *The anti-enlightenment tradition*. New Haven, CT: Yale University Press.

Stieg, M. (1986). *The origin and development of scholarly historical periodicals*. Tuscaloosa, AL: University of Alabama Press.

Subotic, J., & Zarakol, A. (2013). Cultural intimacy in international relations. *European Journal of International Relations*, *19*(4), 915–938.

Swedenburg, T. (1993). *Memories of revolt: The 1936-39 rebellion and the palestinian national past*. Fayetteville, AR: University of Arkansas Press.

Tamari, D. (2011). *Umma Hamushah*. Tel Aviv: Ma'arakhot/Modan.

Tidhar, D. (1949). Schneur Zalman Shazar (Rubashov). *Entsiklopedyah le-halutse ha-yishuv u-vonav* (Vol. 3, pp. 1111–1113). Retrieved from http://www.tidhar.tourolib.org/tidhar/view/3/1111. Accessed on 23 September, 2016.

Tjalve, V. S., & Williams, M. C. (2015). Reviving the rhetoric of realism: Politics and responsibility in grand strategy. *Security Studies*, *24*(1), 37–60.

Tsoref, H., (Ed.). (5768 [2007/2008]). *Zalman Shazar, HaNasi Ha-Shlishi: Mivhar Teudot me-Pirkei Hayav*. Jerusalem: Israel State Archives.

Van Creveld, M. (1998). *The sword and the olive: A critical history of the Israel defense force*. New York, NY: Public Affairs.

Wehler, H. (1985). *The German empire 1871–1918*. Dover, NH: Berg Publishers.

Weiss, M. (2002). *The chosen body: The politics of the body in Israeli society*. Palo Alto, CA: Stanford University Press.

White, H. (1975). Historicism, history, and the figurative imagination. *History and Theory*, *14*(4), 48–67.

Wien, P. (2010). Coming to terms with the past: German academia and historical relations between the Arab lands and Nazi Germany. *International Journal of Middle East Studies*, *42*, 311–321.

Wikipedia [Unsigned]. (2016). *Zalman Shazar*. Wikipedia, The free encyclopedia (Hebrew). Retrieved from https://he.wikipedia.org/w/index.php?title=%D7%96%D7%9C%D7%9E%D7%9F_%D7%A9%D7%96%D7%A8&oldid=18088816. Accessed on March 8.

Wolfson, P. (1956). Friedrich Meinecke (1862–1954). *Journal of the History of Ideas*, *17*(4), 511–525.

Wright, J. K. (2003). History and historicism. In T. M., Porter & D., Ross (Eds.), *The Cambridge history of science: The modern social sciences* (Vol. 7, pp. 113–130). Cambridge: Cambridge University Press.

Yazbak, M., & Weiss, Y. (2011). *Haifa before and after 1948: Narratives of mixed city*. Dordrecht: Republic of Letters.

Yerushalmi, Y. H. (1996). *Zakhor: Jewish history and Jewish Memory*. Seattle, WA: University of Washington Press.

Zertal, I. (1998). *From catastrophe to power*. Berkeley, CA: University of California Press.

Zertal, I. (2006). *Israel's holocaust and the politics of nationhood*. Cambridge: Cambridge University Press.

LATE-VICTORIAN WORLDS: ALFRED MARSHALL ON COMPETITION, CHARACTER, AND ANGLO-SAXON CIVILIZATION

David L. Blaney

ABSTRACT

Duncan Bell's project to restore late-Victorian and Edwardian debates on federative empire or a Greater Britain to international theory emphasizes the "political language" of civilization, race, and character available to fin-de-siècle thinkers on empire. In the process, Bell leaves out the contribution to these debates made by a key figure in the newly emerging discipline of economics: Alfred Marshall. Most recent writings on 19th-century empire similarly ignore the work of late-Victorian economists, as do recent efforts to map the terrain of international theory more broadly. Marshall's writings on federative empire are not referenced by the advocates of Greater Britain that Bell carefully documents, but it is clear that Marshall followed those debates closely. And though he imagined his contribution as distinctly economic, his work unfolded in a similar language of civilization, race, and character, informed particularly by social evolutionary thought. In conclusion, I stress the dangerous

International Origins of Social and Political Theory
Political Power and Social Theory, Volume 32, 127–152

ISSN: 0198-8719/doi:10.1108/S0198-871920170000032006

temptation to sort the relevance of thinkers according to contemporary disciplinary boundaries so that more recent economists and the components of earlier political economic work that might be classed as economics are sifted out of our narratives of political thought. Instead, I see the debates on empire that Bell explores as unfolding in a language that, since the 17th and 18th centuries, has engaged issues of commerce and trade, social change, moral virtue, and the nature of political rule: political economy.

Keywords: Alfred Marshall; civilization; social evolution; federative empire; Greater Britain

INTRODUCTION

Duncan Bell, virtually singlehandedly, has restored late-Victorian and Edwardian debates about, as he puts it, "democracy, empire, race and war" (2014a, p. 648) to scholarly discussion in international political theory. More specifically, Bell (2007a, p. 22) argues that the tendency to focus narrowly on J. S. Mill, either to defend his anti-imperial credentials or to cast him into complicity with the colonial project, leads scholars to overplay Mill's influence and gives short shrift to other figures central to late-Victorian and Edwardian debates on the empire, many of whom remain virtually unknown.[1] This misplaced emphasis also leads scholars to miss the particular contours of late-Victorian political thinking including, importantly, visions of a federative empire or a Greater Britain centered on the Anglo-Saxon world that resonated deeply into the 20th century (Bell, 2007a, 2007b; 2014a, 2014b; 2016, Chapter 8). In recent extension of this work, Bell (2016, especially Chapters 2 and 3) calls for thoroughgoing reexamination of our thinking about liberalism and empire, an examination that bears not only on our understanding of political thought on empire, but also on the very meaning of liberalism as a tradition of thought or a canonical device.

Bell's project turns on attention to the particular "political language" available to *fin-de-siècle* thinkers on empire. Without denying the importance of political language or the possibility of seeing the "political" in rather capacious terms,[2] I believe this frame risks taking for granted the boundary between economics and politics that was being even more finely drawn with the institutionalization of economics as a distinct discipline at this very time. Indeed, it is striking that Bell's careful accounting of the debates on the character of empire and his discussion of liberalism includes few economists, with the exception of representatives of historical economics, Cunningham, Ashley, and Hobson, who were gradually being marginalized within the emerging discipline of economics.[3] This omission of economists seems curious because Bell suggests that the challenges to Britain's dominant economic position serve as a crucial backdrop to the debates he documents (Bell, 2005, 2007a).

Bell's omission is quite consistent with recent work on empire. Whether informed by cultural studies, postcolonial theory, or some combination thereof, "political economy" has been displaced from its determining role (Proudfoot & Roche, 2005, p. 1).[4] The most celebrated recent work on social and political thought and empire, much of which Bell cites, perhaps rightly tends to de-emphasize the role of imperial balance sheets or the rationalizations of sectional interests that had been given too large a place, and emphasize instead the role orientalist tropes, civilizational theories, and practices of racialization play in making sense of and justifying empire (Agnani, 2013; Lowe, 2015; Mehta, 1999; Morefield, 2014; Muthu, 2003; Pitts, 2005; Schultz & Varouxakis, 2005). Through earlier political economists (James and J. S. Mill, Malthus, and Bentham) are often mentioned, the new profession of economics and its major figures are absent from the story.[5]

We find a similar pattern in two recent contributions to the history of international theory. Hobson's (2012) magisterial accounting of the Eurocentrism of international theory encompasses a broad swath of history, beginning with the latter half of the 18th century. Not surprisingly, Adam Smith plays a big role in the early phase of Hobson's book and David Ricardo merits a quick mention. His discussion of the 19th century covers a range of figures, overlapping with Bell and other accounts of imperial political thought, with Mill and Marx given a prominent role. Once he reaches the 20th century, economists, apart from the iconoclastic figure, John Hobson, disappear from the account entirely as if the newly emerging economics discipline did not make contributions to international theory. In a similarly path-breaking book, Vitalis (2015) explores the centrality of race to early-20th-century thinking about the international system, a feature of disciplinary history largely erased by contemporary accounts. Vitalis does note the importance of interdependence (economic and racial) in early texts in the field of international relations, but economists do not figure in the story. We might forgive him for largely ignoring economists' contributions to thinking about international relations, since his audience is a discipline mostly lodged in political science, if Vitalis' account were not also peopled with sociologists, geographers, anthropologists, and historians. Somehow, our interdisciplinary impulses within international relations extend to the social sciences broadly, except for economics.

My goal is to redress this lacuna in a preliminary way by exploring the work of Alfred Marshall, a key figure in what might be called the "neoclassical synthesis" (Reisman, 1990, p. 81) and, by some accounts, the "first professional economist" (Collini, Winch, & Burrow, 1983, p. 312). Yet, Marshall also can be read as a product of this same late-Victorian imperial context and as a representative of liberal "imperial political [economic] thought" (to adapt Bell, 2005, p. 3) in that he brings his new disciplinary understandings to bear not only on debates surrounding import duties and England's competitive position, but also the role of the Anglo-Saxon race and culture within the empire and in world history more generally. Marshall, as various commentators (Hart, 2012, Chapter 1; Reisman, 1990, pp. 92, 93; Samuels, 2001) note, embraces ambivalence and duality in his vision of economics as part of respecting the complexity of social life: Static equilibrium is juxtaposed with dynamics (with analogies shifting from physics to biology), and mathematical precision and abstract deductive systems contend with the messiness of historical and civilizational specificity. More precisely, he attends with great care to the evidence of interconnected economic and civilizational differences and inequalities that were treated as self-evident by a middle-class citizen of the British Empire (Bell, 2016; Burrow, 1966; Stocking, 1987, Chapter 10), and he manages these differences within a complicated understanding of competition among individuals, industrial sectors, nations, and races that explains not only uneven outcomes in one time period, but also human productive and moral advance generally. Here, biological and social evolutionary thinking served as a predominant intellectual assumption (Hart, 2012, pp. 17–28, 63–70; Niman, 1991; Reisman, 1987, Chapter 7), as does a sense of Anglo-American superiority as the height of progress, as we shall see. Marshall's work is striking, then, precisely because this divide between economics and cultural or civilizational analysis appears simultaneously internal to and partly bridged by his work. The position Marshall stakes out in reference to the debates Bell and others document involved *economic, cultural, and political* considerations.

In the section that follows, I sketch Bell's account of the late-Victorian debates around Greater Britain, noting particularly the limited place he gives to economists in his work. I then turn to Alfred Marshall's account of economics as a civilizational/racial science which ultimately serves to understand and contribute to human ethical advance. At various points, Marshall turns to imperial questions, embracing a version of federative Anglosaxondom that appears as a partial rejoinder to the protectionist impulses that motivated some of the Greater Britain thinkers. But Marshall rejects protectionism and supports free trade not so much for their direct material consequences, but because of their cultural and political consequences. His defense of a free-trade federation of Anglo-Saxon nations unfolds in the metaphysical categories of Bell's late-Victorian political thinkers. In the end, I reflect briefly on the continued policing of the politics and economics boundary and suggest that the most encompassing category of language available to modern thinkers remains that of political economy.

LATE-VICTORIAN EMPIRE, GREATER BRITAIN, AND THE MISSING ECONOMISTS

Bell (2007a, 2014a) has painstakingly documented the strains of late-Victorian and Edwardian imperial thought that embrace, in some fashion, a "global state," imagined as an Anglo-Saxon or Anglo-American union or a federative empire: a Greater Britain. He recognizes that renewed interest in empire was a response partly to immediate events, particularly a sense of growing threat to Britain's dominant political and economic position (Bell, 2007a, pp. 27, 34; 2016, pp. 166–167). The fact that empire might be reimagined in a federative form, perhaps prefiguring recent counter- or post-Westphalian scholarly and political projects, turned on a sense that space had been shrunk by new communications and transportation technologies (Bell, 2005, 2014b). Whatever be the catalysts, Bell sees Greater Britain as a distinctly political project. This strand of imperial *political* thought reimagines British political identity as a nation or race dispersed across space, advocates new federative institutions designed to encompass a dispersed Britishness, and justifies this project as much in civic and moral terms as geopolitical. Thus, many of the "colonial unionists" Bell surveys "sought to distinguish themselves sharply from what they saw as the corrosive liberalism of the 'Manchester School' and the utilitarian political economists" (Bell, 2007a, p. 17); they saw economists' dogmatic support for free trade as a cosmopolitanism that undercuts the empire and their blindness to anything but material wealth as contributing to the unraveling of collective moral bonds (Bell, 2007a, pp. 44–45, 118).

But Greater Britain was more than a call for a return to some prior and less cosmopolitan era in which a sense of British national purpose might be rekindled. Rather, following Spencer and Maine, Greater Britain advocates recognized that England's evolutionary advantage was built alongside the extension of social relations and markets across space, but most thinkers fully recognized that these same evolutionary processes entailed the possibility of imperial decline (Bell, 2007b, p. 163). As an alternative to the feared decline of British preeminence, they envisioned a "global" *political* "stage" on which a "trans-continental composite polity" might be built (Bell, 2007a, pp. 55, 261). This political stage remained divided into peoples and races that varying climate and circumstance created and distance perpetuated, in spite of the gradual overcoming of distance by new technologies (Bell, 2007a, pp. 63–91, 117; 2016, pp. 174–175). In short, severe limits to a "global consciousness" remained (Bell, 2007a, p. 260) so that the imagined political state, a Greater Britain, would encompass only Anglo-Saxon peoples: A distinctive racial or national group, in terms often used interchangeably, whose extension across space was effected by English settlements in North America and the Antipodes. This race would lead a Greater Britain, while settlers in Africa, the indigenous peoples of North America and colonized peoples of Asia, with India as the key reference point, would remain subordinated. Thus, the vision of a federated empire was as a narrow, though transnational, "racial polity" (Bell, 2007a, pp. 92, 101, 113–115, 222–226; 2007b, pp. 159–160, 167, 173; 2016, pp. 175–178, 186–196).

Few details were forthcoming about the institutional framework governing the imagined "noncontiguous representative polity." Often the United States served as a loose model for a federated empire (Bell, 2007a, pp. 56, 95, 208, 234), but, as Bell (2007a, p. 8) notes, the idea of a Greater Britain resonated for metaphysical, or perhaps ethical, reasons more than the appeal of any particular institutional configuration. The idea promised, according to its proponents, to restore the vitality of British domestic society by strengthening the bonds of citizenship and refreshing stores of moral energy and civic virtue (Bell, 2007a, pp. 44, 137–139). Bell (2007a, pp. 137–141) calls this "Civic Imperialism," emphasizing the contrast his late-Victorian thinkers drew between themselves and "liberals infected with the 'virus of Manchesterism'." Where "utilitarian reasoning, a narrow obsession with profit, and a debilitating individualism" crippled the spirit of the citizenry, building Greater Britain, these thinkers concluded, would help overcome a sense of selfish isolation, mitigate the conflict of sectional interests, and cultivate a political vision transcending tribe and nation, fostering the development of individual "character" (Bell, 2007a, pp. 141–165).

Bell (2007a, p. 46) does recognize that several "historical economists," W. J. Ashley and William Cunningham the most prominent, joined in support of a colonial federation, but for reasons he sees as distinctive: They saw "empire as the most appropriate unit for enacting economic and social policies, as well as for maintaining British power and prestige," without giving much emphasis to the metaphysical concerns that motivated *political* thinking around Greater Britain. That late-Victorian economists, with their "abstract deductive methods," might have contributed to these discussions of civilization and British power was considered neither by Bell's key figures, nor by Bell himself. Alfred Marshall is interesting precisely because his writings on "great Anglosaxondom" bring to bear both deductive methods and metaphysical concerns, combining a commitment to open trade and the evolving character of national and human civic and moral consciousness.

MARSHALL'S ECONOMICS AS CIVILIZATIONAL/RACIAL SCIENCE

Making Marshall a central figure in this story perhaps requires a stronger defense than given thus far. Though debates about free trade and imperial policy in the middle and late-Victorian era referenced largely Smith, Ricardo, and Mill, that would change gradually as economics was hived off from political economy and institutionalized as degree program and scholarly discipline. As noted, Marshall is central to the institutional birthing of modern economics, though debates about his relative intellectual contribution continue.[6] What is clear is that his *Principles of Economics* becomes the standard English language text after 1890, the final substantially revised version appearing in 1920, until replaced by the work of his student, Keynes. But unlike contemporary "Principles" textbooks since Samuelson set the standard, Marshall's work subordinates the mathematics central to the emerging discipline to a series of "precepts" built around a deeper understanding of history and philosophy (Colander, 2015).[7] Given the mixing of economic analytics, philosophy of history, and social evolutionary thought in Marshall's writings, we might see his economic project, as Peck (2010, p. 41) puts it in another context, as a mixture of "prejudice, practice, and principle." The prejudice may be more relevant than the practice, since Marshall might be thought of more as made by empire than actually making it, though he gave colonial issues substantial attention in his writings and notes (Wood, 1983, pp. 113–134). The prejudices of empire inform his principles: He imagines that economic science may contribute to the expansion of wealth and civilization, and he demarcates his object of analysis in spatial categories inflected by empire (home markets, racial and civilizational units, and industrial zones operating within and beyond colonial space), not in terms of "the economy," a construct that becomes dominant only after his death (Breslau, 2003).

I organize my presentation of Marshall's thought around three broad and intertwined themes. First, I examine his claims in *Principles* that biology, with its understanding of the evolution of the organism, serves as the "mecca" of economic science, not physics, so that he makes competition among individuals and races and the consequent advance of industry and human character central to his economics. Second, and drawing also on his last book, *Industry and Trade* (1919), Marshall intertwines industrial and civilizational advance in his account of the development of England's industrial leadership and its transfer to the United States and the self-governing colonies. Third, over nearly two decades, Marshall publically presents his thinking on colonial policies and empire, including defending the idea of "great Anglosaxondom," though his position serves as an apparent rejoinder to those who see protectionism as necessary to preserving the moral integrity of England and the strength of the empire.

The Biological Analogy, Competition, and Character

Though a key inspiration for an emerging abstract, deductive economic science, Marshall (2009 [1920]) provides clear and quite different guidance, consistent through to the 8th and final edition, for readers of his *Principles* (hereafter cited as *P*). Economics' power as a science, Marshall insists more than once, stems from its focus on "mankind as they live and move and think in the ordinary business of life" (*P*, 12; see also *P*, 1). Since "man's character has been moulded by his every-day work, and the material resources which he thereby procures" (*P*, 1), the "business by which a person earns his livelihood" serves as one of the "great forming agencies of the world's history." Individuals forge their character in their work, establishing the conscious and unconscious habits that give economic life a stability, or what Marshall calls "normal conditions" (*P*, xi). These "normal conditions" are the conditions of possibility of an economic science based on formal or mechanical models of economic behavior.

But Marshall's characterization of normal conditions suggests economic science must find its limits and purpose in historical or civilizational dynamics. Normal conditions apply only to the "city men" (Marshall, 1885, pp. 5, 15) formed by the "conditions of industrial life, and of those methods of production, distribution and consumption, with which modern economic science is concerned" (*P*, xi). Though economists might believe they can adapt "modern economic theory … to the conditions of backward races," by asserting some commonality of "substance" despite the variation in economic "form," the common substance that might be thought to underlie these different economic forms is "not easy to detect" (*P*, 4). What gives his newly founded economic science the hope of any generalized purchase, then, is that humankind moves toward the "economic conditions of modern life" (*P*, 4) through various "stages in social history" (*P*, xiii) or, more strongly, arriving at human nature "constituted as it is at present" (*P*, 416). "The main concern of economics is," Marshall announces, "with human beings who are impelled, for *good and evil*, to *change and progress*" (*P*, xiii; emphasis added).

For economists, then, the real "key-note is that of dynamics rather than statics" (*P*, xiii). The "Mecca of the economist lies," Marshall famously notes, in the complexities of "economic biology" (*P*, xii), so that "[f]ragmentary statical hypotheses are used as temporary auxiliaries to dynamical – or rather biological – conceptions" (*P*, xiii).[8] For Marshall, a mechanical science fails to capture the complexities of specific markets and the path-dependent trajectories of industries with increasing returns (*P*, 284, 415–416), much less providing an exhaustive account of human behavior and character. The everyday life of business competes with "religious ideals" in shaping human character and behavior, and economics must attend not only to the lower faculties, but also to the higher (*P*, 1), including an economic biology attuned to the "more refined and noble life" possible for humankind (*P*, 2). This is crucial because Marshall sees human "patterns of conduct and character as flows, not as stocks" (Reisman, 1987, p. 101); "man's efficiency and character" can no longer be "regarded as a fixed quantity," and the changed conditions of economic life in the 19th century have produced such "rapid changes" in "human nature" that they cannot be ignored (*P*, 631). It should not be surprising, then, that Marshall not only credits authors like Cournot and von Thünen who shaped his understanding of the role of "increments of quantities" in creating "stable equilibrium," but also the influences of Herbert Spencer in suggesting the importance of the biological analogy and Hegel's historical/philosophical studies – the latter two to whom he dedicates *Principles*, but whose influence is felt more strongly in the later *Industry and Trade*,[9] to which we turn below. It is there he applies the biological metaphor to England's economic history.

The historical sweep and social evolutionary content of Marshall's thought is nicely illustrated already in the chapters in Book IV of *Principles* dedicated to industrial organization. He begins Book IV by claiming to combine Adam Smith's account of the division of labor and the biological analogy to understand human progress. For Smith, Marshall (*P*, 200) asserts, advances in division of labor allow larger populations to thrive on a limited territory, but, notably, "the pressure of population on the means of subsistence tends to weed out those races who through want of organization or for any other cause are unable to turn to the best account the advantages of the place in which they live." In this, Smith is claimed to foreshadow the insights of Malthus and Darwin on the role of the struggle to survive in promoting the "development of the organism, whether social or physical." Organismic development, Marshall (*P*, 200–201) claims, "involves an increasing subdivision of functions between its separate parts on the one hand, and on the other a more intimate connection between them. Each part gets to be less and less self-sufficient, to depend for its wellbeing more and more on other parts."[10] Likewise, the "industrial organism" develops by "differentiation" – "of specialized skill, knowledge, and machinery" – and "integration" or a "growing intimacy and firmness of the separate parts" via improved communications and transportation (*P*, 201).[11]

Marshall recognizes that his biological analogy might be greeted with shock by some liberal opinion and he treads carefully. He suggests that the "hard truth" suggested by the "[l]aw of the survival of the fittest" is "softened down by the fact that those races, whose members render services to one another without exacting direct recompense, are not only the most likely to flourish for the time, but most likely to rear a large number of descendants who inherit their beneficial habits" (*P*, 201–202).[12] Marshall argues that any species, no matter how "vigorous in its growth," would not flourish long without a strong measure of "family and race duty." In their "ruder stages," humans render services to others by "hereditary habit and unreasoning impulse," but soon this instinct is supplanted by "deliberate, and therefore moral, self-sacrifice." These moral precepts are refined over time and reinforced by their adaptive success, since the "races in which these qualities are the most highly developed are sure, other things being equal, to be stronger than others in war and in contests with famine and disease, and ultimately to prevail." The "struggle for existence" favors, then, those races in which individuals are most willing to sacrifice themselves for the collective, since they are best able to thrive in their respective environments, thereby contributing to the collective good of moral advance – as if by an invisible hand, I might add.[13]

Marshall makes the movement toward the transcendence of sectional interests a centerpiece of *Industry and Trade* (Marshall, n.d. [1920], hereafter cited as *IT* and volume number). The processes at work – the extension of markets, new industries, increasing application of science – all promote continued advance in the previously developed, or "old countries" as Marshall calls them, and lead the "new countries" to "quickly fall[ ] into line with the old" (*IT* I, p. 5). As he notes, "even stagnant peoples gradually modify their habits and their industrial technique." Key to this is the triumph of "reason" over "tradition" so that the past is displaced as a "guide for the present" by the possibilities shown by "progressive peoples" (*IT* I, pp. 7–9). Partly, we find a growing capacity to "sacrifice ease" in the present in order to gain more in the future and not just for himself but in order "to secure a future provision for his family" (*P*, 566). Paralleling his earlier claims about the adaptability of race duty for individuals and collectives, he sees humans becoming gradually "less selfish," and this "economic chivalry," as he sometimes calls it (Marshall, 1907), begins to extend beyond the family: "there are already faint signs of a brighter time to come, in which there will be a general willingness to work and save in order to increase the stores of public wealth and of public opportunities for leading a higher life" (*P*, 566, 599; see also *IT* I, pp. 6–8). It is this growing spirit of "economic chivalry," not the universal desire for material gain that he associates with a "cosmopolitan point of view" (*IT* I, p. 6).

This transformation in human conduct and character occurs through the operations of "the ordinary business of life" or human beings at work, as we saw above. But, Marshall claims, "economic chivalry" unfolds differently across classes since these divisions create distinct "life chances" and different possibilities for "developing their higher faculties" (Aspers, 2010, p. 151). For example, Marshall (*P*, 219) suggests that the yeoman famers of the United States are especially able and their children "rise rapidly in the world." By contrast, English agricultural laborers, not far removed from "semi-feudal rule," experienced social conditions "that repressed enterprise and even in some degree self-respect," and had very few educational opportunities until recently. But, Marshall (*IT* I, p. 7) asserts, such gaps may be closing since the general expansion of industry coincides with the expansion of education to the working classes, gradually "effacing those distinctions of mind and character between different social strata."

Given his emphasis on competition, he, not surprisingly, devotes great effort to show the gradual evolution of the character of men of business and industry. The kinds of skills necessary to succeed in modern business, Marshall (*P*, 236–252) suggests, force the business "caste" to become expert not only at their particular production process, but to cultivate a spirit of innovation and the general leadership, motivational and organizational skills operative in modern firms. Even when firms increase in size and form, including the rise of joint-stock companies, we see the businessman's continued commitment to innovation and the expansion of organizational skills (*P*, 253; Marshall, 1890, pp. 632–633). But this change in scale prompts, in addition to greater industrial capacity, a shift in the moral character of those involved in business and knowledge production. Increasingly, invention comes to depend less on "experiments" conducted within individual business and more on "the general increase of scientific knowledge" (Marshall, 1890, p. 634). Even when nested in firms, the motivations of scientists, Marshall (1890, p. 634) explains, are never simply tied to monetary rewards but to the quest for knowledge "for its own sake." And where science is recognized as contributing to discoveries that serve as a "collective property" of society, the role of these intrinsic motives as well as the social honor and respect that follows increase in importance. Like scientists, businessmen "have the same 'instincts of the chase' and many of them have the same power of being stimulated to great and even feverish exertions by emulations that are not sordid or ignoble."

Perhaps separating himself from Manchesterism and the utilitarianism despised by some of the Greater Britain advocates, Marshall suggests we err if we obscure these nobler motives by placing too great emphasis on businessmen's "desire to make money." And to the extent that they seek monetary rewards for their contributions to the world, it is because money serves as an imperfect, yet best available and most socially resonant, measure of their success (Marshall, 1890, p. 635). Greater attention to the value of our contributions as a social good intensify, Marshall (1890, p. 637) believes, in an era where "public opinion" or "the desire of men for the approval of their own conscience and the esteem of others is an economic force of the first order of importance." This tendency to think beyond simply the "personal" and the "private" to "public and national" issues only intensifies with the wider and deeper "diffusion of knowledge." Marshall (1890, pp. 638–639) points to the growing diffusion of knowledge and increased role of public opinion in improving colonial administration and turning labor struggles to the advantage of workers. In short, domestic reform depends more on general industrial advance spurred by international competition than on turning inward.

Here, Marshall (1890, p. 635) is answering his own concern that competition produces "inequalities of wealth" that "prevent human faculties from being turned to their best account." Perhaps thinking of Smith's own critique of the technical division of labor, Marshall (*P*, 218–219) considered the charge that monotony of work is a key impediment to the development of worker's "human faculties," though he redefines it as about monotony of life. Today's factory work, he says, is less debilitating than earlier forms, because working hours are shorter and "the social surroundings of factory life stimulate mental activity in and out of working hours," so that "factory workers," even in the most monotonous of occupations, "have considerable intelligence and mental resources." Yet, Marshall (*P*, 599) recognizes that the "low earnings of the poorest classes" limit the capacity of many to meet their needs but also inhibit the kinds of leisure "activities" that ennoble life.

The gradual advancement of human industrial capacity might in time raise the living standards of workers and provide greater leisure, but he also points to the possibilities of greater attention to social reform. The advance in a chivalrous attitude to "the community as a whole" leads to greater attention to the health of public space, prompting the creation of parks and museums. These benefit all, but the chivalric spirit is also called to "co-operate with the State ... in relieving the suffering of those who are weak and ailing through no fault of their own." Marshall includes supporting old-age assistance and schemes to compel and correct those "who have lost their self-respect" so that they may "reform their own lives, or, at all events, to cease to drag their children down with them" (Marshall, 1907, p. 14). It is, for Marshall (*P*, 599–600), "the young whose faculties and activities are of the highest importance." The duty of each generation is to "provide for the young such opportunities as will both develop their higher nature, and make them efficient producers." This requires freeing children from work so that they possess "abundant leisure for school and for such kinds of play as strengthen and develop the character." But, as quoted above, Marshall sees these educational opportunities become possible on a general basis only with the industrial advance of a country and, therefore, the general advance of countries around the globe. He urges the social reformer, then, to be patient. We cannot advance the human species too quickly: Human progress is "slow" but "solid" (*P*, 600–601).

Industrial/Civilizational Advance and English Leadership

In *Industry and Trade*, Marshall signals his concerns with human civilization as a whole by placing the motto, "The many in the one, and the one in the many," on the title page. Reisman (1987, p. 350) sees in this phrase a debt to Spencer, but it might as well be Hegel. For both of these thinkers the advance of the parts, particularly the advance of certain peoples or civilizational zones, is an advance for human civilization, just as advance for the whole is an advance of the parts (except perhaps those sacrificed on the slaughter bench of history). Likewise, Marshall maps relevant similarities and differences in "industrial technique," "business organization," and the "distribution of benefits thence arising" (*IT* I, p. 5) onto complicated geoeconomic spaces, including, as we have seen and shall see, industrial sectors, nations/races, home, colonial, and foreign markets, and the globe. And he locates these spaces in developmental time, where industrial leaders reshape inherited productive capacities into progress that humanity inherits. For Marshall, whatever other units or scales appear useful for a particular analysis or for identifying abstract principles, in the end, it is the whole – human civilization – that gives the analysis its political and ethical meaning.

Despite this interest in the progress of human civilization as a whole, Marshall, writing just after the Great War, suggests at the beginning of *Industry and Trade* that we should quickly "turn from the cosmopolitan point of view to the national" (*IT* I, p. 6); the time is not yet ripe for a fully cosmopolitan vantage point. Short of a "Pax Cosmopolitana enforced by an international peace," the "shadow of war" requires that countries turn industrial advance to military advantage (*IT* I, p. 5). The national point of view, with its emphasis on social intercourse not only between individuals in a country, but also among nations, is partly subsumed then by "essential" reference to "an international point of view" (*IT* I, p. 21). Though largely dedicated to addressing Britain's efforts to maintain "industrial leadership" in the face of growing challenges (*IT* I, p. 6), Marshall's narrative sustains reference to all three points of view, which appear in part as a succession in time. The sequence, however, generally runs from the mercantile international to the national and, only then, to an intensification of international interactions so that, in some future era that nonetheless appears visible from the present, the cosmopolitan viewpoint reemerges.[14]

Marshall makes it clear that an advanced country's industrial capacity is never a product simply of its own efforts; it always assumes the mantle of industrial leadership by building on earlier efforts. Difference as uneven development is visible, though always in conjunction with universal processes in play. For instance, England inherited mechanical inventions and industrial skills from earlier industrial leaders: Medieval city states and, especially, Holland (ship-building) and France (displaced Huguenot weavers) (*IT* I, pp. 28–29). Yet, national traits remain critical to Marshall's story of England's leading role. While not discounting natural endowments (and tropical climates appear an insuperable barrier to civilization; *IT* I, p. 112), Marshall (*IT* I, p. 30) lays greater emphasis on matters of national character or spirit, in England's case certain "qualities of body and character": "firm will, self-determination, thoroughness, fidelity and love of freedom" (see also Marshall, 1890, p. 630). These traits appear distinctively combined so that Marshall exclaims that England has pursued its course "so independently and steadily," so harmoniously blending economic and political institutions, that the English "stand out now as the leading type of continuous development" (*IT* I, p. 30). The one, in this case England, conditions the prospects for the many. The implication is that industrial leadership is relational: not only does it show the future to followers who might emulate its industrial practices, but it also sets the baseline for additional industrial advance.

But Marshall's story is not of single countries advancing in isolation and only later connecting in the social intercourse of international trade. The one and many co-mingle continually, so that the progress of interconnected internal industries develops only along with and largely as a consequence of foreign trade. Though the traits comprising English "economic nationality" date to a misty past (*IT* I, pp. 28–29), the "Mercantile Age" of trade and internal development forged the country "into an economic unity," where these national traits and industrial leadership could be profitably expressed, and leading eventually to dominance in markets for industrial goods in "the highly civilized parts of the East," in the extraction of the natural resources of "ignorant people," and in the development of colonial "plantations" (*IT* I, pp. 30–33). As perhaps for Bell's figures, the unity of the one of England emerges in the context of the many of empire.

Marshall recognizes that the progress of the one and many is neither even nor seamless, as in today's notions of uneven and combined development. He believes that any moral evaluation of uneven progress requires turning to the kinds of complex assessments common in Smith's work (*IT* I, p. 36). For Smith progress involves apparent costs, some of which can be mitigated, others revalued as actually advantages, but others accepted as necessary (Blaney & Inayatullah, 2010, Chapter 2). Marshall seems to apply roughly this strategy, with an emphasis on identifying the necessary costs. He recognizes that the freeing of capital and labor from traditional bounds destroyed old duties and obligations, though leaving "odours, some sour and some sweet" (*IT* I, p. 36). "The enclosure of the commons" is a case in point. It expanded the land and raw materials open to use by industry and diffused a sense of the new opportunities widely in the population; it was "excellent ... from a broad national view." But the costs were so high, that many, "with some justice," opposed it (*IT* I, pp. 36–37). Slavery comes in for a similar assessment. What Marshall calls "primitive civilization" (read: Africa and much of Asia) is held back, as was England earlier, by the bonds of mutual dependence that resist "new ideas." Thus, "the institution of slavery sometimes came to the aid of progress, by forcibly breaking down the prescriptions of custom" (*IT* I, p. 137). This harsh reading is justified when we consider that Marshall, in the sentence that follows his comments on slavery, draws a general lesson: "progress has owed much to the subordination of the masses of the population to the will of a dominant race, whose minds have not been occupied with petty cares." But he immediately promises eventual redemption for common people, since "mankind will not have achieved their destiny till the masses can pioneer for themselves" (*IT* I, p. 137).

Great Anglosaxondom and Preserving the Empire

Marshall makes Anglo-Saxon leadership central to this narrative of human progress in *Industry and Trade*, as we shall see below, but, as we shall also see below, he had been pondering the relative role of England and its former and self-governing colonies for some time. The nearly invariable catalyst for his attention to the empire was on-going debates about customs duties and imperial trade. Marshall rarely weighed in on public debates, but he did editorialize against coal duties (Marshall, 1901) and, in 1903, along with other prominent economists, signed a letter to *The Times* opposing tariff-reform proposals designed to protect English trade with its colonies. Soon after, Marshall was asked by a private secretary to the Chancellor of the Exchequer to draft a memorandum on the fiscal implications of the proposals to impose customs duties, but the document, "The Fiscal Policy of International Trade," was not published for five years and only after substantial revision (Marshall, 1908).[15]

Though beginning with a measured but largely negative assessment of the prospects for improving England's fiscal position through customs duties, Marshall's case for free trade turned, in the end, on a defense of the empire. Marshall generally defended free trade, though he was open to infant-industry arguments and traveled to the United States with the express purpose of studying the impact of protectionist policies in US industrial advance (Jha, 1973, p. 31; Wood, 1983, pp. 121–122). Marshall (1908, p. 2) opened the memo with the claim of policy neutrality: that his concern was simply to explore the issues involved from the point of view of a "student of economics." He suggests that the burden of duties is "borne almost exclusively by the consumers. But there is no absolute rule in the matter" (Marshall, 1908, p. 3). Rather, the impacts of the proposed duties can be decided only by examining Britain's vulnerability and bargaining power relative to major competitors, including the United States and Germany (Marshall, 1908, pp. 6–10). Though Marshall (1908, pp. 11–13) concludes that taxes on agricultural imports might shift some of the costs onto exporters, the idea that protectionist duties could revive England's flagging competitiveness is misplaced. England's position as "*a* leader," though not "*the* leader," in industry depends instead, he argues, on "keeping her markets open," because that "increases the alertness of her industrial population in general, and her manufactures in particular" (Marshall, 1908, pp. 21–23). Leadership might be sustained despite growing manufacturing imports from her colonies and elsewhere, since the colonies remained "thirsty for capital" and England maintained a surplus position. And England rules the seas: Her "battleships" secure shipping routes for trade against "several restless nations" in the Pacific and Atlantic (Marshall, 1908, p. 26).

But Marshall ends the memo with a justification of free trade in the very metaphysical terms supposedly lacking, as Bell's thinkers asserted, in liberal economists. England, he suggests, may need to sacrifice "something of material gain for the sake of a high ideal. Imperial unity is a high ideal. A well-to-do Englishman who is not prepared to sacrifice something for it appears to be hardly worthy of his age." Less well-to-do Englishmen might also be called on to sacrifice for "posterity," but only in proportion to their means and only with the promise that "their present sacrifice would redound in a greater benefit to their descendants." England is called thereby to "promote general intercourse throughout the Empire" (Marshall, 1908, pp. 25–27) and to avoid a turn to protectionism, because such

> schemes appear to me likely to breed more of disappointment and friction between England and her Colonies than of goodwill and the true spirit of Imperial unity. And if appraised in a spirit of greed, rather than of self-sacrifice, they are likely to rouse animosity in other lands, and to postpone the day at which it may be possible to work towards a federated Anglo-Saxondom, which seems to be an even higher ideal than Imperial unity. (Marshall, 1908, p. 29)

Marshall makes clearer the reasoning behind the claim that a federated Anglosaxondom stands as higher ideal in a speech at the Institute of Bankers in 1903 in which he defends policies that respect the interests of other countries. He explains:

> Since the Empire is not geographically continuous, Imperial Federation could not have the economic advantages which resulted from the German Zollverein. But it is a high aim in itself; while material wealth is merely a means towards ends. And yet, in my humble judgement, it is far from being our highest aim. That highest aim is, I submit, the development of a common feeling and of common interests throughout our race .... The United States contain many or more of our race than do all of our colonies and dependencies together .... Our true ideal is to be found not in little Anglosaxondom, but in great Anglosaxondom. (quoted in Reisman 1987, p. 24)

Marshall clearly saw the ties of race within and beyond the empire as crucial and as containing the possibility of an "economic unity" (Reisman, 1990, p. 251). Yet, his vision extended beyond just economic unity, since, as he argued, a federated Anglosaxondom could not be built on the kinds of protectionist policies embraced by some of Bell's key figures.

Marshall continued this line of thought in *Industry and Trade*, though conditioned by Anglo-American cooperation during the Great War. He devotes much attention to recounting England's global economic impact over the past century or more, though, coming to the 20th century, he highlights the role of "England's children beyond the seas" (*IT* I, Chapter 4, p. 63). England's colonies are able to assume a leading role because they benefitted from a relatively enlightened, and increasingly chivalrous, Imperial policy, that eschewed protectionism and fostered competition (*IT* II, pp. 233, 234; Marshall, 1890, pp. 615–619). Like Adam Smith before him, he reflects on the somewhat stifling limits earlier placed on the American colonies that were designed to secure monopolies for "Englishman ... of those manufacturing industries without which no modern country can be in the first rank of civilization." And, yet, these restrictions didn't forestall "the higher development of the colonies." But "this selfishness" did "lower the moral character of Englishmen" and completely undermined the "industrial instincts" of the Irish (*IT* II, p. 218).[16] Thus, he praises "the grandeur and moral strength" of Smith's "large Imperialism, where he proposed that England's chief Colony should become the kernel of a great empire, in which [England] should play a leading, but not dominant role" (*IT* II, p. 219).

When Marshall looks out at the world of the one and many in his times, he sees the mantle of civilizational/racial leadership being passed on to the United States. Its "spirit of youth" (*IT* I, p. 97), its greater individualism, and the "restless energy and the versatile enterprise of a comparatively few very rich and able men who rejoice in that power of doing great things by great means that their wealth gives them" (Marshall, 1890, pp. 621–622) were brought to the forefront, all in a context that allowed the "natural selection of singular efficiency" and made the United States the "chief leader" in industrial production (*IT* I, pp. 97, 105). The particular basis of US industrial leadership is mastery of techniques of "multiform standardization": mass production of standardized goods and with increasingly standardized capital tools (*IT* I, p. 97). And the new American industries find an abundant supply of relatively unskilled, especially immigrant, labor to man the factories. "In spite of some racial differences," the "methods of living" of the population are generally homogeneous, especially since the country came "under effective control of an advanced western people" and despite "new strains of immigrants of excitable temperament" (*IT* I, pp. 97–99). With all these advantages, Marshall believed that the United States now showed the future to England and the world, establishing the base on which additional industrial advance may rise.

But Marshall's model remains Smith's "large Imperialism" with England in a key role in a globalized Anglo-Saxon axis. The United States may have inherited the advances made by Holland, France, and now England, and will in the future be seen as "the parent" of other races, but England retains a leadership role in relation to her own colonies: Australia, New Zealand, and South Africa. Canada and Australia both house "natural riches" and "alert populations," though Australia's distance inhibits a leadership role and Canada is likely to emerge only as a US "partner." South Africa shows promise, with its diamonds and "the solid strength of the British and Dutch population, now happily united," but needs to "pioneer new and more successful methods of intimate cooperation between white and black races" (*IT* I, pp. 109–111). Nor can non-European races provide leadership. Japan shows strength, but lacks the scale of the United States. India lacks unity and sources of energy. Russia and China are large countries, but instability seems to "obscure the outlook" (*IT* I, pp. 111–112). Though Marshall (*IT* I, pp. 109, 112) suggests there is no basis for believing "that industrial leadership will remain always with the same races," it is clear that his "slight speculations as to the future homes of industrial leadership" forecast an Anglo-Saxon-centered world.

Marshall locates his position short of a full cosmopolitanism, the time for which has not yet arrived, despite the establishment of the League of Nations. Yet, he points to an arena beyond England as a national "aggregate" of interests or bounded territory (*IT* I, pp. 5–6; II, p. 166), gesturing to the idea of a "British Confederation of Nations," in which England would play the role of "eldest sister" for English-speaking peoples. Though England continues to be a source of capital and a market for its colonies' raw materials, her "daughters beyond the sea" are beginning to be "recognized in their turn as industrial centers" (*IT* I, pp. 72–73). Under these circumstances, England's "industrial leadership is in the process of being fulfilled and merged in that of the British Federation of Nations; the younger members of which are learning much from the present leadership of her first great colony." Marshall believes he can speak with such confidence about continued leadership because "Britain surprised the rest of the world, if not herself, by the energy which she has shown in the World-war: and the English-speaking peoples of the four continents have proved themselves to be united in spirit and in truth." He announces, then, the punch line of his inquiry: "Britain's industrial leadership is to be measured by the achievements of Britons in their new homes as well as in their old" (*IT* I, p. 72). The empire remains crucial, nevertheless, though in a newer form: a "larger, though looser, grouping ... suggested by the active alliances in support of freedom which have been developed during the World-war." This "looser" grouping may indicate a model something short of a federative Greater Britain, but the point is that Marshall imagines less of a free-trade cosmopolitanism, the bugaboo of Bell's Greater Britain thinkers, and more a vision of a "great Anglosaxondom" as an economic, cultural, and political space.

FINAL REFLECTIONS

Marshall's thought on federative empire may not have been referenced by the major advocates of a Greater Britain, as Bell indicates in recent correspondence, but it is clear from his own writings that he followed those debates. This fact seems to vindicate Bell's claim of the importance of this neglected episode in the history of liberal imperial thought. But it also raises questions about Bell's framing of the Greater Britain debate as unfolding in a distinctly "political language." It seems unlikely that Marshall would recognize himself or his work in that description. He framed his own contribution to the debate as the standpoint of a "student of economics," a discipline he was working to establish as a distinctive science, although, as we have seen, his account of the promise of economics encompasses language we might associate with anthropology and sociology. And Marshall stressed, by contrast with many early economists, the continuity of his work with classical political economy (Reisman, 1990, pp. 100–105).

Admittedly, the discipline Marshall helped build now depends for its identity on policing the boundaries between itself and other disciplines, disconnecting, for example, the economic from other domains of motive and action, including ethics (Dupré, 2001; Glaze, 2015; Sen, 1987). Or, in Buck-Morss' more charged terms, the minimalist vision of neoclassical economics impoverished the "*philosophy* of political economy" without regret (Buck-Morss, 1995, pp. 464–465), and must do so, because, as Gilpin (2001, pp. 51–54) notes, undue attention to cultural difference or spatial specificity undermines nomothetic explanation, since, as economists proudly insist, economic laws operate without regard to time and space.

But I am somewhat less concerned with the well-known and intractable narrowness of economics than I am with the fact that contemporary critical scholars also help drive this wedge between economy and matters cultural and political/ethical. Thrift (2003, p. 692) warns that the growing emphasis on meaning and discourse leads many to take "remarkably little ... note of economics." The neglect is endemic because the opposition of culture and economics is constitutive of the cultural turn itself: "Culture was culture because it had been purified of the taint of the economic" (Thrift, 2003, pp. 698–699). I sense a similar reluctance in Bell to engage the economists, since past work on empire and imperial thought has given precedence to economic factors and he hopes to recover a distinctly "political language" informing liberal imperial thought. The dangerous temptation is to sort the relevance of thinkers according to contemporary disciplinary boundaries, so that more recent economists and the components of earlier political economic work that might be classed as economics are sifted out of the narrative. Instead, I would see the debates on empire that Bell explores as unfolding a language that, according to Pocock (1975, Chapter 13), has, since the 17th and 18th centuries, engaged together issues of commerce and trade, social change, moral virtue, and the nature of political rule: "political economy."

NOTES

1. Bell gave this as justification for his choices in recent correspondence.
2. As Bell suggested we should in recent correspondence.
3. See Hodgson (2005) and Reisman (1990, Chapter 7) for sketches of that story.

4. The idea that economics serves empire and empire economics once seemed commonplace to critical scholars in IR/IPE. See Mommsen (1980), Semmel (1993), and Brewer (1990). Bell, in recent correspondence, suggests that his goal in recovering the specifically political language of empire was to redress earlier work that emphasized economic motives.

5. As Bell warns, this work attends only to early and mid-19th-century thinkers. For Mehta (1999), James and John Stuart Mill are key protagonists, with Burke as unlikely hero, and later liberal thinking about empire receives no attention. Pitts (2005) documents the embrace of empire by early and mid-19th-century liberals, highlighting Bentham, J. S. Mill, and Tocqueville. Lowe (2015) makes J. S. Mill central, but sees him as heir to Smith, Bentham, and Ricardo. Essays in Schultz and Varouxakis (2005) canvas views of utilitarian thinkers on race and empire, beginning with Bentham and emphasizing Mill, and reaching only the later Victorian figure, ethicist and political economist Henry Sidgwick. It appears that public debates on empire in the late-Victorian era were conducted partly in reference to earlier thinkers, such as Mill, but also Smith (Palen, 2014), yet Wood (1983) documents the role of neoclassical economists, including Marshall and Jevons, though few follow his example.

6. His intellectual insights, along with Jevons, Clark, Pigou, Edgeworth, Walras, Menger, and Pareto, shaped the new, more formal, and "scientific" character of economic studies, though the priority of each is disputed (Blaug, 1973; Hutchison, 1955; Stark, 1944, pp. 1–3). But his position within the history of economics owes as much to his personal role in establishing departments, curriculum, and associations (Kadish, 1993; Maloney, 1985; Reisman, 1990, Chapters 3 and 4). Despite this central role in the new discipline, many have seen his thinking as incoherent, the broader, and social historical elements necessarily ignored or abandoned as part of recovering a systematic economics as a deductive science (Hart, 2012, pp. x, 1; Mirowski, 1990, pp. 61–63; O'Brien, 1990, p. 82).

7. I counted roughly 15 graphs spread across 600 pages of the main body of the 1920 edition and these appear in footnotes or as an appendix to a chapter. The only mathematics in the text appears in an appendix.

8. Marshall admits his "volume on Foundations must … give relatively large place to mechanical analogies," including "frequent use" of the term "'equilibrium', which suggests something of statistical analogy" useful for policy making in the normal conditions of a particular time (*P*, xii).

9. On the influence of Spencer and Hegel, see Hart (2012, pp. 17–28), Reisman (1990, pp. 7, 118–120, 278–279), Groenewegen (1990), Niman (1991), and Cook (2009).

10. Marshall's reading of Darwin back into Smith is problematic. Both are read through his growing fondness for Spencer. See Hodgson (1993) and Glassburner (1955).

11. The resemblance to later modernization theory is more than coincidental. Parsons (1949) combines Marshall with Pareto, Durkheim, and Weber to create an image of modern society as a structurally differentiated but functional whole, which served as the basis of modernization theory (Inayatullah and Blaney, 2004, Chapter 3).

12. Descendants inherit habits, it might be noted, not only through passing on of culture, but also heredity. Marshall favored Lamarckian views of evolution and sought confirmation in his wide correspondence with biologists (Hart, 2012, pp. 63–70).

13. Yet Marshall (*P*, 203–204) warns that the fact that a race thrives relative to others over is not prima facie evidence of its positive contribution to mankind; some are parasitical (Jews and Chinese) and others pass on love of warfare or desire for money without respect for hard work and saving.

14. Reisman (1990, p. 239) suggests a more complicated set of sequences: "from family and tribe to unit individual, social convention to selfish interest, mercantilist direction to free trade, nationalism to cosmopolitanism."

15. Marshall's memo is considered by some as one of the greatest examples of economic policy analysis (Wood, 1980, p. 482, fn 4). Wood (1980, 1983, Chapter 6) and Jha (1973, Chapter IV) describe in greater detail the events surrounding its drafting, revision, and publication.

16. But the need for Imperial restrictions seems to vary by race. Colonial monopolies gradually became mostly "obsolete" for the most advanced nations, but those in the earlier stages of development lack forward-looking faculties and need direction from a central authority in order to stimulate industrial advance. Here, Marshall includes not only "regulation of [external] trade" but also internal industrial policy and "regulation of the ... social order of the population" (*IT* II, 219–222).

ACKNOWLEDGMENTS

Thanks to Duncan Bell and all the members of the workshop on "The International Origins of Social and Political Theory" for their careful and constructive reading of this article. I am especially grateful to Tarak Barkawi and George Lawson for bringing the workshop participants together.

REFERENCES

Agnani, S. M. (2013). *Hating empire properly: The two indies and the limits of enlightenment anticolonialism*. New York, NY: Fordham.

Aspers, P. (2010). Alfred Marshall and the concept of class. *The American Journal of Economics and Sociology*, *69*(1), 151–169.

Bell, D. (2005). Dissolving distance: Technology, space, and empire in British political thought, 1770–1900. *Journal of Modern History*, *77*, 523–562.

Bell, D. (2007a). *The idea of greater Britain: Empire and the future of world order, 1860–1900*. Princeton, NJ: Princeton University.

Bell, D. (2007b). The Victorian idea of a global state. In D. Bell (Ed.), *Victorian visions of global order: Empire and international relations in nineteenth-century political thought* (pp. 159–185). Cambridge: Cambridge University.

Bell, D. (2014a). Before the democratic peace: Racial utopianism, empire, and the abolition of war. *European Journal of International Relations*, *20*(3), 647–670.

Bell, D. (2014b). Beyond the sovereign state: Isopolitan citizenship, race and Anglo-American Union. *Political Studies*, *62*(2), 418–434.

Bell, D. (2016). *Reordering the world: Essays on liberalism and empire*. Princeton, NJ: Princeton University.

Blaney, D. L., & Inayatullah, N. (2010). *Savage economics: Wealth, poverty, and the temporal walls of capitalism*. London: Routledge.

Blaug, M. (1973). Was there a marginal revolution? In R. D. Collinson Black, A. W. Coats, & Cranford D. W. Goodwin (Eds.), *The marginal revolution in economics: Interpretation and evaluation* (pp. 3–14). Durham, NC: Duke University.

Breslau, D. (2003). Economics invents the economy: Mathematics, statistics, and models in the work of Irving Fisher and Wesley Mitchell. *Theory and Society*, *32*, 379–411.

Brewer, A. (1990). *Marxist theories of imperialism: A critical survey*. London: Routledge.

Buck-Morss, S. (1995). Envisioning capital: Political economy on display. *Critical Inquiry*, *21*, 434–467.

Burrow, J. W. (1966). *Evolution and society: A study in Victorian social theory*. Cambridge: Cambridge University.

Colander, D. (2015). Economic theory has nothing to say about policy (and principles textbooks should tell students that). *Eastern Economic Journal*, *41*, 461–465.

Collini, S., Winch, D., & Burrow, J. (1983). *That Noble science of politics: A Study in Nineteenth-Century Intellectual History*. Cambridge: Cambridge University Press.

Cook, S. J. (2009). *The intellectual foundations of Alfred Marshall's economic science*. Cambridge: Cambridge University.

Dupré, J. (2001). Economics without mechanism. In U. Mäki (Ed.), *The economic worldview: Studies in the ontology of economics* (pp. 308–332). Cambridge: Cambridge University.

Gilpin, R. (2001). *Global political economy: Understanding the international economic order*. Princeton, NJ: Princeton University.

Glassburner, B. (1955). Alfred Marshall on economic history and historical development. *The Quarterly Journal of Economics*, *69*(4), 577–595.

Glaze, S. (2015). Schools out: Adam Smith and pre-disciplinary international political economy. *New Political Economy*, *20*(5), 679–702.

Groenewegen, P. (1990). Marshall and Hegel. *Economie Appliquée*, *XLIII*(1), 63–84.

Hart, N. (2012). *Equilibrium and evolution: Marshall and the Marshallians*. London: Palgrave Macmillan.

Hobson, J. (2012). *The Eurocentric conception of world politics: Western international theory, 1760–2010*. Cambridge: Cambridge University.

Hodgson, G. M. (1993). The Mecca of Alfred Marshall. *The Economic Journal*, *103*(417), 406–415.

Hodgson, G. M. (2005). Alfred Marshall versus the historical school. *Journal of Economic Studies*, *32*(4), 331–348.

Hutchison, T. W. (1955). Insularity and cosmopolitanism in economic ideas, 1870–1914. *The American Economic Review*, *45*(2), 1–16.

Inayatullah, N., & Blaney, D. L. (2004). *International relations and the problem of difference*. New York, NY: Routledge.

Jha, N. (1973). *The age of Marshall: Aspects of British economic thought 1890–1915* (2nd ed.). London: Frank Cass.

Kadish, A. (1993). Marshall and the Cambridge economics tripos. In A. Kadish & K. Tribe (Eds.), *The market for political economy: The advent of economics in British university culture, 1850–1905* (pp. 137–161). London: Routledge.
Lowe, L. (2015). *The intimacies of four continents*. Durham, NC: Duke University.
Maloney, J. (1985). *Marshall, orthodoxy, and the professionalization of economics*. Cambridge: Cambridge University.
Marshall, A. (1885). *The present position of economics*. London: Macmillan.
Marshall, A. (1890). Some aspects of competition. *Journal of the Royal Statistical Society, 53*(4), 612–643.
Marshall, A. (1901). An export duty on coal. *The Economic Journal, 11*(42), 265–267.
Marshall, A. (1907). Social possibilities of economic chivalry. Retrieved from http://la.utexas.edu/users/hcleaver/368/368MarshallChivalrytable.pdf. (pp. 1–15).
Marshall, A. (1908). Memorandum on the fiscal policy of international trade. Stationery Office of the House of Commons, London. Retrieved from https://books.google.com/books?id=mL4nAAAAYAAJ&pg=PA1&lpg=PA1&dq=Alfred+Marshall,+Memorandum+on+the+Fiscal+Policy+of+International+Trade+House+of+Common&source=bl&ots=OhkTSqG3dA&sig=yz5nVNrywM2quERJGUFMxm2GO0U&hl=en&sa=X&ved=0ahUKEwjT7pbMxNfMAhVI44MKHZW5CH0Q6AEIITAB#v=onepage&q=Alfred%20Marshall%2C%20Memorandum%20on%20the%20Fiscal%20Policy%20of%20International%20Trade%20House%20of%20Common&f=false
Marshall, A. (2009 [1920]). *Principles of economics* (8th ed.). New York, NY: Cosimo.
Marshall, A. (n.d. [1920]). *Industry and trade* (3rd ed., Vol. I). Kissimmee, FL: Signalman Publishing.
Mehta, U. S. (1999). *Liberalism and empire: A study in nineteenth-century British liberal thought*. Chicago, IL: University of Chicago.
Mirowski, P. (1990). Smooth operator: How Marshall's demand and supply curves made neoclassicism safe for public consumption but unfit for science. In P. M. Tullberg (Ed.) *Alfred Marshall in retrospect* (pp. 61–90). Aldershot: Edward Elgar.
Mommsen, W. J. (1980). *Theories of imperialism* (P. S. Falla, Trans.). Chicago, IL: University of Chicago.
Morefield, J. (2014). *Empires without imperialism: Anglo-American decline and the politics of deflection*. Oxford: Oxford University.
Muthu, S. (2003). *Enlightenment against empire*. Princeton, NJ: Princeton University.
Niman, N. B. (1991). Biological analogies in Marshall's work. *Journal of the History of Economic Thought, 13*(1), 19–36.
O'Brien, D. P. (1990). Marshall's industrial analysis. *Scottish Journal of Political Economy, 37*(1), 61–86.
Palen, M.-W. (2014). Adam Smith as advocate of empire, c. 1870–1932. *The Historical Journal, 57*(1), 179–198.
Parsons, T. (1949). *The structure of social action*. New York, NY: Free Press.
Peck, J. (2010). *Constructions of neoliberal reason*. Oxford: Oxford University.
Pitts, J. (2005). *A turn to empire: The rise of imperial liberalism in Britain and France*. Princeton, NJ: Princeton University.
Pocock, J. G. A. (1975). *The Machiavellian moment: Florentine political thought and the Atlantic republican tradition*. Princeton, NJ: Princeton University.

Proudfoot, L., & Roche, M. (2005). Introduction: Place, network, and the geographies of empire. In L. Proudfoot & M. Roche (Eds.), *(Dis)Placing empire: Renegotiating British colonial geographies* (pp. 1–11). Aldershot: Ashgate.

Reisman, D. (1987). *Alfred Marshall: Progress and politics*. London: Macmillan.

Reisman, D. (1990). *Alfred Marshall's mission*. London: Macmillan.

Samuels, W. J. (2001). Alfred Marshall and neoclassical economics: Some insights from his correspondence. In A. K. Dutt & K. P. Jameson (Eds.), *Crossing the mainstream: Ethical and methodological issues in economics* (pp. 247–274). South Bend, IN: Notre Dame University.

Schultz, B., & Varouxakis, G. (Eds.). (2005). *Utilitarianism and empire*. Lanham, MD: Lexington Books.

Sen, A. (1987). *On ethics and economics*. Oxford: Blackwell.

Stark, W. (1944). *The history of economics in relation to social development*. New York, NY: Oxford University.

Stocking, G. W. Jr. (1987). *Victorian anthropology*. New York, NY: Free Press.

Thrift, N. (2003). Pandora's box? Cultural geographies or economies. In G. Clark, M. Feldmann, & M. Gertler (Eds.), *The oxford handbook of economic geography* (pp. 689–702). Oxford: Oxford University.

Vitalis, R. (2015). *White world order, black power politics: The birth of American international relations*. Ithaca, NY: Cornell University.

Wood, J. C. (1980). Alfred Marshall and the Tariff-Reform Campaign of 1903. *The Journal of Law and Economics*, *23*(2), 481–495.

Wood, J. C. (1983). *British economists and the empire*. New York, NY: St. Martin's Press.

EPISTEMIC RUPTURES: HISTORY, PRACTICE, AND THE ANTICOLONIAL IMAGINATION

Ricarda Hammer

ABSTRACT

Examining the work of Frantz Fanon and Stuart Hall, this article argues that their biographic practices and experiences as colonial subjects allowed them to break with imperial representations and to provide new, anticolonial imaginaries. It demonstrates how the experience of the racialized and diasporic subject, respectively, creates a kind of subjectivity that makes visible the work of colonial cultural narratives on the formation of the self. The article first traces Fanon's and Hall's transboundary encounters with metropolitan Europe and then shows how these biographic experiences translate into their theories of practice and history. Living through distinct historical moments and colonial ideologies, Fanon and Hall produced theories of historical change, which rest on epistemic ruptures and conjunctural changes in meaning formations. Drawing on their biographic subjectivities, both intellectuals theorize cultural and colonial forms of oppression and seek to produce new knowledge that is based on practice and experience.

Keywords: Anticolonial thought; empire; theory; race; practice

International Origins of Social and Political Theory
Political Power and Social Theory, Volume 32, 153–180

ISSN: 0198-8719/doi:10.1108/S0198-871920170000032010

INTRODUCTION

> The disaster of the man of color lies in the fact that he was enslaved. The disaster and the inhumanity of the white man lie in the fact that somewhere he has killed man [...] But I as a man of color, to the extent that it becomes possible for me to exist absolutely, do not have the right to lock myself into a world of retroactive reparations. I, the man of color, want only this: That the tool never possess the man.
>
> (Fanon, 2008, p. 180)

> Diaspora is a loss. It's not forever, it doesn't mean that you can't do something about it, or that other places can't fill the gap, the void, but the void is always the regretful moment that wasn't realized. History is full of what is not realized, and I feel that about it. Whenever I go back, I think I'm at home but still I'm not at home.
>
> (Hall & Back, 2009, p. 668)

To study systems of cultural oppression requires a particular kind of imagination. This article argues that the specific biographic, subjective, and affective experiences of anticolonial thinkers provide insight into how colonial epistemic frameworks operate. If, as analysts, we start from the subjective experience of the colonized, the racialized, or the diasporic subject, we adopt a perspective that captures the workings of racial hierarchies and imperial representations. Of a long tradition in anticolonial thought, this article focuses on the work of Frantz Fanon and Stuart Hall specifically. Both intellectuals were born in the Caribbean but left for Europe, and Fanon later for Africa. The article suggests that these "transboundary experiences" were profound, affective, biographic instances which shaped their intellectual work (see Introduction, this volume): Frantz Fanon recognized and felt the racializing structures of colonialism upon encountering white Europe, witnessed the dehumanizing colonial violence in Algeria and sought to explain his life experience as a racialized subject. Stuart Hall, a former colonial, then a diasporic subject in Britain, experienced the feelings of being out of place or perpetually displaced, which, I argue, fueled his anticolonial imagination.

What we know is positioned, arising from our particular, socially constructed standpoint (Go, 2016). Fanon's and Hall's anticolonial subjectivity allowed them to theorize not only how power structures operate, how dominant regimes of representation reproduce themselves and affect the subject, but they also identify openings in history and opportunities to break with conventional "ways of seeing the world." While cultural sociology has long theorized the work of ideology and symbolic domination, the anticolonial tradition adds insights into the racializing and imperial structures of modernity. Fanon and Hall focus on a specific subjective experience within empire, that of the racialized and the displaced subject. For Fanon, the colonized is enveloped in a system of discourses that profoundly affect his sense of self and render him inferior. Hall puts his focus on the subjective experience of belonging, the migrant and the diaspora, and shows how, for the colonized subject, this sense of self always seems to be somewhere else. Both put forth a theory of history and propose that new knowledge – and indeed, epistemic ruptures – can emerge out of practice and experience.

There are also interesting differences in Fanon's and Hall's anticolonial imaginations. While Fanon gives us a theory of racialization, Hall theorizes displacement and identity fragmentations. This may be because they were embedded in distinct colonial ideologies. For example, France considered its colonies as extensions of the French nation state, aimed to standardize language, laws, and institutions across the territories, thereby upholding the illusion that all subjects within the territories were equal (Ahluwalia, 2010). This pernicious myth, which, Césaire writes, associated "in our minds the word France and the word liberty" and bound "us to France by every fiber of our hearts and power of our minds" (Césaire quoted in Hall, 1995), broke for Fanon upon realizing that he had been fixed as black. Colonial subjects in the British Empire similarly looked to Britain as the motherland, but there was little pretense to elevate colonial subjects to equality. Instead, ideology was built on tutelage for an endlessly delayed self-determination. For Fanon, racialization excluded him from France and humanity itself, while for Hall, displacement was the central experience to modernity. In what follows, I describe these biographic interactions with empire before showing how Fanon and Hall theorized history, practice, and openings for change. In sum, I hope to show that the anticolonial tradition provides an example for how the unity of practice, theory, and subjectivity can challenge epistemic oppressions.

TRANSBOUNDARY EXPERIENCES: FRANTZ FANON

His father a slave descendant and his mother of mixed French heritage, Frantz Fanon was born to a middle class family in 1925 in Fort-de-France, the French colony of Martinique. Early on, Fanon was influenced by the anticolonial writer Aimé Césaire and his teachings on colonial racism in the Martiniquan Lycée Schoelcher (Alessandrini, 2005; Gibson, 2003; Gordon, 2015). Looking back on the paradigmatic experience of the Antillean black schoolboy, Fanon recounts how much the boy sees himself as belonging to and identifying with France: "Forever talking about 'our ancestors, the Gauls', [the schoolboy] identifies himself with the explorer, the bringer of civilization, the white man who carries truth to savages – an all-white truth. There is identification – that is, the young Negro subjectively adopts a white man's attitude" (Fanon, 2008, p. 114).[1] The Antillean subject's identification with metropolitan France is particularly strong when compared to other subjects in the French Empire. For example, the image of the black man – created in colonial tales and ideologies – is associated with "the African," located on the African continent. "When in school he has to read stories of savages told by white men, he always thinks of the Senegalese. As a schoolboy, I had many occasions to spend whole hours talking about the supposed customs of the savage Senegalese" (Fanon, 2008, p. 114). In short, the Antillean does not think of himself as black. "Subjectively, intellectually, the Antillean conducts himself like a white man. But he is a Negro" (Fanon, 2008, p. 114).

This colonial paradox becomes apparent once the Antillean moves to Europe: Through the encounter with white Europe, the Antillean colonial subject learns that the category of "the Negro" in fact includes him just as much as the Senegalese. Leaving Martinique, the young Fanon joined the French resistance against occupying Nazi Germany, and it was during his time in the French military that he experienced racial hierarchies and racism on a daily basis: White soldiers, fighting alongside black soldiers, addressed blacks with the informal "tu" as opposed to the respectful "vous," white French villagers – for whom black soldiers had risked their lives – mistreated them, and white women preferred Italian, fascist prisoners over black soldiers who had liberated them (Go, 2013a, 2013b; Gordon, 2015, p. 12). In a famous incident in *Black Skins, White Masks*, Fanon (2008) recounts the crystalizing moment, when he understood that his skin color, ranked at the bottom of the racial hierarchy, trumped any feelings of belonging to France. Fixed as a racial other in the gaze of a young white French boy, Fanon describes the psychological, affective reaction he felt upon recognizing the child's dehumanizing gaze.

While traveling in France, Fanon encounters a mother with her young child. Upon seeing Fanon, the young boy turns to his mother and exclaims: "Look a Negro ... Mama, see the Negro! I'm frightened!" (Fanon, 2008, p. 84). In the glance of the boy, Fanon writes, he had been fixed as something other: something outside Europe, Frenchness, whiteness, civilization, and outside the bounds of those who belong. Recognizing the power of this gaze, Fanon reacts, feeling the burden of history on his shoulders. "I could no longer laugh, because I already know there were legends, stories, history and above all *historicity* .... Then assailed at various points, the corporal schema crumbled its place taken by a racial epidermal schema ... I was responsible for my body, for my race, for my ancestors" (Fanon, 2008, p. 84, italics in original). Inscribed in his skin color and physical features, was a history of racial slavery and colonial ideologies that marked him as entirely other. Thus, even though the colonial subject feels himself as a part of France, he gets fixed outside it.

The colonial condition is inherently contradictory (Go, 2013a, 2013b). Hailed as a free French citizen from Martinique to metropolitan France, Fanon realizes that his black skin prevents him from truly belonging to the French republic. The racialized subject is called to inhabit a contradictory reality, a fragmented space, as the "white man's other" (Sardar, 2008). "The movements, the attitudes, the glances of the other fixed me there, in the sense in which a chemical solution is fixed by a dye. I was indignant; I demanded an explanation. Nothing happened. I burst apart. Now the fragments have been put together again by another self" (Fanon, 2008, p. 109). His identity and sense of self is placed in a space of nonbeing, which is perpetually external to the ideals held up by colonialism.[2] Even though France is "his" country, the racialized subject is made to feel different to other people (Fanon, 2008, p. 115). Moreover, this contradictory situation forces itself into the realm of the intimate: Since the Antillean family has little connection with "national" France, the Antillean subject is faced with a choice between his family and European society and its ideals of civilization and whiteness. Seeking to attain the status of the white, the Antillean "tends to reject his family – black and savage – on the place of imagination" (Fanon, 2008, p. 115).

This encounter with the white world is powerful on a psychological level. "When the Negro makes contact with the white world, a certain sensitizing action takes place. If his psychic structure is weak, one observes a collapse of the ego. The black man stops behaving as an *actional* person" (Fanon, 2008, p. 119). Instead of being one's own person, the black man instead strives to emulate the European because that is what is valued, socially, but also subjectively. That is, in order to attain a measure of self-worth, the black man wants and needs to be white. It is Fanon's own trans-boundary encounter, the encounter with the racialized gaze that made apparent to him the profound psychological effects this immersion can have. Succumbed to the weight of history, stories, language and meanings of a white world, the racialized subject loses his agency, he stops being *actional*. While the inferiority of the colonized subject is felt inside him, as a form of personal weakness or inferiority complex, Fanon asserts over and over that the subject is in fact "*made* inferior" (Fanon, 2008, p. 115, my italics). The immersion of inferiorizing narratives, tales, and languages produces inside him this feeling in inferiority. However, once he recognizes that the ideals of the colonial world are beyond his attainability, the process of developing his true self begins.

Philosophically, Fanon's conception of the human builds on phenomenology's assertion of being-in-the-world. Oriented to explain one's lived experience, phenomenology considers consciousness as inseparable from the body, with the body "at all times invaded by consciousness" (Hudis, 2015, p. 8). The universal, for Fanon, is a world of mutual recognitions, where the I is the we and the we is the I, but racism distorts the possibilities for true recognition. Racial schemas fix us into whiteness and blackness, where the other, in the words of Lewis Gordon, fails "to be seen through being seen" (Gordon, 1995, p. 58). Fixed into an entirely over-determined blackness, the racialized subject feels himself alien to himself. Yet, unable to escape how the world "sees" his body, the black subject must engage with the world through this bodily schema. Here, Fanon leaves room for the agency of the black subject: Consciously deciding on this engagement with the white world, while racially fixed, the racialized subject can do so at his own terms, not as an object, but as an embodied subjectivity.

It is futile and, in fact, counterproductive to separate Fanon's biographic experiences from his theoretical writings. His subjective experiences of *encountering* white Europe, of *feeling* the gaze of a young boy and of *internalizing* the discourses of inferiority the white world had produced around him, were the impetus for his scholarship. What is more, precisely this subjective experience gives us an insight into the relationship between self-formation and racializing structures and the consequences of being a racialized subject in a colonial system. Fanon's description of the psychological effects of colonialism and racial structures contrasts any theory that seeks to neatly distinguish the objective and the subjective. Starting with the subjective experience of the racialized subject, enveloped in a system of discourses and knowledge that structurally render him inferior, then allows us to understand the radical break historical change requires.

Experiences in Colonial Struggle

After the War, Fanon studied medicine and psychiatry and began to use psychoanalytic tools to understand the effects of racialized schemas on blacks' sense of self-perception and self-worth. The 1950s in France brought together a series of African freedom fighters who met in the metropole in order to discuss independence. This particular time and place was thus replete with revolutionary philosophies. In 1953, precisely when Algeria was on the brink of anticolonial struggle against France, Fanon was offered a job at Joinville Hospital outside Algiers. In Algeria, Fanon witnessed first-hand the violence and dehumanizing effects of colonial relations. In fact, he treated both, colonized and colonizers, which made clear to him that the colonial relationship is dehumanizing for both parties (Fanon, 2008). By 1956, he resigned and officially joined the National Liberation Front (FLN). While located in Tunis, Fanon founded the radical magazine *Moudjahid*, and became one of the most influential ideologues of the Algerian revolution. However, stricken by leukemia, Fanon died on December 6, 1961, and never lived to see Algerian independence (Alessandrini, 2005; Gibson, 2003; Gordon, 2015; Hudis, 2015).

Given his biographic experience and the context of anticolonial revolutionary struggles, Frantz Fanon's work was always born out of practice and he, in turn, sought to influence worldly events. The context of colonial violence in Algeria as well as later decolonization struggles throughout Africa fed his theoretical development, just as much as his writings sought to propel struggle and call the black man to action. *The Wretched of the Earth*, written in the months before his death, for example, is explicitly oriented as a text for practice, while proposing a profound analysis of colonialism's knowledge structures. It is important to keep in mind that this kind of historical context not only endangered his physical existence, but also profoundly shaped his mind, soul, and humanity (Sardar, 2008).

The anticolonial struggle, Fanon exclaims, demands new concepts and new forms of knowing, because not only are epistemic structures and action linked, but they also inform and feed off each other. Europe's involvement in the colonial project suggests that it has a racist structure, which operates on the social as well as the symbolic level. Manifested in discourses, knowledge structures, practices, and ways of thinking, this racist structure maintains colonial dominance (Fanon, 2008, p. 68). For example, given that the colonizer not only acts in the world but also constructs the narrative and history of this action, the colonized subject finds his inferiority written into history. In other words, science, discourses, and ways of knowing are not outside history but in fact developed hand in hand with social structures. For example, referring to comic books where black men are villains and white men are heroes, Fanon writes, even "the magazines are put together by white men for little white men" (Fanon, 2008, p. 103). Colonial structures are *held up* and reproduced through the frameworks in which we view the world, which allows us to take the white man as the master of the world for granted. Consequently, the revolutionary struggle demands new ways of knowing, new concepts, through which we can think the new reality.

Breaking with Knowledge Structures through Practice

Fanon proposes a new kind of universalism that does not yet exist and cannot be formulated out of existing dominant discourses. He rejects the blind imitation of European Enlightenment thought just as much as a valorization of existing essentialist Black identities that are nothing more than images and representations produced by Europeans. New forms of knowing cannot be conjured up by existing, dominant knowledge structures. Instead, for Fanon, newness arises in practice and revolutionary struggle. In *The Wretched of the Earth* (2007), he calls on the colonized to act, to bring into existence a *new man*. Put differently, his theorizing is neither aimed for knowledge production nor critique, it is composed to incite action. His emphasis on colonial agency is clear: "Man is what brings society into being. The prognosis is in the hands of those who are willing to get rid of the worm-eaten roots of the structure" (Fanon, 2008, p. 4). He calls upon anticolonial revolutionaries to bring into creation a new man, and the only way that practice and the idea of a new humanism can become reality is through action: "The 'thing' colonized becomes a man through the very process of liberation" (Fanon, 2007, p. 2).

Importantly, decolonization, for Fanon has a very distinct meaning. An escape from colonialism inevitably involves struggle. In other words, true decolonial agency is very different from accepting the colonizer's gifts. This rests on Fanon's theory of colonial subjectivity: The only way the colonized can rid themselves of their inferiority complexes, imposed by European, dominant, cultural understandings, is through struggle and anticolonial actions. For example, if the colonized accept *recognition* based on the colonizer's terms, this recognition always rests on the gifting of recognition by Europeans (see also Coulthard, 2014). While recognition may thus objectively improve their economic or social situation, *subjectively* the colonized remain in an inferior position. Fanon does suggest, alongside other Marxists of his day, that economically exploitative relations within colonialism need to end, but if recognition is the colonizer's gift, emancipation will always be incomplete.

Here, Fanon's biographic, subjective, and affective practices shape his understanding of colonialism in distinct ways. The kind of recognition Fanon advocates, one that levels the playing field and allows the colonized to escape from their position of inferiority, involves struggle. Put differently, the colonized cannot expect to eat at the master's table, without confronting the *terms* on which they gain recognition. They cannot accept European ways of knowing, images, and representations, for neither the colonized nor the colonizer will fully break with their dehumanizing relationship. Instead, the colonized subject has to find her own ways of being, acting, and knowing. In short, Fanon is asking for a much more profound form of action. As such, he urges the colonial subject not to seek "equality" or "freedom" in the replication of European civilization, in trying to imitate because that ideal hides behind a moving bar.

Moreover, the colonial relationship cannot be broken simply by European withdrawal. The only thing that can break the colonial relationship is the creation of a new man: He who was formerly colonized must transform himself into an active, thinking historical being, "to rise above this absurd drama that others have staged around me ... to reach out to the universal" of reciprocal recognition (Fanon, 2008, p. 197). If the colonized subject is not recognized, he is not fully human, for as long as the colonized "has not been effectively recognized by the other, that other will remain the theme of his actions. It is on that other being, on recognition by that other being, that his own human worth and reality depend. It is that other being in whom the meaning of his life is condensed" (Fanon, 2008, p. 169). As long as the colonized subject is not seen as human, he will *always* depend on the actions of Europeans, so only through reciprocal recognition can the colonial relationship be broken.

What are the tools and resources the black subject can draw on in this quest for liberation? First, Fanon implores the colonized to recognize how representations of black identity and black inferiority are constructions. Moving beyond self-loathing, the racialized subject needs to "rise above the absurd drama" to work for a new kind of human being (Fanon, 2008, p. 153). This recognition is the first step in a process to find one's own agency amidst colonial structures of oppression. In other words, in a situation where colonial subjects live-in-death, the long process of finding their own agency, which had been written, defined, and determined from elsewhere, is a painful and violent process. Given this over-determination from the outside, there is no "ontology of blackness" and the black subject is faced with the task to construct an identity out of absence. The colonized has to overcome his own powerless position, most importantly, by overcoming his own sense of inferiority that had been externally imposed. Without waiting to be recognized as a black man, he must "make [himself] known" (Fanon, 2008, p. 95), thereby regaining historical agency. Importantly, Fanon departs from Negritude thinkers in that the affirmation of blackness can only be one step on the road to universality. As a next step, decolonization must move beyond racial schemas to create a "new man." This would not only bring decolonization, but also allow us to break from the relationship between colonizer and colonized: "For Europe, for ourselves and for humanity, comrades, we must turn over a new leaf, we must work out new concepts, and try to set afoot a new man" (Fanon, 2007, p. 239).

Yet, action does not automatically follow from thought. To make the colonized into a social, reflexive, actionable being, the colonized need aspirations. It is here where the anticolonial intellectual can provide guidance and stability. Fanon's own texts were written to promote this sense of practice and vision. In short, the imaginary, the creation, the invention of the new man can benefit from the work of an intellectual, but this intellectual labor has to stand in an interactive relationship with the practical struggle. If the intellectual fails to actively engage in practice, he may become nothing more than a colonial protégé. Influenced by European universalisms and systems of thought, he is just as much a product of the colonial system (Fanon, 2007, p. 46). To contribute to the anticolonial struggle, the intellectual must conduct self-analysis (Fanon, 2007, p. 211) and engage with the people's struggle: "[T]he colonised intellectual who is lucky enough to bunker down with the people during the liberation struggle, will soon discover the falsity of this theory. Involvement in the organization of the struggle will already introduce him to a different vocabulary [...] the colonised intellectual witnesses the destruction of all his idols: egoism, arrogant recrimination, and the idiotic, childish need to have the last word" (Fanon, 2007, p. 11). Without this grounding in the liberation struggle, the intellectual finds himself rootless, without a compass that anchors his vision.

Practice against History

The black subject is confronted with a dilemma. A history of colonialism and racial slavery has brought with it a system of representations, tales, images, stories, and narratives that mark the black subject's place in the world. Enveloped in these discourses, "[t]he black man wants to be like the white man. For the black man there is only one destiny. And it is white. Long ago the black man admitted the unarguable superiority of the white man, and all his efforts are aimed at achieving a white existence. Have I no other purpose on earth, then, but to avenge the Negro of the seventeenth century?" (Fanon, 2008, p. 178). The burden of history manifests itself in epistemic structures. How then, despite this historical weight, can the colonized subject break with the weight of history? Fanon very much acknowledges the cultural and structural impediments that hold the colonized subject in his place, but he emphasizes over and over again, that "I am not a prisoner of history" (Fanon, 2008, p. 179). While decolonization does need a certain amount of historical rewriting, Fanon's emphasis lies on forging new imaginaries. The colonized cannot succumb to the historical process that is "pre-given," written for him. Instead, Fanon states: "The body of history does not determine a single one of my actions. I am my own foundation. And it is by going beyond the historical, instrumental hypothesis that I will initiate the cycle of my freedom" (Fanon, 2008, p. 180).

In order to grasp Fanon's theory of history and the necessity for an epistemological break, it is important to remember the urgency of his writings. Amidst colonial revolution, it is this historical watershed moment that introduces "invention into existence" (Fanon, 2008, p. 179). While acknowledging the life-in-death condition of the colonial subject that has historically been placed in a space of nonexistence, Fanon calls for the "leap," that breaks with the structures of history. "I am a Negro, and tons of chains, storms of blows, rivers of expectoration flow down my shoulders. But I do not have the right to allow myself to bog down. I do not have the right to allow the slightest fragment to remain in my existence. I do not have the right to allow myself to be mired in what the past has determined. I am not the slave of the Slavery that dehumanized my ancestors" (Fanon, 2008, p. 179).

Furthermore, Fanon underlines that the colonial relationship not only dehumanizes the colonized but also implicates the white man. "The disaster of the man of color lies in the fact that he was enslaved. The disaster and the inhumanity of the white man lie in the fact that somewhere he has killed man" (Fanon, 2008, p. 180). In other words, the colonizer, just as much as the colonized, has lost his humanity through being implicated in violence and torture. The radical break must therefore not only reposition the black man as an actional being, but also transform the relationship between the colonizer and the colonized. It is through this new creation that we can create mutual recognition. Fanon's vision of this world, breaking with Manichean colonial reality, is a reimagining of social relations between men: "Superiority? Inferiority? Why not the quite simple attempt to touch the other, to feel the other, to explain the other to myself?" (Fanon, 2008, p. 181). In order to overcome the fixing of the racialized subject in a position of exteriority, Fanon envisions a new form of relating between people that works through dexterity, emotion, and a radical form of knowing each other.

Fanon's anticolonial imagination points to a new kind of social relationship that escapes prewritten social hierarchies. This insight was made possible due to his own affective and subjective experiences of being-in-the-world. Recognizing how colonial and racialized structures dehumanize the racialized subject, Fanon suggests that a break from these hierarchies needed to be based on a transformation of the racialized subject. To become an "actional" person, to break from epistemic structures that define one's sense of self, the racialized have to act. Due to Fanon's own biographic and practical experiences in a colonial system, he was able to understand how deeply colonial structures shape the humanity of all involved. To escape from this colonial situation and to obtain veritable recognition and self-determination, struggle was necessary.

"Decolonisation never goes unnoticed, for it focuses on and fundamentally alters being, and transforms the spectator crushed to a nonessential state into a privileged actor, captured in a virtually grandiose fashion by the spotlight of History" (Fanon, 2007, p. 2). Witnessing the decolonizing struggle, Fanon suggests that (Algerian) combat gives rise to "new attitudes, to new modes of action, to new ways" (Fanon, 1965, p. 64). Yet, national consciousness, just as much as racial pride, is solely one stage to a new society, for national consciousness has to give way to social and political consciousness. Aware of possible deadends following decolonization, Fanon warned of one-party states, the power of national bourgeoisies, or reifications of nationalism, as they deter from his universal vision. Only by transcending national consciousness could we aim for deep-seated transformation and a new humanity.

Fanon's writings were always deeply implicated in current political situations, drawing from contemporary events and subsequently seeking to influence them (Fanon, 1969). Most importantly, for him, culture and ideas could reflect both, the failures of social change and also the possibility for social change. In order to create a new world, a new man, an actional subject, what is needed is a radical break from old systems of representations. For Fanon, the anticolonial intellectual has the task to articulate a vision for anticolonial revolutionaries, never as an outside observer, but always linked to practice. Then, the intellectual can put forth a "new history of man," a system of knowledge categories that ceases to reproduce European domination. Only by breaking with epistemic foundations that position the white man at the top of the hierarchy will we stop taking his position for granted.

In short, this epistemic break, brought about through struggle and historical rupture, can produce the conditions for a new humanity (Bogues, 2005). Fanon, through his intellectual practice, attempted to inspire this structural break.

Fanon's realization that, as a racialized subject, he could never really be a part of France was a profound biographic experience, which in turn inspired his analyses of racialization: the need to break from racial fixations, to assert himself as a human being, and to create a new conception of man that allows for mutual recognition. Deeply shaped by historical context and his engagement in decolonization struggles, Fanon's call for a new humanity and a clear epistemological break makes up his anticolonial imagination. Importantly, neither Fanon nor Hall – whom I turn to next – write about race as a subcategory, but instead theorize how imperial and racializing schemas are a constitutive element of the modern world. Hall's anticolonial imagination differs from Fanon's as he wrote from a different historical moment. However, influenced by his upbringing in colonial Jamaica and his transboundary experience as a diasporic intellectual in Britain, Hall is similarly positioned to analyze the pervasiveness of dominant, imperial representations: He recenters displacement as a modern experience, includes the other in a national political imaginary, and illuminates for us ways to intervene in dominant cultural meaning systems.

TRANSBOUNDARY EXPERIENCES: STUART HALL

Stuart Hall was born on February 3, 1932, in the British colony of Jamaica. He grew up, in his words, "in a lower-middle class family that was trying to be a middle class Jamaican family trying to be an upper-middle class Jamaican family trying to be an English Victorian family" (Hall, 1987, p. 45). Colonialism marked not only the political context of his early life, but also Hall's family life. This means that the objective condition of colonialism created contradictory subjectivities: On the one hand, his family wanted to belong to the metropole and on the other, the racial hierarchies of colonial Jamaica meant that his skin being darker than his family's was "the first social fact" he knew (Akomfrah & Hall, 2014). Hall's early years were marked by a refusal to live up to the dominant metropole-oriented aspirations presented to him. For him, the objective and subjective could not be separated, because the objective, colonial contradictions produced intense subjective feelings and anguish, breaching into the private sphere

(Hall & Chen, 1996). Hall recalls that his mother in particular aspired to British-ness, and "thought the world would disappear with the departure of the British" (Hall & Back, 2009, p. 662). After winning a Rhodes scholarship to study at Oxford, Stuart Hall left for Britain in 1951, leaving Jamaica 12 years before it reached independence (Back & Tate, 2015).

"I felt out of place in Jamaica, and when I came to England I felt out of place in Merton College, Oxford, and I feel out of place even now. I feel out of place in relation to the British, which might sound a very strange thing because I've lived here for 50-something years" (Hall & Back, 2009, p. 669). The sense of displacement marked Hall's early childhood experiences, just as much as his adult life. As a colonized subject, he writes, one is always "displaced from the center of the world" (Hall in Meeks, 2007, p. 272). This center of the world is represented as *elsewhere*, and one feels out of place with the people as well as the conditions one finds himself in. Moving to Britain perpetuated this sense of displacement. "It is my home in a certain kind of way. But I will never be English – never. I can't be, because traces in my life, and the traces in my memory and the traces in my history of another place are just ineradicable. I can't get them out of my head. I don't want to have a fight about it, but that's just how one is. So being displaced, or out of place, is a characteristic experience of mine. It's been all throughout my life" (Hall & Back, 2009, p. 669).

The sociological imagination, as Mills (2000) reminds us, is a bringing together of biography, structure, and history. Stuart Hall's biographic experiences and affective relationship pertaining to displacement, profoundly shaped his analysis of social structures and of history. His biographic experience of "being displaced" as a "place of identity," as a state of being that is consistently in motion, is an affective state he became familiar with long before he learnt about it through scholarship. Displacement as a defining factor of one's identity means "[l]iving with, living through difference" (Hall, 1987, p. 45). Hall notes that in the midst of anticolonial struggles, many intellectuals from across the British Empire came together in Britain to discuss the end of empire. Upon sharing his own experiences with others, he understood that this feeling of displacement was in fact very wide spread: Everyone had come to London, escaping from the throes of colonial society and seeking a way to "become modern subjects." To become modern, one had to leave behind the colony, to go elsewhere, to start the process of "becoming," to become, in the words of George Lamming, "a native of my person" (Hall in Meeks, 2007, pp. 272, 273).

Hall settled in Britain throughout the period of decolonization and became a founding figure of and in British cultural studies. He contributed to the emergence of the New Left and became the editor of the *New Left Review*, all the while reflecting on the meaning of "we" in the New Left, given his diasporic position within it (Hall & Chen, 1996). Throughout the 1980s and 1990s, Hall's voice was heard on British radio and television, and he became Britain's foremost public intellectual of multiculturalism. To this day, his critical work on Thatcherism provides one of the most profound analyses of changing culture in Britain. In his writings, he documented the experience of the diaspora, the experience of being black in Britain, and analyzed the changing configurations of class and race in British society (Hall, 1988, 1997). Throughout his life, his theoretical interventions always came from a particular standpoint, that of a diasporic Caribbean intellectual. Knowledge, he argued, is always deeply shaped by one's positionality, and his way of looking at British culture started through the "prism of his Caribbean formation" (Hall in Meeks, 2007, p. 271). Not simply a Caribbean intellectual, but as a diasporic Caribbean intellectual, Hall's intellectual life was marked by an attempt to understand his own biography.

His way of looking at the world was defined by movement, displacement, dislocation, the sense of not quite belonging, and the question of where to find meaning without having an easy answer to the question of "origin." In a larger quest to understand culture and society Hall placed the people of the diaspora front and center. Seeking to learn "who they think they are, where they want to go, where have they come from, what's their relation to the past, what's their memories, [and] how they express their creativity, how they express where they want to go to next" (Hall & Back, 2009, p. 662), Hall did not view displacement as somehow "outside" the nation state or the boundaries of the body politic, but definitive of the modern world. The answer to the question of where one is from, in a time defined by movement, he thought, merits "a long story" (Akomfrah & Hall, 2014). It is this positionality, this diasporic biography, I argue, that has shaped Stuart Hall's intellectual practice, his theory of history, and his view of the world in a global, relational ontology.

Diasporic Insights

Due to his own sense of displacement, Stuart Hall centered the migrant in his analyses of postwar Britain. Hall's experience of "never-quite-belonging" marked his own identity, an identity which "depended on the fact of being a migrant, on the difference from the rest of you" (Hall, 1987, p. 44). He recounts, that having been through the British colonial school system, having been immersed in English literature, and having his mother's aspirations oriented toward England, "I knew England from the inside. But I'm not and never will be 'English'" (Hall & Chen, 1996, p. 490). This position of knowing a place but not being of that place, not being wholly of either place, "that's exactly the diasporic experience, far away enough to experience the sense of exile and loss, close enough to understand the enigma of an always-postponed 'arrival'" (Hall & Chen, 1996, p. 490). In a sense, Hall's biography and subjectivity mirrors a larger British colonial ideology that not only ruled British subjects but also permanently delayed their arrival to modernity.

Yet, Hall's own biographic experiences allow him to recognize this sense of displacement as a very wide spread condition of contemporary times. Displacement, migration, and movement are not a marginal phenomenon, but in fact the story of many people's lives, a kind of collective cultural experience. Biographically displaced, always "somewhere else," the colonial subject is able to shatter essentialized claims to identity, homogeneity, and stability. What is more, with today's prevalence of global flows and movement, everyone's identity is fragmented, and many can empathize with the subjective feeling of not quite belonging. Ironically, it is his diasporic, colonial experience of not quite belonging that makes Hall the paradigmatic modern subject. In this age, he writes "you all feel so dispersed, I become centered. What I've thought of as dispersed and fragmented comes, paradoxically, to be *the* representative modern experience" (Hall, 1987, p. 44).

Hall's focus on movement and the diaspora has at least three analytical consequences: First, it forces us to think about belonging as a complex story that cannot be contained in nation state boundaries or one "origin." Belonging is created and recreated in the movement itself, and this movement has become the norm in modern life. Second, it explodes the ideal of a homogeneous, bounded nation, and highlights the empire's constitutive nature in nation-building and all seemingly "local" histories. This standpoint also recreates a kind of national imaginary that finds room for "the other." Third, if our lives and senses of attachment cross nation state boundaries or emerge within the empire, we must conduct analyses that are themselves relational and "contrapuntal" (Go, 2016; Said, 1993). For the analyst, adopting the category of the nation state is restrictive at best and inaccurate at worst, particularly if it fails to portray a holistic, transboundary experience of migrants, the diaspora, travelers, refugees, and the displaced.

Stuart Hall's experience in the diaspora thus gave him very unique insight into the contemporary cultural experience. Akin to Simmel's stranger, Hall suggests, the diasporic subject also gains a kind of insight into his host culture. Through the "shock" of translation, he may be able to see what others do not see or simply take for granted. Drawing on C. L. R. James, the diaspora is "in but not of Europe" and may be able to create knowledge from this distinct position (Hall & Back, 2009). That is, the experiences of the diaspora suggest that the world is made up of "overlapping territories" and "intertwined histories." As a result, Hall was sensitive to Britain's history of empire and related knowledge formations and discourse. He argued against "imperial amnesia" and critiqued the surprise the British public felt regarding the "sudden" arrival of a black population in Britain.

Failing to appreciate Britain's intertwined, imperial history, the British public came face-to-face with the fact that Britain had a black population and that this black population was here to stay. For Hall, this "surprise" was misconstrued. Caribbeans had not only "recently" become part of Britain and the Windrush generation was not the "first" to belong to Britain, but Caribbeans and their ancestors had always been "the sugar at the bottom of the English cup of tea" (Hall, 1991, p. 48). Having grown up in colonial Jamaica, Hall was able to intertwine the history of two distinct points in the British Empire: the history of his birthplace, colonial Jamaica, and the history of his residence, metropolitan Britain. Through this transboundary, biographic experience, Hall overcame analytic bifurcations, be that methodological nationalism, external/internal, or domestic/international distinctions. His biographic practice allows him to recenter questions of immigration, to focus on the experience of the migrant himself, to reconstruct historic linkages, and to map imperial cultural representations. This recentering makes imperial legacies more apparent, does not mark immigrants as always already external to the body politic of the nation state, and focuses our attention to traces in racial representations. In short, Hall's subjective experience alerts us to systems of oppression that were previously hidden.

Identification and the Making of the Subject

On a visit to Jamaica in the early 1960s, after the first wave of immigration to Britain, Stuart Hall recounts an interaction with his mother. She remarked: "I hope they don't think you are one of those immigrants over there!" Hall states that in this moment he understood who he was – an immigrant. The narrative of migration brought to light one part, one version, of his own identity. He turned to his mother and said: "Of course,

I'm an immigrant. What do you think I am?" She responded "in that classic Jamaican middle class way, 'Well, I hope the people over there will shove all the immigrants off the long end of a short pier'" (Hall, 1987, p. 45). Again, Hall draws on his subjective life experience – his encounter with his mother who had bought into the British colonial ideology – to build a larger theoretical narrative: ideas, discourses, and narratives shape who we are, where we belong, and how we can change.

Motivated to understand his own identity, Hall developed the concept of "identification." He defines identification as "the process of subjectification to discursive practices, and the politics of exclusion which all such subjectification appears to entail" (Hall, 1996f, p. 3). In other words, the process of identification was one of "becoming, rather than being." If identity, then, is about "becoming rather than being," identity can change; but it is also dependent on concrete historical and institutional sites and the cultural resources made available to us. Identities are "constituted within, not outside representation" (Hall, 1996a, p. 4). Who we are is formed in interaction with the narratives we find available to us. There is no "essence," or fixed, ahistorical part to our identity. Subjectively, we may think that identity arises from inside, but "who we are" is in fact the result of one's long conversation with the world around us. We are, in part, how others see us (Akomfrah & Hall, 2014). Therefore, to understand the materials through which identities are created, we need to analyze the specific, historical resources that are made available to us (Hall, 1996a, p. 4). Subjective experiences interact with the narratives of history and continuously make and remake who we are.

Drawing on his own biographical practice, Hall notes that the identity of being "an immigrant" is an unstable place to be. Once Hall recognized his identity as an immigrant, Hall embarked on an identification process to learn that he was "black." This identification as a black intellectual comes at a very specific historical moment, connected to the rise of British Black cultural politics (Alexander, 2009). The category "black" in itself is not a stable label, but it is also culturally, politically, and historically constituted. While, to outsiders, Jamaicans may "appear black," they themselves never spoke of themselves as "black," and never saw themselves as black. The black identity, therefore, particularly for people in the British diaspora, has to be recognized through, what he calls, political education (Hall, 1987, p. 45). Hall writes: "Many, many people in Jamaica, including lots of people who were black, did not think of themselves in the way in which people after the late 60s came to think of themselves as black. So it was a discovery for me, a rediscovery of the Caribbean in new terms, and a rediscovery of my thinking about culture, and a rediscovery of the black subject" (Hall & Back, 2009, p. 662). While Hall draws attention to the importance of narratives that serve as resources for our identification, he also emphasizes that to adopt a position means "staking a place in a certain discourse or practice" (Hall in Meeks, 2009, p. 282). This *act* of taking a position is important. Assuming a certain identity allows us to not only speak from that particular position, but it also allows us to – under a different set of circumstances – actively modify this position.

Here, it makes sense to juxtapose Hall's theory of subject-making with Althusser's. In fact, neither Fanon nor Hall thought that we are mere products of ideological interpellation. Hall rejects Althusser's interpellation and the top-down making of the subject and instead defines identities as "the meeting point, the point of *suture*, between on the one hand the discourses and practices which attempt to 'interpellate', speak to us or hail us into place as the social subjects of particular discourses, and on the other hand, the processes which produce subjectivities, which construct us as subjects which can be 'spoken'" (Hall, 1996f, p. 5, 6). Hall emphasizes the importance of agency on the part of the subject in recognizing oneself in a web of meanings offered to us by ideologies. Identities are never simply "produced" from the top down, but rather come into existence through the subjects' temporary attachments to particular positions in society; they are not "hailed" but they have to invest in a particular position.

This solves what Hall calls Althusser's problem of "correspondence," the fact that the theory cannot explain whether the interpellated subject is somehow predisposed to subject and "fall into" a particular situation in the social order (Hall, 1996f, p. 8). Hall formulates a theory of articulation, which analyzes which discourses are *received* by their subjects. The perceived unity of a discourse is really a particular articulation of specific elements that can be rearticulated in different ways. Articulation is "the non-necessary link, between a social force which is making itself, and the ideology or conceptions of the world which makes intelligible the process they are going through, which begins to bring onto the historical stage a new social position and political position, a new set of social and political subjects" (Hall, 1996f, p. 144). A subject then has to invest in a particular position by thinking of it as *articulation* of self rather than as imposed designation (Hall, 1996f, p. 6). Enunciated practices productively *make* the subject and are explicitly situated in concrete historical situations.[3]

To go back to Hall's example of discovering himself as "black," we can recognize that only because the category is historically and culturally constituted does not mean that it is "less real." The symbolic is the space where the subject enters into a dialogue with available cultural narratives. Even though these narratives are fragmented and ever unfinished, the subject – one's "self" – relates to these narratives as a set of histories, histories that are very much real. Narratives *represent* reality and also allow individuals to situate themselves as particular subjects. We position ourselves in relation to a particular discourse, with real effects. This interplay between the narrative and our investment in it suggests that cultural identities also undergo constant transformations. The idea that at some point we will "secure" our sense of self in a fixed way is false. If narratives change, if we retell history in a different way, the way we relate to this narrative also changes. Identities, in short, are "subject to the continuous 'play' of history, culture and power" (Hall, 1990, p. 225).

Hall's theory of identification captures racial and colonial symbolic systems of oppression, attached to *real* histories. The colonial subject identifies with the Victorian family and enters this process of becoming. The subject positions himself in relation to colonial cultural narratives. As a result, the colonial subject's identity is perpetually "somewhere" else. In fact, the subject is doubly displaced: displaced in his relationship to the narrative (not there) and displaced from making and constituting the narrative altogether (Hall, 1987). It is from his theory of identification that Hall seeks to uncover the trauma of the colonial experience: The colonized find themselves confronted with a set of narratives, subjected to dominant regimes of representation that normalized their position of inferiority (Hall, 1990, p. 225). This leads Hall to underline the importance of representation, particularly with regard to being black in Britain and to explore the problem of ideology.

Ideology, Conjunctures, and Ruptures

Hall's cultural theory consistently underlines the importance of narratives that are available to us, that help us define who we are and how we articulate who we are. His writings on identification make clear that our identity construction is a two-way process between subjection and investment. To have meaningful choices available to us leads us to the question of ideology. What happens if "perpetually displaced subjects" do not participate in the construction of narratives? What if they cannot draw on productive narratives to define themselves? And how do systems of representation contribute to the fact that we take the world, as it is, for granted? Representations, to Hall, are crucial because they form the reservoir of available narratives. Precisely when dominant discourses fail to represent, for example, the black presence in Britain, Hall turned to an examination of black cinema or everyday practices (Hall, 1980, 1996a, 1996b, 2006). Thus, to him, social ideas manifest themselves not just in top-down bourgeois ideology, but also in practice and in the everyday – just as much as in intellectual, theoretical knowledge frameworks (Hall, 1996e, p. 27).

To understand how Hall's diasporic insight into – what one might call – "subversive representations" shapes his theory of history, we need to discuss his writings on ideology. In short, similar to the fragmented nature of his writings on identity, Hall also saw the cultural system as fragmented. While ideology produces powerful dominant frameworks, there are always spaces – in the everyday, in art, film, or everyday practices – that challenge this dominance. Stuart Hall defines ideology as the "mental frameworks – the languages, the concepts, categories, imaginary of thought, and the system of representation," that are available to us to make intelligible, define, and make sense of the world around us (Hall, 1996e, p. 26; Hall, 1992). The problem of ideology, then, is the way in which dominant mental frameworks define the way we interpret particular historical moments. These ruling ideas allow us to delineate what seems rational or reasonable and they give us a vocabulary that allows us to interpret and give meaning to particular actions. Akin to Sewell's duality of history (Sewell, 1992, 2005), Hall's concept of ideology takes on an interactive role with the material: While ideology is symbolic, it takes on "material force." No practice, action, or material structure can ever be outside the realm of the symbolic. Instead, all practices are always enveloped in a system of meaning that allows us to orient ourselves in this world (Bogues, 2005; Hall, 1996e). To understand how and why social change occurs, he argues, we need to account for how social ideas arise (Hall, 1996e, p. 26).

In his analysis on Thatcherism, for example, Hall proposes that Thatcher changed the "currency" of political thought. Freedom came to be equated with the free market, and society was not deemed a relevant category of thought. The point here is that Thatcherism not only changed Britain's structural make-up, but also the way we interpret and give meaning to everyday interactions (Bogues, 2005; Hall, 1982, 1988). Politics is always also a symbolic formation. Therefore, if we want to think about social change, and the ways in which history proceeds, we need to focus on the semiotic struggles that underlie how we interpret social events. In short, a theory of change rests on understanding how meanings change over time and decipher openings for new meaning formations. To do so, Hall urges us to pay attention to historical specificity and the analysis of conjunctures.

Openings for "newness," where a challenge to ideology can take place, rest in historical conjunctures. A conjuncture is the combination of distinct long-term social and historical processes that articulate themselves with great intensity at a given historical moment. Conjunctures may be historically specific because they are enunciated in distinct discursive forms. An analysis of historical conjunctures thus seeks to understand "how the new replaces the old" and how, in turn, we learn to take the new for granted (Akomfrah & Hall, 2014). The old, however, never quite goes away; the break with history is never complete. Compared to Fanon's envisioned radical break, Hall conceptualizes change as a "reconfiguration" of elements that belong to the past with some that are new. In his words, the present always has an incomplete, and to some extent an unfinished, relationship to the past. To study ideology within a given historical configuration, then means to understand how the symbolic "stabilizes" particular forms of domination (Hall, 1996e, p. 27). Hall's articulation forms the connection between ideology (the symbolic) and the social, but not in an economic deterministic manner; that is, not "as one *necessarily* given in socioeconomic structures or positions, but precisely as the result of an articulation" (Hall, 1996c, p. 145).

To give an example, to Hall, the lasting presence of the British Empire was always evident, be that in ways in which identities were configured or how the British interpreted the presence of their black population. The way "race" is articulated in Britain fed off a particular "reservoir of unconscious feelings about race," but this reservoir gets articulated in distinct ways (Hall & Back, 2009, p. 677). Historical long-term processes are thus very much at play and always influence the present, but dominant discursive formations *change* in specific historical circumstances. For the analyst, that means that pointing to the mere "legacy of empire" is insufficient; instead, one has to understand the *specific* configurations of meaning and articulations for each unique historical conjuncture. Importantly, ideology is never all-encompassing and totalizing, but always fragmented and contested. This means that historical change cannot solely be based on an analysis of structural logics, but must take into account how narratives relate to the social and how subjects articulate and position themselves in society at large. If people invest in a particular narrative, it is with this moment of recognition that a political change can occur.

Given the importance of narratives, cultural representations, and meaning-creation in history, the task of the intellectual is also never "outside" history. Instead, Hall suggests, intellectual labor should aid us to understand specific historical conjunctures *and* seek to make an intervention.

First, the intellectual traces how a particular conjuncture emerges, configures itself out of distinct elements, and creates a historically specific, new element. Second, critical intellectual work seeks to intervene in a particular historical conjuncture in order to shift its outcome. In understanding how various ideologies come together and in proposing a given narrative, there may always be a possibility to reshift how we make sense of our reality. Importantly, this intervention is only ever possible if we seek to carefully understand the specific historical conjuncture, for, "[e]ach time that comes, it does require a change of perspective" (Akomfrah & Hall, 2014). Since ideologies are fragmented, the opening for radical politics is always a possibility. It is important to note that this kind of intellectual work forces us to orient our critical practice not toward the blind reproduction of academic disciplines, but to engage in a kind of cultural practice that mirrors what Gramsci called the work of the organic intellectual (Gramsci, 1971).

To sum up, Stuart Hall's diasporic and colonial experience allowed him to formulate a theory of identification, subject-making, and historical change. Akin to his writings on identity – the ever unfinished process through which we define who we are and stake our position within historically constructed narratives – his theory of cultural systems is also always in motion. While he was very aware of the powers of hegemonic ideologies – particularly under Thatcherism – and the importance of ideologies in the constitution of subjects, he similarly emphasized the availability of *openings* in history (Bogues, 2005). Cultural forms, he wrote, are never fully closed. Instead, it is in these openings, that he sought to intervene as a public intellectual and put forth systems of interpretation that may lead to a change in social relations. As a diasporic intellectual, displacement and movement was central to his own life experience, so his search for movement and temporary openings in the midst of historical conjunctures mirrors these subjective experiences.

A British subject growing up in colonial Jamaica, Hall's positionality made him very aware of the dominance of empire, not just in structural, political manifestations, but also in terms of epistemic forms of domination. Writing from this particular position, Hall combated British imperial amnesia, be that in recentering how we think about the presence of Britain's black population – as always already there – or in focusing on the prevalence of diasporic experiences and narratives of displacement as a modern experience. The colonial experience of always being displaced to "somewhere else" and always awaiting the postponed arrival allowed Hall to create a distinctly anticolonial imaginary that recenters those at the margins and make space for Britain's others. Even though he turned to the study of race only later in his career, the focus on displacement spans his entire oeuvre and is profoundly anticolonial.

Hall's and Fanon's anticolonial imagination is distinct, due to differing colonial structural experiences and ideologies, but also because they were born into two distinct historical moments. While Fanon wrote in dialogue with decolonization movements, Hall's writings were interventions, aiming to shift British postwar political and cultural discourse, seeking to provide new imaginaries and new spaces of representation for black artists and marginal voices. Moreover, in contrast to Fanon, looking back on anti-colonial revolutions, Hall gives us a theory of history that accounts for the durability of old elements and their powerful grasp on people's minds. Yet, he always maintained that through careful analysis of historical conjunctures, new knowledge and meaning systems may emerge – ideas that allow for shifts in history (Bogues, 2005; Wilder, 2014).

CONCLUSION

This article proposed that Frantz Fanon and Stuart Hall were able to draw on their formative transboundary experiences in order to break with dominant, colonial categories of thought. Because they lived in distinct historical moments, Fanon amidst anticolonial revolutions and Hall in post-World War II Britain, they put forth distinct theories of practice, history, and social change. Yet, despite their different historical contexts, both intellectuals' subjective experiences allow for a particular kind of epistemic rupture. Fanon's focus on the colonized's subjectivity and the psycho-affective effects of colonial structures led him to argue for a radical break, not only with socioeconomic colonial relations, but also epistemic colonial frameworks. It is through his attention to psychological colonial structures and the impossibility to fully develop one's humanity as a racialized person that he suggests a radical creation of the new, *actional* being. Stuart Hall put his focus on the experience of the diaspora, the migrant, and displacement, which not only makes a global relational analysis possible, but also allowed him to argue against fixed, essentialist identities. Identities are fragmented, much like the cultural system: Despite dominant ideological frameworks, Hall was able to look for openings in history, conjunctures, in which newness can emerge. Both placed front and center the constitutive nature of empire, colonialism, and racialization to modern societies, seeking to make space for and truly recognize "the other."

Consistently uniting theory and practice, anticolonial writers not only positioned their intellectual labors as a form of political practice aimed at social change, but also sought to understand how history could provide openings for ideas to create this kind of change. Fanon proposed that it is in revolutionary practice through which the colonized subject can break with the burdens of history and find his own ways of acting, thinking, and knowing. Hall theorized how history has an always incomplete relationship to the present and how thought can intervene in these ruptures. Both produced ideas that were intended to influence action and produce social change. In other words, intellectual production is not "outside" history, but exists in a dialectical relationship with the everyday and revolutionary practice. For Hall, theory can play an important role in articulating and extrapolating the meaning of specific historical conjunctures, while for Fanon, the intellectual – in dialogue with practice – can enunciate visions for a new humanism and aid in the anticolonial struggle.

The tradition of anticolonial thought may particularly speak to cultural sociology. Influenced by the "practice turn" (Bourdieu, 1977; Bourdieu & Eagleton, 1992; Dirks, Eley, & Ortner, 1994; Ortner, 2006; Sewell, 1992, 2005), cultural sociologists have largely worked to collapse the distinctions between theory, practice, and history, and theorized the symbolic realm. They have turned to the study of practices and meaning-making as theory-generating exercises, seeking to overcome a conception of theory as ahistorical, apolitical, and abstracted from the life world. With the turn, culture – ideas, orienting conceptual frameworks, and meaning-giving interpretations – was no longer seen as a "product" or "reflection" of other determinants but formed part of the social itself (Somers, 1995). Sewell called this the duality of structures – emphasizing that history is simultaneously composed of meaning-conferring, virtual schemas, and material resources which sustain each other (Sewell, 1992, p. 136; Somers & Gibson, 1994). Given the dialectic between virtual schemas and material resources, ideas and intellectual practice consistently influence social change. It is here where the anticolonial tradition may push cultural sociology further.

Anticolonial thought is marked by a double bind: it is itself part of the world, but seeks to break with dominant frameworks and to imagine the world differently. As this article showed with the example of Fanon and Hall, anticolonial thinkers aim to create knowledge that breaks with colonial and racial hierarchies, based on practice and experience. In particular, Fanon and Hall create epistemic ruptures by focusing on the *subjectivity* of the colonized or the diasporic subject. Showing how colonial histories and representations of these histories dehumanize or continuously displace the colonized or racialized, Fanon and Hall both make a case for new narratives. Based on their own biographies, they are able to grasp the operation of empire, based on how its knowledge categories shape what we know, what we deem reasonable, and how we construct human difference. While cultural sociology has a long tradition of ideological critique, anticolonial thought points to the epistemic realities of empire and shows us a way to recenter the racialized, inferiorized, or displaced self. Based on their practice, colonized and diasporic subjectivity, Hall and Fanon proposed distinct ways to capitalize on ruptures in history that allow for an escape from racialized structures of oppression.

NOTES

1. Fanon's language is a product of his time and hence does not use gender-neutral expressions. Without seeking to make gendered statements, in this article, I adopt Fanon's language for clarity.

2. Fanon's theorization of self-formation in racialized societies is similar to W. E. B. Du Bois' "double consciousness." Du Bois also points out how the racialized subject has to contend with the dehumanizing structures of racialized societies in his self-formation.

3. As a sidenote, Hall never equated society "with text" but used these concepts as an analogy to uncover subjects' meaning-making practices (Hall, 1996f).

REFERENCES

Ahluwalia, P. (2010). *Out of Africa: Post-structuralism's colonial roots*. London: Routledge.

Akomfrah, J., & Hall, S. (2014). *The Stuart Hall project*. British Film Institute, London.

Alessandrini, A. C. (Ed.). (2005). *Frantz Fanon: Critical perspectives*. London: Routledge.

Alexander, C. (2009). Stuart Hall and 'race'. *Cultural Studies*, *23*(4), 457–482.

Back, L., & Tate, M. (2015). For a sociological reconstruction: WEB Du Bois, Stuart Hall and segregated sociology. *Sociological Research Online*, *20*(3), 15.

Bogues, A. (2005). Working outside criticism: Thinking beyond limits. *Boundary 2*, *32*(1), 71–93.

Bourdieu, P. (1977). *Outline of a theory of practice*. Cambridge: Cambridge University Press.

Bourdieu, P., & Eagleton, T. (1992). Doxa and common life. *New Left Review*, *191*, 111–121.

Coulthard, G. (2014). *Red skin, white masks*. Minneapolis, MN: University of Minnesota Press.

Dirks, N. B., Eley, G., & Ortner, S. B. (Eds.). (1994). *Culture/power/history: A reader in contemporary social theory*. Princeton, NJ: Princeton University Press.

Fanon, F. (1965). *A dying colonialism*. New York, NY: Grove Press.

Fanon, F. (1969). *Toward the African revolution: Political essays*. New York, NY: Grove Press.

Fanon, F. (2007). *The wretched of the earth*. New York, NY: Grove Press.
Fanon, F. (2008). *Black skin, white masks*. New York, NY: Grove Press.
Gibson, N. C. (Ed.). (1999). *Rethinking Fanon: The continuing dialogue*. New York, NY: Humanities Books.
Gibson, N. C. (2003). *Fanon: The postcolonial imagination*. Cambridge: Polity Press.
Go, J. (2013a). Fanon's postcolonial cosmopolitanism. *European Journal of Social Theory*, *16*(2), 208–225.
Go, J. (2013b). For a postcolonial sociology. *Theory and Society*, *42*(1), 25–55.
Go, J. (2016). *Postcolonial thought and social theory*. Cambridge: Cambridge University Press.
Gordon, L. R. (1995). *Fanon and the crisis of European man*. London: Routledge.
Gordon, L. R. (2015). *What Fanon said: A philosophical introduction to his life and thought*. New York, NY: Fordham University Press.
Gramsci, A. (1971). *Selections from the prison notebooks* (Vols. 1–3), London: Lawrence & Wishart.
Hall, S. (1980). Cultural studies: Two paradigms. *Media, Culture and Society*, *2*(1), 57–72.
Hall, S. (1982). The rediscovery of ideology: Return of the repressed in media studies. In M. Gurevitch, T. Bennett, J. Curon, & J. Woolacott (Eds.), *Culture, Society and the Media* (pp. 56–90). New York, NY: Methuen.
Hall, S. (1987). Minimal selves. In L. Appignanesi (Ed.), *Identity 6* (pp. 44–46). London: ICA.
Hall, S. (1988). The toad in the garden: Thatcherism among the theorists. In C. Nelson & L. Grossberg (Eds.), *Marxism and the interpretation of culture* (pp. 35–57). London: Macmillan.
Hall, S. (1990). Cultural identity and diaspora. In J. Rutherford (Ed.), *Identity* (pp. 222–237). London: Lawrence & Wishart.
Hall, S. (1991). Old and new identities, old and new ethnicities. In A. King (Ed.), *Culture, globalization and the world-system* (pp. pp. 41–68). London: Macmillan.
Hall, S. (1992). The West and the rest: Discourse and power. In R. Maaka & C. Anderson (Ed.), *The indigenous experience: Global perspectives* (pp. 165–173). Toronto: Canadian Scholars' Press Inc.
Hall, S. (1995). Negotiating Caribbean identities. *New Left Review*, January–February 2009. Retrieved from https://newleftreview.org/I/209/stuart-hall-negotiating-caribbean-identities
Hall, S. (1996a). Cultural identity and cinematic representation. In H. A. Baker Jr., M. Diawara, & R. H. Lindeborg (Eds.), *Black British cultural studies: A reader* (pp. 210–223). Chicago, IL: University of Chicago Press.
Hall, S. (1996b). New ethnicities. In H. A. Baker Jr., M. Diawara, & R. H. Lindeborg (Eds.), *Black British cultural studies: A reader* (pp.163–173). Chicago, IL: University of Chicago Press.
Hall, S. (1996c). On postmodernism and articulation: An interview with Stuart Hall. In D. Morley & K.-H. Chen (Ed.), *Stuart Hall: Critical dialogues in cultural studies* (pp. 131–150). New York, NY: Routledge.
Hall, S. (1996e). The problem of ideology: Marxism without guarantees. In D. Morley & K.-H. Chen (Ed.), *Stuart Hall: Critical dialogues in cultural studies* (pp. 24–46). New York, NY: Routledge.
Hall, S. (1996f). Who needs 'identity'? In S. Hall & P. Du Gay (Eds.), *The Question of Cultural Identity* (pp.1–17). London: Sage.

Hall, S. (1997). Subjects in history: Making diasporic identities. In W. Lubiano (Ed.), *The house that race built* (pp. 289–299). New York, NY: Pantheon.
Hall, S. (2006). Black Diaspora artists in Britain: Three 'Moments' in post-war history. *History Workshop Journal, 61*(1), 1–24.
Hall, S., & Back, L. (2009). At home and not at home. *Cultural studies, 23*(4), 658–688.
Hall, S., & Chen, K.-H. (1996). The formation of a diasporic intellectual: An interview with Stuart Hall. In D. Morley & K. H. Chen (Eds.), *Stuart Hall: Critical dialogues in cultural studies* (pp. 486–505). London: Routledge.
Hudis, P. (2015). *Frantz Fanon: Philosopher of the barricades*. London: Pluto Press.
Meeks, B. (2007). *Caribbean reasonings: Culture, politics, race and diaspora: The thought of Stuart Hall*. Kingston: Ian Randle Publishers.
Mills, C. W. (2000). *The sociological imagination*. Oxford: Oxford University Press.
Ortner, S. B. (2006). *Anthropology and social theory: Culture, power, and the acting subject*. Durham, NC: Duke University Press.
Said, E. W. (1993). *Culture and imperialism*. New York, NY: Vintage.
Sardar, Z. (2008). *Preface in Black skin, white masks*. New York, NY: Grove Press.
Sewell Jr, W. H. (1992). A theory of structure: Duality, agency, and transformation. *American Journal of Sociology, 98*(1), 1–29.
Sewell Jr, W. H. (2005). *Logics of history: Social theory and social transformation*. Chicago, IL: University of Chicago Press.
Somers, M., & Gibson, G. (1994). Reclaiming the epistemological 'Other': Narrative and the social construction of identity. In C. Calhoun (Ed.), *Social theory and the politics of identity* (pp. 37–99). Cambridge, MA: Blackwell.
Somers, M. R. (1995). What's political or cultural about political culture and the public sphere? Toward an historical sociology of concept formation. *Sociological Theory, 13*(2), 113–144.
Wilder, G. (2014). *Freedom time: Negritude, decolonization, and the future of the world*. Durham, NC: Duke University Press.

EMPIRE AND VIOLENCE: CONTINUITY IN THE AGE OF REVOLUTION

Jeppe Mulich

ABSTRACT

When the 13 colonies in North America, the slave colony of Saint-Domingue, and the colonial territories of the Portuguese and Spanish Americas all rose against their imperial rulers, a new postcolonial order seemingly emerged in the Western Hemisphere. The reality of this situation forced political theorists and practitioners of the early 19th century to rethink the way in which they envisioned the nature and dynamics of international order. But a careful analysis of this shift reveals that it was not the radical break with prior notions of sovereignty and territoriality, often described in the literature. This was not the emergence of a new postimperial system of independent, nationally anchored states. Rather, it reflected a creative rethinking of existing notions of divided sovereignty and composite polities, rife with political experiments – from the formation of a new multi-centered empire in North America to the quasi-states and federations of Latin America. This moment of political experimentation and postcolonial order-making presented a distinctly new world repertoire of empire and state-building, parts of which were at least as

International Origins of Social and Political Theory
Political Power and Social Theory, Volume 32, 181–204

ISSN: 0198-8719/doi:10.1108/S0198-871920170000032007

violent and authoritarian as those of the old world empires it had replaced. The most radical ideas of freedom and liberty, championed by the black republic of Haiti, remained marginalized and sidelined by more conservative powers on both sides of the Atlantic.

Keywords: Age of revolution; empire; hierarchy; slavery; sovereignty; state formation

INTRODUCTION

This article is less about origins than it is about continuity. While the revolutionary decades around the turn of the 19th century have often been posited as a pivotal moment of transformation – the period in which the nation-state either originated or cemented its place in international relations and political thought – I argue that it was as much a period of continuity as one of radical change. While revolutions swept across the Atlantic and altered the political landscape of the Western Hemisphere, these changes did not discard the basic elements of existing political order. That is to say, the foundational view of how the political world should be organized changed relatively little. In particular, international thought continued to operate to a large extent within an older, imperial, repertoire of composite polities and layered sovereignty (Benton, 2010, pp. 30–32; Burbank & Cooper, 2010, pp. 16–17; Stern, 2008). This was a period rife with experimentation with the state form to be sure, but such experimentation primarily took place within an imperial imagination and only in rare instances did it break out of a hierarchical mode of organizing power and institutions that owed much to earlier regimes.

National states as the organizing units of interpolity relations were almost entirely contained within Europe, and even here they solidified and spread only incrementally over the course of the 19th century. The new polities of the Americas took many different forms, from the multicentric republican empire of the United States to the short-lived city-states and federations of Spanish South America, but common to all of them was the lingering influence of older conceptions of sovereignty, territory, and constitutionalism. Although a break took place with the specifics of European colonialism in the new world, political order both between and within polities continued to be envisioned within a predominantly imperial register.

Of the ruptures that did take place during this period, the most radical had less to do with nationhood and anti-imperialism than they had with the specifics of racial hierarchy and notions of a very particular freedom – freedom from enslavement. The spread of these notions was more limited than the general wave of revolutions, however, and their advocates and thinkers have in many cases been less well remembered, sidelined as bit players in the dominating historical narratives that cast abolition and emancipation as white reformist projects, rather than black revolutionary ones.

Perhaps paradoxically, historical sociology as a field has been particularly reluctant to engage with the central role of empire in the history of the state.[1] A number of influential sociological accounts have told differing stories about the development of the state, from the classic Marxist analysis by Eric Hobsbawm to the explicit critique of historical materialism by Anthony Giddens, the majority of which have focused heavily on the early modern and modern periods of European history (Ertman, 1997; Giddens, 1985; Hobsbawm, 1962; Mann, 1993).[2] This focus on European metropoles, combined with a preoccupation with the origins of a particular form of "modern" nation-state, often ideal-typically defined along Weberian lines, have led historical sociologists to pay disproportionate attention to national, rather than imperial, polities.[3] Given this tendency, therefore, it is not surprising that the age of revolution and its immediate aftermath has overwhelmingly been read by historical sociologists as signifying a critical juncture on the path toward nation-states, rather than a more subtle shift within the framework of empire (Giddens, 1985, pp. 32–34, 255–257; Hobsbawm, 1962, pp. 1–7; Skocpol, 1979, pp. 174–205). Pushing back on this particular Eurocentric and nation-centered reading of the age of revolution is thus one way of compelling the field to more carefully consider the role of empire in the historical processes of state formation, revolution, and interpolity order.

This article contributes to the larger concerns of the special issue by illuminating a specific example of the entanglement of practice and theory at a very particular moment of transnational history (Barkawi & Lawson, 2017). This moment – the revolutionary decades at the turn of the 19th century – was fundamentally one of transboundary interaction, not just within large imperial polities but also between different empires. While I argue that it was not an origins moment per se, it was nonetheless a key period of political experimentation and theorizing of the state form, theorizing that came directly out of international or transboundary events driven forward by actors who were practitioner-theorists in their own right. Indeed, the distinction between practitioners and theorists mattered little to those engaged in the revolutionary upheavals at the turn of the century. For these men and women, thinking about the state and its place in the world was part of a larger effort of implementing reforms and enacting new repertoires of political practice – forging institutions and reshaping legal and political frameworks in the process.

READING PRACTICE AS THEORY

This article does not follow the traditional approach of viewing the history of political ideas through the optic of great canonical thinkers and their body of work. Rather, it adopts an approach that insists not only on the entanglement of theory and practice but on the necessity of reading practitioners as theorists, fashioning their own view of the dynamics of the world around them through their actions and policies.

Two related trends in intellectual and legal history have paved the way for this particular approach. The first is the time-honored historical method of focusing on the practical and political context within which influential works of theory have been written (Hunter, 2013; Van Ittersum, 2006). The other trend is of a more recent date. A number of scholars have begun to focus on political and legal practitioners as theorists in their own right, highlighting the way in which judges, politicians, and magistrates argued for their particular interpretations of imperial law (Fitzmaurice, 2014; Pitts, 2012). A slew of recent works on the history of empire have combined these two approaches, effectively writing the history of imperial practices and the history of imperial theoretical and legal justifications as one and the same (Benton & Ford, 2016; Benton & Straumann, 2010; Mantena, 2010).

The approach advocated here goes beyond a search for the historical origins of particular theories or an insistence on the importance of historical context (Pocock, 1957; Skinner, 1969). Instead, it argues that practices themselves constitute a certain type of theorizing. It is no coincidence that such an approach has been particularly fruitful in legal history, since legal documents and rulings contain within them justifications and analyses which have the potential to make broader claims about the political or social world based on the details of specific cases. But the insights are not limited to legal history; indeed, much political practice can be read as theory when looked at from a certain vantage point. Does a head of government or a revolutionary leader have to write down a doctrine for us to be able to say that their policies constitute a particular view of the world? Surely a careful reading of their actions and policies can provide some insights into their perspective on the political landscape that surrounds them.[4]

Constitutions and declarations of independence are arguably among the most potent examples of specific political theories articulated within practice-oriented frameworks, whether authored by individuals or by committees (Armitage, 2008; Lane, 1996). Such texts represent the way in which the elites of new polities conceive of themselves, including crucially their relationship to other states and their position in interstate politics. They are not just documents meant for governance or targeted at internal audiences, but also messages being broadcast to the other powers of the world, signaling goals, ambitions, and attitudes. In one sense, then, declarations of independence and founding constitutions are the products of very specific marriages between pragmatic politics and aspirational ideological frameworks, encapsulated into documents with lasting historical consequences. When studied on their own terms, they can be revealing windows into these moments of political turmoil, potentially illuminating the *weltanschauung* of their composers.

A REVOLUTIONARY MOMENT

Since R. R. Palmer's influential work in the 1950s, historians of Western Europe and the Atlantic world more broadly have referred to the decades surrounding the 19th century as the age of revolution (Palmer, 1959/1964).[5] This particular moment has been seen historiographically as a defining turning point in the emergence of not only nationalism but also the "nation-form" – the progenitor of the 21st century nation-state model – whether this emergence has been located on one side of the Atlantic (Bell, 2001; Sewell Jr., 2004) or the other (Anderson, 2006; Brading, 1993). Indeed, much of the historiographical debate of the past two decades has centered on the origin points of this new mode of politics, the central question being whether the old imperial metropoles or the colonies of the new world were the more important spaces for turning revolutionary ideals into political transformations. To put it somewhat crudely, this was a debate between Paris and Port-au-Prince (Dubois, 2004; Geggus, 2010).

Of notable importance for this debate has been Benedict Anderson's magisterial account of nationalism and, in particular, his notion of a certain kind of revolutionary creole nationalism originating in the colonial

Americas (Anderson, 2006, pp. 49–67). The creole elites of Anderson's story pioneered the idea of modern nationalism in the decades leading up to their revolutionary struggles against European imperial metropoles, and the formation of autonomous postcolonial republics in South America was essentially the culmination of this process. This creole nationalism, Anderson argues, contained a particularly modular notion of what exactly a nation meant, making it all the more easy for the intellectual framework to circulate and take root across the globe during the following century (Anderson, 2006, pp. 80–82).

A number of European historians have pushed back against Anderson's account, arguing that the revisionist views of the origins of nationalism have gone too far in decentering European politics from the intellectual origins of a modular nation-form. Such critiques include arguments focusing on the importance of the French Revolution for articulations of the nation as a political project (Sewell Jr., 2004) as well as arguments for locating the origins of nationalism far earlier, in 17th-century Northwestern Europe (Gorski, 2000; Pincus, 1999). In recent years the field seems to have moved toward a more complex and multifaceted understanding of the period, focusing more on the circulation of revolutionary ideas and practices across the ocean than on the somewhat one-sided search for specific points of origin (Klooster, 2009).

The various historical narratives of the age of revolutions, whether they place their emphasis on one side of the Atlantic or the other, have been immensely important for our conceptions of the development of the international system. As indicated above, the period has typically been read in both historical sociology and international relations as heralding the beginnings of a global shift away from premodern polity types and toward the modern nation-state.[6] However, when looking more carefully at the revolutionary upheavals at the turn of the 19th century, and especially at the political reforms and reorientations of their immediate aftermath, it becomes clear that this is less the story of a ground-breaking shift in perceptions and more one of continuity and experimentation within existing modes of political ordering. While European political thinkers gradually began to operate with the nation-form as a central unit of analysis, political thought and practice outside the narrow confines of Western Europe looked quite different. What revolutionaries and republicans in the Caribbean and the Americas championed was not a new political entity easily recognizable as the nation-state of the 20th or 21st century. Autonomy did not mean nationhood and revolution did not spell the end of empire.

CONSTITUTIONAL THOUGHT AND POLITICAL EXPERIMENTS

The major revolutionary powers of the Western Hemisphere – the United States, Haiti, Gran Colombia, the United Provinces of the Río de la Plata, and Brazil – all followed distinct paths to independence and adopted quite disparate strategies once autonomy had been achieved. The US endeavored to build a new empire to rival those of the European powers, with multiple different centers and interests in partial competition with each other; the Spanish American states struggled to forge new alliances, both with each other and with foreign imperial actors, simultaneously resisting and welcoming outside influences, while experimenting with federation and autonomy in the process; Brazil attempted to replace Lisbon as the center of the Lusophone colonial world; and Haiti created an autonomous space not driven by ambitions of nationhood or expansion, but rather by notions of racial equality and abolition, whether within the French Empire or outside of it. Despite these differences, they all shared a number of common features in their approach to fashioning a stable political order.

The historiography on US empire has been far more developed than any of the other cases examined here, in part because of the very visibility of imperial ambitions in American politics during the early republican period. Indeed, notions of empire were built into the US Constitution itself, positioning the young republic as a political contender among the powers of the earth while retaining important continuities with the legal and political framework of the British Empire in North America (Hulsebosch, 2005, pp. 203–258; Lawson & Seidman, 2004). In one influential reading of this founding document, the Constitution is seen as a "peace pact" between the disparate polities that made up the United States, ensuring that they would unite as a single empire, rather than wage war against one another over the territory and resources of North America (Hendrickson, 2003). This imperial ambition was carried forward into the administration of the third US president, Thomas Jefferson, who put both expansion and intervention at the heart of his foreign policy with the Louisiana Purchase, the Barbary War, the "civilizing program" of assimilating Native Americans into the empire, and continued westward expansion being prime examples (Golay, 2003; Hendrickson & Tucker, 1990; McCoy, 1980).

The Monroe Doctrine, a set of policy propositions authored by American President James Monroe and Secretary of State John Quincy Adams in 1823, became a turning point of sorts for the 19th century political division of the Atlantic world into a western and an eastern half. This document made it clear that the Western Hemisphere was first and foremost a space of new world empires, and would from now on be outside the reach of old world colonialism:

> ... with the Governments who have declared their independence and maintain it, and whose independence we have, on great consideration and on just principles, acknowledged, we could not view any interposition for the purpose of oppressing them, or controlling in any other manner their destiny, by any European power in any other light than as the manifestation of an unfriendly disposition toward the United States.[7]

The doctrine would, of course, later become a rationale the for the United States' own interventions in Latin America, but even in its original form it was arguably more about demarcating spheres of influence than about rejecting the notion of imperialism (Murphy, 2009).

The United States was an interesting example of a multicentric imperial polity. Given its origins as 13 distinct colonies and the reading of the constitution as a peace pact given above, it should come as no surprise that there were different centers of political power in the early republic. At the turn of the century, three cities in particular competed over the informal seat of imperial power – New York, Philadelphia, and Washington – the country's newly erected capitol. Each of these cities presented their own ambitious imperial projects, focusing in particular on major infrastructure and legislation meant to project American power across the continent (Kanhofer, forthcoming). Later, in the first half of the 19th century, the internal competition for empire shifted to the north–south divide that would become so critical for the future of the union.

Imperial expansion was of particular importance to the Southern states, as this provided an opportunity to spread the institution of slavery to new parts of the growing American empire, especially important given the rising power of northern abolitionist movements. The most obvious targets for colonial enterprises of this sort were the plantation islands of the Caribbean, but Southern elites also had their eyes on expansion into Central and Western America and the remnants of New Spain (May, 1989). This coalesced with the general American trend of westward expansion, culminating in the late 1830s and 1840s with the notion of manifest destiny, a particularly American form of settler colonialism that came to dominate much of the country's political discourse (Graebner, 1955; Haynes & Morris, 1997; Rifkin, 2009).

While the different political centers of the United States had competing visions of what an American empire ought to look like, these ambitions often came together to shape what was in general an outward-looking policy of intervention and expansion. In this way the United States proved to be both a competitor with and an inheritor of the British Empire to which its founding colonies had belonged. The obsession with empire building continued within influential strands of US policy throughout the 19th and into the 20th century, with practitioner-theorists at various times looking eastward to the Caribbean, south toward Central America, and westward to the Pacific Ocean (Heffer, 1995; Hendrickson, 2009; Magness & Page, 2011).[8]

The revolutions in the Spanish Americas were not initially about rejecting empire as much as about contesting the centers of legitimacy and authority within the empire itself. The initial impetus for the revolutions was the fall of the House of Bourbon during the Napoleonic Wars and the establishment of the Supreme Central and Governing Junta in 1808, which claimed to rule all of the Spanish Empire overseas (Rodríguez, 1998). Several competing juntas were established across the colonies, growing rapidly following the defeat of the Central Junta by Napoleon's forces in 1810, and a decade of conflict between the various juntas and between the juntas and the Spanish Empire took place over the next decade. The early state projects of Latin America were wrought by internal tensions between loyalists and republicans – those who saw the old European metropoles as disseminators of political legitimacy and those who would replace those symbols with a new world republican federalism, itself evolved from an older imperial political imagination (Adelman, 2006).

These conflicts brought together a diverse cast of political actors, including influential creole revolutionaries such as Simón Bolívar, born in Caracas, and José Gervasio Artigas, born in Montevideo, as well as many royalists who continued to see themselves as imperial subjects first and foremost and who, while ready to reject a Napoleonic puppet regime, were less eager to embrace complete independence from the empire. Such men came to the ascendance during the brief but bloody Reconquista – the Spanish Empire's attempt to regain control of its American colonies following the restoration of Ferdinand VII in 1814. As defeating the returning Spanish forces, the majority of who were American royalists rather than Europeans, became the key aim for republicans, revolutionary regimes moved toward consolidating their power and forging new continental alliances amidst these internal conflicts. This consolidation led to more organized experiments aimed at replacing the formal imperial authority of Spain with new unitary cosmopolitan federations, gathering together provincial juntas and city-states that shared similar visions of autonomy and self-control.

In attempting to consolidate power and establish a sustainable postrevolutionary political order in the former Spanish territories, men like Bolívar and Artigas acted as practitioner-theorists in their own right. While they did not leave behind large bodies of tracts and monographs, as some of their predecessors and contemporaries in North America had done, they nonetheless formulated clear theories of statecraft and governance, visible in declarations and speeches such as Artigas' Instrucciones del año XIII or Bolívar's Angostura Address (Bushnell, 2003; Street, 1959).

Perhaps the clearest and most famous example of such texts was Bolívar's so-called Jamaican Letter, a letter written in 1815 to one Henry Cullen of Jamaica. In it, Bolívar not only analyzed the recent history of the Latin American struggles for independence, including the failure of the Second Republic of Venezuela the previous year, but also framed these conflicts within a wider context of transimperial upheaval across the Western Hemisphere, aligning the fates of Caribbean, South American, and North American subjects. The letter also highlighted the unequal and unfair differentiation of subject groups by the Spanish Empire, while making it clear that this colonial legacy would continue to play a central role in the new Latin American polities:

> ... we, who preserve only the barest vestige of what we were formerly, and who are moreover neither Indians nor Europeans, but a race halfway between the legitimate owners of the land and the Spanish usurpers – in short, being Americans by birth and endowed with rights from Europe – find ourselves forced to defend these rights against the natives while maintaining our position in the land against intrusion of the invaders.[9]

There was thus little space for the rights of indigenous populations in Bolívar's America. Indeed, the ideology shaping these new state projects was not so much a universal liberalism as it was a certain kind of constitutionalism, one that drew directly on and contributed to the growing body of federalist and confederalist thought coming out of the American Revolution.

One of the key components of this federalism was also an important characteristic of earlier imperial rule – the notion of divisible and layered sovereignty. The principle of layered sovereignty was built into the constitutions of both Gran Colombia, the republican successor to the Spanish colony of New Grenada, and the United Provinces of the Río de la Plata, which replaced the colonial Viceroyalty of the Río de la Plata following the May Revolution of 1810. Cities and provinces such as Buenos Aires and Santa Fe in the Río de la Plata and Bogotá and Quito in Gran Colombia were autonomous or semiautonomous political units in their own right, enjoying a degree of sovereign control layered below the overarching sovereignty of the political federations to which they belonged.[10] While the political experiments of the new world ran from relatively revolutionary republicanism to monarchical neoauthoritarianism, all of these state-building projects thus involved ideas of multilayered sovereignty and were founded on remnants of the imperial administrative order of the ancien régime (Chiaramonte, 2004; Rodríguez, 1998). In the words of Benton and Ford, these were "Republican visions built on structures of colonial and imperial bureaucracy, including and especially systems of law" (2016, p. 165).

As new republics emerged out of the ruins of the first Latin American federations in the 1830s, the involvement of old European empires on the continent also became more formalized. While the initial involvement of, especially, the British Empire in the Americas had been a matter of strong dispute within creole elites, with arguments ranging from ambivalent rejection by Artigas to the very direct embrace of imperial interventions by Carlos Alvear (Benton & Ford, 2016), the 1830s saw a more unambiguous invitation of European commercial power into the Western Hemisphere. While European policy-makers did their best to use this opening to influence Latin American political processes in what has often been termed a strategy of "informal empire" (Gallagher & Robinson, 1953), such diplomatic maneuverings were rarely very successful, and the American republics generally managed to retain a great deal of independence while gradually becoming more integrated into emerging global markets (Mclean, 1995, pp. 39–65).

Parallel to and at times entangled with the struggles over autonomy in Spanish South America was the internal strife that shook the Portuguese Empire in the 1810s and 1820s. During Napoleon's occupation of Portugal, the seat of the Portuguese monarchy relocated to Brazil. As Portugal regained its independence following the defeat of Napoleon in 1815, a schism broke out between those in the royal family who returned to Europe and those who remained in Brazil, namely the Prince Regent Dom Pedro (Adelman, 2006, pp. 220–257, 340–342). This schism was in part a struggle between the older generation, favoring a continuation of absolute monarchy, and the younger supporters of constitutionalism, eventually leading to the revolution of 1820 and to the establishment of the Empire of Brazil by Dom Pedro, now Pedro I, in 1822.

The Braganza monarchy in Brazil became independent of the Portuguese branch of the royal dynasty, ruling over its own version of a federal empire in the Americas and rivaling Lisbon as a seat of power and authority in the wider Lusophone world (Hamnet, 2013). The Brazilian Empire was thus, despite its embrace of constitutional rather than absolute monarchy, a new world inheritor to one of Europe's longest-lived anciens régimes and no less imperial than its older Portuguese progenitor (Paquette, 2013). Crucially, it continued to operate within an imperial register of rule, relying on differentiation of subject groups and a hierarchical political order internally and expansionism and colonialism externally.

The revolution in Saint-Domingue was not initially an attempt to forge a new polity independent of the French Empire. Rather, it was an attack upon the social order of the colony, founded as it was on systemic racial violence, the exploitation of black slaves, and the partial disenfranchisement of the island's free people of color. This was a multifaceted revolution with different groupings and different aims, which were not always entirely overlapping. After a tumultuous decade of fighting and infighting, which included interventions or attempted interventions by both the Spanish and the British empires, the revolutionary leader and former slave Toussaint Louverture took control of the island colony at the turn of the century.

Louverture's initial constitution was in some ways a radical document, but it did not break with the fundamental institution of empire. It was drafted by the island's constitutional assembly, mostly consisting of white planters, and was approved by Louverture in July of 1801. This was not in any way a call for national sovereignty, but specifically a constitution for "the French colony of Saint-Domingue," which together with "other adjacent islands constitute the territory of a single colony that forms part of the French empire, but which is subject to particular laws." A colony with a certain level of legal and political autonomy, in other words, but a colony nonetheless, to be administered by "a governor, who will correspond directly with the metropolitan government regarding everything concerning the interest of the colony." In one important area this was, however, a radical document: the third article stated, with no caveats or exceptions, that "there can exist no slaves in this territory; servitude therein is forever abolished."[11]

After a brief period of restoration of French imperial authority in Saint-Domingue, enforced by Napoleon's forces and resulting in the deportation and death of Louverture, Jean-Jacques Dessalines declared Haitian independence on the first of January 1804. In contrast to the relatively conservative constitution of the Louverture government, Dessaline's constitution of May 1805 definitively severed Haiti's ties to the French Empire, declaring in Article 12 that "no white man of whatever nation he may be, shall put his foot on this territory with the title of master or proprietor, neither shall he in future acquire any property therein."[12] Perhaps more interesting for the issue of imperialism in general, as opposed to the specifics of European powers, was the Haitian commitment not to engage in any expansionist or interventionist policies. Article 36 of the Dessaline constitution thus read: "The Emperor shall never form any enterprize with the views of making conquests, nor to disturb the peace and interior administration of foreign colonies." While Haiti was to be the first black empire of the Western Hemisphere, it was deliberately designed by its founders to be a nonexpansionist and noninterventionist power, in part to reassure the other powers of the Atlantic world.

These self-imposed restraints on expansionist policies were eventually abandoned, with then-President Jean-Pierre Boyer's invasion of the Eastern half of Hispaniola in 1822 signaling a new and more aggressive role in the region. The Spanish colony of Santo Domingo had gone through its own revolution the previous year, with the revolutionary junta of what was now known as the Republic of Spanish Haiti (later the Dominican Republic) attempting to join forces with Gran Colombia and the government of Simón Bolívar. This union never materialized, however, and following a bloodless military invasion all of the island of Hispaniola came under the rule of Boyer for the next two decades. Not surprisingly, given Haiti's own history, one of the first acts by Boyer's government was the total and unconditional emancipation of the slaves of Santo Domingo.[13] While this period of Haitian rule was closer to territorial expansion than colonial occupation, it did result in decidedly hierarchical political relations between the two constituent polities, with considerable internal pressure for independence brewing among Dominican elites.[14]

Haitian independence had important reverberations, both in the Western Hemisphere and in Europe. Haiti's influence on the ideas of certain European political philosophers, in particular Hegel, has been well documented (Buck-Morrs, 2009), but the more practical political consequences of Haitian independence have only recently been scrutinized by historians. One of the first comprehensive accounts of the Haitian Revolution to appear in Europe was Michael Rainsford's *An historical account of the Black Empire of Hayti*, which painted Louverture as an idealistic revolutionary and a benevolent emperor. As the title of his book implies, Rainsford described Haiti not as a nation or a colony but as a black Atlantic empire (Rainsford, 1805). This sympathetic narrative represented one end of the spectrum of European reactions, with the majority of commentators and onlookers being far more hostile toward the very notion of an empire forged by slaves. European imperial elites were particularly worried, as the prospects of further slave uprisings in the wake of 1801 loomed large (Mulich, 2013). Such fears led to some Caribbean colonies moving in the opposite direction, imposing tightened control over their populations and moving toward ever more draconian and hierarchical rule (Ferrer, 2014).

The Haitian governments of the first decade and a half of independence were themselves important in spreading notions of black liberty and emancipation throughout the region, in part through their dealings with other revolutionary leaders. Indeed, rulers such as Alexandre Pétion demanded from their allies, namely Bolívar, that they emancipate the slaves of their own territories as well as those enslaved Africans they captured through privateering (Ferrer, 2012). In this and other ways, the ideals of Haiti were not just important influences on Atlantic and Caribbean political thought, but were advanced concretely and strategically by Haitian elites in their dealings with foreign powers (see also Gaffield, 2015; Smith, 2014).

Haitian relations with the French Empire shifted over the course of the postindependence period. Initially refusing to accept Haitian independence at all, the French government eventually agreed to recognize the former colony as a sovereign republic only if it would pay France 150 million francs as compensation for the loss of men and territory incurred by the revolution. Importantly, this claim for compensation was based in part on the claims made by individual plantation owners who demanded recompense for land and slaves lost to the revolution.[15] Haiti also landed in trouble with the Spanish Empire, as the government granted asylum to Bolívar and assisted him with resources during his fight against the Spanish Empire. Yet, despite all these struggles with the old European empires, and despite the betrayed promises of political liberty within the territory of Haiti itself, the very idea of the Haitian state remained a beacon of hope in the black Atlantic. In the 1840s a commentator in the *Jamaica Tribune*, witnessing Spain's recolonization of Santo Domingo, put it thus: "Where, we ask, is France? Or England, the champion of universal freedom? ... Haiti is without a doubt the only place on earth that can truly be called the homeland of the African race" (quoted in Smith, 2014, p. 109).

THE CONTINUITY OF EMPIRE

Throughout the age of revolution, empire continued to be the dominant mode of ordering the political sphere, both within and between polities. The political imagination and theoretical framework of many policymakers and intellectuals in the Western Hemisphere continued to be characterized at least in part by imperial structures well into the 19th century, even within the most ardently independent polities of the Americas. What took place at the dawn of the 19th century, then, was not a shift away from imperial states and toward nation-states, but instead a messy process of replacing the repertoires of ancien régime empires with those of the newly autonomous polities of the new world, many of which were expansionist empires in their own right. What drove these breaks with the old order was not a newfound desire for nationhood in any of the cases examined here – rather, the breaks were driven by a complex set of causes and pressures that came together to spark social and political revolutions. These factors included the desire for increased political representation and a reconfiguration of colonial ties in North America; a demand for a more just racial order in Saint-Domingue; and clashes over the sources of sovereignty in the Spanish and Portuguese Americas. In the messy aftermath of such upheavals, new modes of organizing were forged and many old ones were retained.

The four cases examined in the previous section displayed different degrees of parting with the old order, from the staunchly conservative Brazilian Empire to the more radical Haitian governments, but all of them shared aspects of the political modality of empire. In terms of racial parity, Haiti was no doubt the most revolutionary, followed by the republics of the Spanish Americas, at least in their first years of independence. In terms of democratic constitutionalism and narrowly dispersed civil rights, the United States was arguably the most innovative, drawing on both new and old world political philosophy. Even when clear breaks were made with imperial and colonial forms of government, the first half of the 19th century saw several polities undo such ruptures. The clearest and most startling example to contemporaries was the Spanish recolonization of Haiti's eastern neighbor, Santo Domingo, but a more widespread trend was the reneging on earlier promises of emancipation across much of Latin America and the Caribbean. While the Law of Wombs was passed in the United Provinces of the Río de la Plata in 1813, promising that no one could be born into bondage, general slavery was not ended in the region until it was written into the Argentine Constitution of 1853, a full four decades later. Similar protracted processes of abolition and emancipation took place in Gran Colombia, Venezuela, and Mexico. Brazil, for its part, remained one of the last bastions of slavery, refusing to enact full emancipation until the adoption of the so-called Golden Law in 1888.

At the center of the forging of new states in the Western Hemisphere stood a particular breed of revolutionary practitioner-theorists. Through their actions, policies, and writings these leaders drew on and contributed to new notions of republicanism, constitutionalism, and federalism. The circuits through which such ideas traveled were inherently transboundary, facilitating dialogues that not only crossed the divide between North and South America but also crossed the Atlantic, shaping political and intellectual landscapes on both sides of the ocean. The experiments of leaders such as Artígas, Bolívar, and Louverture were born out of necessity, forged in the fires of transboundary conflict and crisis, but they were also influenced by novel ideas of how to organize polities and how to govern colonial and postcolonial societies. This marriage of pragmatism and ideology in many ways formed the foundation of new world state-building.

At the constitutional level, political experimentation did not preclude the continuation of empire. The new polities of Spanish South America were republics to be sure. But as the United States had already shown in recent memory, and the Dutch and Roman empires had proven decades and centuries before, there was no inherent dichotomy between republicanism and imperialism. More radical, perhaps, were the experiments with city-states and continental federations, which dominated Latin American politics in the first two decades after independence, especially on the eastern coast, but even these creative endeavors carried with them particular notions of composite polities and layered sovereignty inherent in imperial modes of ordering politics.

Other experiments within the new Atlantic polities were of a fundamentally conservative or authoritarian nature, concerned with enacting social control rather than with bestowing new political liberties. These new imperial repertoires included first and foremost a reaffirmation and partial rearticulation of the hierarchical racial order. Slavery persisted for considerably longer in the new world empires than in most of the old European empires, not because of a newfound benevolence on the part of slave owners or any less desire to throw off their shackles on the part of slaves, but in no small part due to innovative new systems of control and violence.[16]

A prominent example of such regimes was to be found in the United States, where a series of slave uprisings and the specter of the Haitian Revolution led to an increased obsession with race and a large-scale expansion and reinforcement of the institution of slavery itself (Baptist, 2014; Johnson, 2013; White, 2010). Legal reforms restricting the mobility and political agency of black subjects, and outlawing miscegenation, grew over the course of the 19th century, especially in the Southern states, eventually resulting in the one-drop rule, which legally defined anyone with even a single ancestor of African descent as "black." Thus, the Florida Assembly passed an act in 1865 that legally defined "every person who shall have one-eight or more of negro blood" as a "person of color."[17]

Other polities in the Western Hemisphere not directly touched by revolutionary upheavals went through similar authoritarian reforms, often increasing or extending the reach of their state apparatus to stave off the potential for political instability. Cuba was an obvious example of this process, witnessing its own "counterrevolution of slavery and racism" during the last part of the Haitian Revolution, providing the colonial "antithesis" to that new black empire (Ferrer, 2014, pp. 187, 338). Similar examples of racial prejudice infusing political and legal regimes could be found throughout the Spanish Caribbean, including in Puerto Rico (Kinsbruner, 1996).

Given these circumstances, it should come as no surprise that Haiti was the polity of the ones here examined that struggled the most with gaining interstate recognition following its successful bid for independence. It represented an explicit dismissal of white supremacy and became a beacon of black empowerment within a political region that was explicitly built on racial hierarchies and violence enacted upon black bodies.[18] Haitian leaders continued to speak words of liberty into a political vacuum that refused to listen. While empire and sovereignty were malleable and flexible categories with room for experimentation and interpretation, the racial dimensions of social ordering in the Atlantic world proved much harder to disrupt. The window of emancipation that had opened up in the years surrounding the turn of the century soon closed, and, as mentioned above, the majority of newly independent polities either reversed or limited their initial moves toward full emancipation, leading to a much longer and more protracted process of black liberation than had initially seemed likely. It would take another three decades after Haitian independence before the slaves of the British Empire were emancipated, in an act that was ultimately framed as one of white benevolence rather than black empowerment.[19]

While this might have been a postcolonial moment for many states in the Western Hemisphere, it was far from a postimperial one. Unlike the classic narratives of the age of revolution that cast the early decades of the 19th century as a new dawn for the international system, this article has argued that the period was in fact characterized as much by continuity as by transformation. What changes did take place in the interstate system had more to do with the specifics of border drawings and centers of power than they did with revolutionizing the state form itself, and much of the experimentation that took place never fully broke free from the framework of imperial ordering. Only in a few cases did imperial modes of rule collapse entirely, and only after prolonged struggles to return to the status quo. And these cases had, despite their historical significance, relatively little impact on the way in which ruling elites and practitioner-theorists envisioned their political world. As such, the most radical theories of racial equity and black empowerment that emerged out of the wreckage of the age of revolutions were largely ignored and their advocates were, for the most part, speaking into the wind.

NOTES

1. There are some notable recent exceptions to this tendency, in particular the work of Go (2011, 2013) and Adams and Steinmetz (2015).

2. The obvious geographical exception here is Anderson (2006), discussed in further detail below. It is worth noting that Mann has subsequently acknowledged the absence of empire in his earlier work and made some attempts at rectifying it (2012, p. vii).

3. For a general critique of the project of defining "modern" states and state systems, see Cooper (2005, pp. 113–149).

4. In some cases such actors did indeed document their thoughts in a more coherent and systematic fashion, but given the vagaries of historical scholarship and the passage of time, these texts have not always been submitted to careful scholarly analysis. See for example the rich sources left behind by Toussaint Louverture, including his short memoir explicitly defending his political program as governor of Saint-Domingue (Girard, 2013, 2014).

5. Palmer's original work was notably Eurocentric, relegating the revolutions in Latin America to a few sentences and leaving the Haitian Revolution entirely untouched.

6. For example, Hobsbawm (1962), Giddens (1985), Mayall (1990), Mann (1993), and Reus-Smit (2013). In their account of the political transformations of the 19th century, Buzan and Lawson avoid making a similar claim by limiting most of their discussion of the nation-form in the international system to the last decades of the century (2015, pp. 35, 117, 118).

7. Message of President James Monroe at the commencement of the first session of the 18th Congress, December 2, 1823, Records of the United States Senate 1789–1990, the National Archives.

8. A different but parallel strand of US imperialism was carried out by relatively autonomous agents on the ground, stretching from Panama to Canton, with little direct involvement by political authorities (Blaufarb, 2007; Brown, 1980; Downs, 1997; McGuinness, 2009; Warren, 1943). For the long trajectory of US interventionism abroad, see Williams (1980).

9. "The Jamaican Letter: Response from a South American to a Gentleman from This Island," printed and translated in Bushnell (2003, p. 18). The letter is of further interest because it had as its secondary subject the government of the British Empire, serving as a call for recognition and support of the new Spanish American polities.

10. Such relationships were not always without tension, of course, and led to multiple internal conflicts in the 1810s and 1820s, resulting ultimately in the demise of these large federations. For the long-term rivalries of regional hubs such as Montevideo and Buenos Aires that carried over into the republican period, see Prado (2015).

11. *Constitution de la colonie française de Saint-Domingue*, Paris, 1801. This print is held at the Rare Book Division, New York Public Library. Even emancipation in Haiti was a long-term process with important antecedents in the period of French colonial rule, and the debates over slavery and liberation in the 1790s and 1800s frequently referred to the older Code Noir, underscoring the continued relevance of imperial legal frameworks (Ghachem, 2012).

12. This translation is taken from the *New York Evening Post*, July 15, 1805. Dessalines' declaration of April 28, 1804, which was in many ways a predecessor to the constitution proper, put it in even clearer terms vis-à-vis empire: "Never shall any colonist or European set foot on this land as a master or a proprietor" (Jean-Jacques Dessalines to the Inhabitants of Haiti, in the National Archives of Britain, Colonial Office 137/113). For more on the constitution in general, see Gaffield (2007, pp. 81–103).

13. This had previously been done in 1801 when Louverture took control of the territory, but was quickly reversed by the Spanish Empire.

14. The clearest example of these sentiments was the formation of La Trinitaria, a Dominican secret society with the aim of overthrowing Haitian rule over eastern Hispaniola. It is worth noting that once this goal had been accomplished in 1844, the new ruler of the Dominican Republic, Don Pedro Santana, almost immediately betrayed La Trinitaria and invited the Spanish Empire to return to the island, in effect recolonizing Santo Domingo (Matibag, 2003).

15. These claims mirrored similar ones made by British slave owners during the 1830s when the British Empire abolished slavery within its colonies. In the British case such demands were met, with compensations totaling 20 million pounds sterling.

16. Other crucial factors leading to the divergence of slave regimes in European and American empires in the early 19th century were related to the politics of abolitionist activism and the strength of public moral and religious movements in Europe (Brown, 2006).

17. "An act in addition to an act entitled an act to amend the act entitled an act concerning marriage licenses approved January 23, 1832," passed during the Fourteenth Session of the General Assembly of the State of Florida, 1865.

18. In the eyes of white practitioner-theorists in the 19th century, the notion of a Black Atlantic did not stretch any further than the coastal waters of West Africa. See in particular the work of Trouillot on the unthinkable nature of Haitian independence to European writers and philosophers (1995, pp. 70–107). On the notion of the Black Atlantic in general, see also Gilroy (1993), Thornton (1998), and, more recently, Diouf and Prais (2015).

19. Of course there was a significant disconnect between the way such things were talked about among imperial practitioners and theorists and the way it looked from the ground in many colonial territories. The way in which the slaves of the Danish West Indies were freed – by a desperate act of concession by the local

governor-general in the face of a forceful black uprising, later retold as a carefully deliberated and compassionate political decision – is but one example (Hall, 1992, pp. 208–227).

REFERENCES

Adams, J., & Steinmetz, G. (2015). Sovereignty and sociology: From state theory to theories of empire. *Political Power and Social Theory*, *28*, 269–285.

Adelman, J. (2006). *Sovereignty and revolution in the Iberian Atlantic*. Princeton, NJ: Princeton University Press.

Anderson, B. (2006). *Imagined communities* (new ed.). London: Verso.

Armitage, D. (2008). *The declaration of independence: A global history*. Cambridge, MA: Harvard University Press.

Baptist, E. E. (2014). *The half has never been told: Slavery and the making of American capitalism*. New York, NY: Basic Books.

Barkawi, T., & Lawson, G. (2017). The international origins of social and political theory. *Political Power and Social Theory*, *32*, 1–8.

Bell, D. A. (2001). *The cult of the nation in France: Inventing nationalism, 1680–1800*. Cambridge, MA: Harvard University Press.

Benton, L. (2010). *A search for sovereignty: Law and geography in European empires, 1400–1900*. New York, NY: Cambridge University Press.

Benton, L., & Ford, L. (2016). *Rage for order: The British Empire and the origins of international law, 1800–1850*. Cambridge, MA: Harvard University Press.

Benton, L., & Straumann, B. (2010). Acquiring empire by law: From Roman doctrine to early modern European practice. *Law and History Review*, *28*(1), 1–38.

Blaufarb, R. (2007). The Western question: The geopolitics of Latin American independence. *American Historical Review*, *112*(3), 742–763.

Brading, D. A. (1993). *The first America: The Spanish monarchy, creole patriots and the liberal state* (pp. 1492–1866). Cambridge: Cambridge University Press.

Brown, C. H. (1980). *Agents of manifest destiny: The lives and times of the filibusters*. Chapel Hill, NC: University of North Carolina Press.

Brown, C. L. (2006). *Moral capital: Foundations of British abolitionism*. Chapel Hill, NC: University of North Carolina Press.

Buck-Morrs, S. (2009). *Hegel, Haiti, and universal history*. Pittsburgh, PA: University of Pittsburgh Press.

Burbank, J., & Cooper, F. (2010). *Empires in world history: Power and the politics of difference*. Princeton, NJ: Princeton University Press.

Bushnell, D. (Ed.). (2003). *El Libertador: Writings of Simón Bolívar* (F. H. Fornoff, Trans.). Oxford: Oxford University Press.

Buzan, B., & Lawson, G. (2015). *The global transformation: History, modernity and the making of International Relations*. Cambridge: Cambridge University Press.

Chiaramonte, J. C. (2004). *Nación y estado en Iberoamérica: El lenguaje político en tiempos de les independencias*. Buenos Aires: Editorial Sudamericana.

Cooper, F. (2005). *Colonialism in question: Theory, knowledge, history*. Berkeley, CA: University of California Press.

Diouf, M., & Prais, J. (2015). "Casting the badge of inferiority beneath black people's feet": Archiving and reading the African past, present, and future in world history. In S. Moyn & A. Sartori (Eds.), *Global intellectual history*. New York, NY: Columbia University Press.

Downs, J. M. (1997). *The golden ghetto: The American commercial community at Canton and the shaping of American China policy, 1784–1844*. Bethlehem, PA: Lehigh University Press.

Dubois, L. (2004). *Avengers of the new world: The story of the Haitian Revolution*. Cambridge, MA: Harvard University Press.

Ertman, T. (1997). *Birth of the leviathan: Building states and regimes in medieval and early modern Europe*. Cambridge, MA: Harvard University Press.

Ferrer, A. (2012). Haiti, free soil, and antislavery in the revolutionary Atlantic. *American Historical Review, 117*(1), 40–66.

Ferrer, A. (2014). *Freedom's mirror: Cuba and Haiti in the age of revolution*. New York, NY: Cambridge University Press.

Fitzmaurice, A. (2014). *Sovereignty, property and empire, 1500–2000*. Cambridge: Cambridge University Press.

Gaffield, J. (2007). Complexities of imagining Haiti: A study of national constitutions, 1801–1807. *Journal of Social History, 41*(1), 81–103.

Gaffield, J. (2015). *Haitian connections in the Atlantic world: Recognition after revolution*. Chapel Hill, NC: University of North Carolina Press.

Gallagher, J., & Robinson, R. (1953). The imperialism of free trade. *The Economic History Review, 6*(1), 1–15.

Geggus, D. (2010). The Caribbean in the age of revolution. In D. Armitage & S. Subrahmanyam (Eds.), *The age of revolutions in global context, c. 1760–1840* (pp. 83–100). New York, NY: Palgrave Macmillan.

Ghachem, M. W. (2012). *The old regime and the Haitian revolution*. New York, NY: Cambridge University Press.

Giddens, A. (1985). *The nation-state and violence: Volume two of a contemporary critique of historical materialism*. Berkeley, CA: University of California Press.

Gilroy, P. (1993). *The black Atlantic: Modernity and double-consciousness*. Cambridge, MA: Harvard University Press.

Girard, P. H. (2013). Un-silencing the past: The writings of Toussaint Louverture. *Slavery & Abolition, 34*(4), 663–672.

Girard, P. H. (Ed. and Trans.). (2014). *The memoir of general Toussaint Louverture*. Oxford: Oxford University Press.

Go, J. (2011). *Patterns of empire: The British and American Empires, 1688 to the present*. Cambridge: Cambridge University Press.

Go, J. (2013). For a postcolonial sociology. *Theory and Society, 42*(1), 25–55.

Golay, M. (2003). *The tide of empire: America's march to the Pacific*. Hoboken, NJ: Wiley.

Gorski, P. S. (2000). The mosaic moment: An early modernist critique of modernist theories of nationalism. *American Journal of Sociology, 105*(5), 1428–1468.

Graebner, N. A. (1955). *Empire on the Pacific: A study in American continental expansion*. New York, NY: Ronald Press Company.

Hall, N. A. T. (1992). *Slave society in the Danish West Indies: St. Thomas, St. John, and St. Croix*. Mona: The University of the West Indies Press.

Hamnet, B. (2013). Themes and tensions in a contradictory decade: Ibero-America as a multiplicity of states. In M. Brown & G. Paquette (Eds.), *Connections after colonialism: Europe and Latin America in the 1820s* (pp. 29–45). Tuscaloosa, AL: University of Alabama Press.
Haynes, S. L., & Morris, C. (Eds.). (1997). *Manifest destiny and empire: American antebellum expansion.* College Station, TX: Texas A&M University Press.
Heffer, J. (1995). *Les États-Unis et le Pacifique: Histoire d'une frontière.* Paris: Albin Michel.
Hendrickson, D. C. (2003). *Peace pact: The lost world of the American founding.* Lawrence, KS: University of Kansas Press.
Hendrickson, D. C. (2009). *Union, nation, or empire: The American debate over international relations, 1789–1941.* Lawrence, KS: University Press of Kansas.
Hendrickson, D. C., & Tucker, R. W. (1990). *Empire of liberty: The statecraft of Thomas Jefferson.* New York, NY: Oxford University Press.
Hobsbawm, E. J. (1962). *The age of revolution: Europe, 1789–1848.* London: Weidenfeld & Nicholson.
Hulsebosch, D. (2005). *Constituting empire: New York and the transformation of constitutionalism in the Atlantic World.* Chapel Hill, NC: University of North Carolina Press.
Hunter, I. (2013). Kant and Vattel in context: Cosmopolitan philosophy and diplomatic casuistry. *History of European Ideas*, *39*(4), 477–502.
Johnson, W. (2013). *River of dark dreams: Slaver and empire in the Cotton Kingdom.* Cambridge, MA: Harvard University Press.
Kanhofer, D. (forthcoming). *The chimerical scheme of a canal: Controlling land, water, and people in mid-Atlantic North America, 1720–1830.* PhD dissertation. New York University.
Kinsbruner, J. (1996). *Not of pure blood: The free people of color and racial prejudice in nineteenth-century Puerto Rico.* Durham, NC: Duke University Press.
Klooster, W. (2009). *Revolutions in the Atlantic world: A comparative history.* New York, NY: NYU Press.
Lane, J. E. (1996). *Constitutions and political theory.* Manchester: University of Manchester Press.
Lawson, G., & Seidman, G. (2004). *The constitution of empire: Territorial expansion and American legal history.* New Haven, CT: Yale University Press.
Magness, P. W., & Page, S. N. (2011). *Colonization after emancipation: Lincoln and the movement for black resettlement.* Columbia, MO: University of Missouri Press.
Mann, M. (1993). *The sources of social power, vol. 2: The rise of classes and nation states, 1760–1914.* Cambridge: Cambridge University Press.
Mann, M. (2012). *The sources of social power, vol. 3: Global empires and revolution, 1890–1945.* Cambridge: Cambridge University Press.
Mantena, K. (2010). *Alibis of empire: Henry Maine and the ends of liberal imperialism.* Princeton, NJ: Princeton University Press.
Matibag, E. (2003). *Haitian-Dominican counterpoint: Nation, race, and state on Hispaniola.* New York, NJ: Palgrave Macmillan.
May, R. E. (1989). *The southern dream of a Caribbean empire, 1854–1861.* Athens, GA: University of Georgia Press.
Mayall, J. (1990). *Nationalism and international society.* Cambridge: Cambridge University Press.

McCoy, D. R. (1980). *The elusive republic: political economy in Jeffersonian America*. Chapel Hill, NC: University of North Carolina Press.

McGuinness, A. (2009). *Path of empire: Panama and the California gold rush*. Ithaca, NY: Cornell University Press.

Mulich, J. (2013). Microregionalism and intercolonial relations: The case of the Danish West Indies, 1730–1830. *Journal of Global History*, *8*(1), 72–94.

Murphy, G. (2009). *Hemispheric imaginings: The Monroe Doctrine and narratives of U.S. empire*. Durham, NC: Duke University Press.

Palmer, R. R. (1959/1964). *The age of democratic revolution: A political history of Europe and America, 1760–1800* (Vols. 1–2), Princeton, NJ: Princeton University Press.

Paquette, G. (2013). *Imperial Portugal in the age of Atlantic revolutions: The Luso-Brazilian world, c. 1770–1850*. New York, NY: Cambridge University Press.

Pincus, S. (1999). Nationalism, universal monarchy, and the glorious revolution. In G. Steinmetz (Ed.), *State/culture: State-formation and the cultural turn* (pp. 182–210). Ithaca, NY: Cornell University Press.

Pitts, J. (2012). Empire and legal universalisms in the eighteenth century. *American Historical Review*, *117*(1), 92–121.

Pocock, J. G. A. (1957). *The ancient constitution and the feudal law: A study of English historical thought in the seventeenth century*. Cambridge: Cambridge University Press.

Prado, F. (2015). *Edge of empire: Atlantic networks and revolution in Bourbon Río de la Plata*. Berkeley, CA: University of California Press.

Rainsford, M. (1805). *An historical account of the black empire of Hayti: Comprehending a view of the principal transactions in the revolution of Saint Domingo; with its ancient and modern state*. London: J. Cundee.

Reus-Smit, C. (2013). *Individual rights and the making of the international system*. Cambridge: Cambridge University Press.

Rifkin, M. (2009). *Manifesting America: The imperial construction of U.S. national space*. New York, NY: Oxford University Press.

Rodríguez, J. E. (1998). *The independence of Spanish America*. Cambridge: Cambridge University Press.

Sewell, Jr., W. H. (2004). The French Revolution and the emergence of the nation form. In M. Morrison & M. Zook (Eds.), *Revolutionary currents: Transatlantic ideology and nationbuilding, 1688–1821* (pp. 91–125). New York, NY: Rowman and Littlefield.

Skinner, Q. (1969). Meaning and understanding in the history of ideas. *History and Theory*, *8*(1), 3–53.

Skocpol, T. (1979). *States and social revolutions: A comparative analysis of France, Russia and China*. Cambridge: Cambridge University Press.

Smith, M. J. (2014). *Liberty, fraternity, exile: Haiti and Jamaica after emancipation*. Chapel Hill, NC: University of North Carolina Press.

Stern, P. J. (2008). 'A politie of civill & military power': Political thought and the late seventeenth-century foundations of the East India Company-State. *Journal of British Studies*, *47*(2), 253–283.

Street, J. (1959). *Artigas and the emancipation of Uruguay*. Cambridge: Cambridge University Press.

Thornton, J. (1998). *Africa and Africans in the making of the Atlantic world, 1400–1800* (2nd ed.), Cambridge: Cambridge University Press.

Trouillot, M. R. (1995). *Silencing the past: Power and the production of history*. Boston, MA: Beacon Press.

Van Ittersum, M. (2006). *Profit and principle: Hugo Grotius, natural rights theories and the rise of Dutch power in the East Indies, 1595–1615*. Leiden: Brill.

Warren, H. G. (1943). *The sword was their passport: A history of American filibustering in the Mexican revolution*. Baton Rouge, LA: Louisiana State University Press.

White, A. (2010). *Encountering revolution: Haiti and the making of the early republic*. Baltimore, MD: Johns Hopkins University Press.

Williams, W. A. (1980). *Empire as a way of life: An essay on the causes and character of America's present predicament, along with a few thoughts about an alternative*. Oxford: Oxford University Press.

SUPERFLUOUS INJURY AND UNNECESSARY SUFFERING: NATIONAL LIBERATION AND THE LAWS OF WAR

Helen M. Kinsella

ABSTRACT

During the four years of preliminary meetings that led to the 1977 Protocols Additional I and II governing internal armed conflict, the prohibitions against superfluous injury and unnecessary suffering – two concepts that gird the regulation and moderation of war and limit the use of certain means and methods of warfare – were invoked as a means of calling into account the actions of imperial states. These meetings took place in the context of the conflicts in Southeast Asia, following the wars of decolonization and national liberation in the 1950s and 1960s. The participants in these meetings were freedom fighters and liberation movements who used this forum, which was open to them for the first time, to push for a wider understanding of the concepts of superfluous injury and unnecessary suffering. Their intention was to hold imperialism and imperial states accountable for suffering and injury beyond that of physical death or wounding and to recognize the violence of colonization and the

International Origins of Social and Political Theory
Political Power and Social Theory, Volume 32, 205–231

ISSN: 0198-8719/doi:10.1108/S0198-871920170000032008

social and cultural devastation it brought. These interventions were a critical attempt to broaden and deepen the meaning of the laws of war, to make them responsive to more than established sovereign state violence, and to ensure that they reflected the experience of colonization/decolonization. This episode matters because the prohibitions against unnecessary suffering and superfluous injury are two elements that detail the general prohibition first codified in 1907 Hague Convention IV, Article 22, namely that the "the right of belligerents to adopt means of injuring the enemy is not unlimited." However, the history and formulation of these two concepts has yet to be fully explored, the meaning of each is debated, and taken together the two are among "the most unclear and controversial rules of warfare."

Keywords: Laws of war; national liberation; self-determination; superfluous injury; imperialism; Ranciére

INTRODUCTION

Every present moment is a tangle of emergent and residual forms.

Cole (2015, p. 809)

In this article, I examine a fundamental dictate of international humanitarian law, or the laws of war, namely the prohibition against superfluous injury and unnecessary suffering. Accepted as both customary and positive law, the prohibition against superfluous injury and unnecessary suffering is codified in the 1977 Protocol Additional I to the Geneva Conventions of August 12, 1949, girds the regulation and moderation of war, and limits the use of certain means and methods of warfare. The laws of war govern the use of force in international politics and are the oldest system of international law informing and constituting relations among states and other entities. The laws of war are also a constellation of discourses and debates, practice and procedures, through which the legitimacy and meaning of violence takes shape and form and, as such, provide an extensive archive for considering the relations of history and theory, especially in regards to the formulation of what Ann Stoler calls "rubrics of rule" in colonial and imperial contexts (Stoler, 2009, p. 4).

I argue that it was during the four years of Diplomatic Conferences on the Reaffirmation and Development of International Humanitarian Law

Applicable in Armed Conflict which led to the 1977 Protocol Additional I that the interpretation of superfluous injury and unnecessary suffering were detailed and debated because they were invoked as a means for calling to account the actions of imperial states. This matters significantly because the prohibitions against unnecessary suffering and superfluous injury are two elements that detail the general prohibition first codified in 1907 Hague Convention IV, Article 22, namely that the "the right of belligerents to adopt means of injuring the enemy is not unlimited." That is, there is a limit on the exercise of force in the pursuit of victory. However, the history and the formulation of these two concepts – superfluous injury and unnecessary suffering – has yet to be fully explored, the meaning of each is debated, and taken together the two are among "the most unclear and controversial rules of warfare" (Cassese, 2008, p. 193).

The Diplomatic Conferences took place from 1974 to 1977 at the time of conflicts in Southeast Asia, Latin and Central America, and Lusophone Africa, following the wars of decolonization and national liberation in the 1950s–1960s. The conferences were directly informed by the experiences of these wars and the diverse and contentious "transnational culture of Third World liberation" generated by such wars (Chamberlin, 2011, p. 5). Newly decolonized states and national liberation movements used the Diplomatic Conferences, which were officially open to them for the first time, to push for a larger conceptual understanding of superfluous injury and unnecessary suffering to hold imperialism and imperial states accountable for suffering and injury beyond that of physical death or wounding and to recognize the violence of colonization and the social and cultural destruction it brought.

While the origins of the prohibition were deeply rooted in and "generated by problems relating to colonial order," its scope and substance were reconfigured by the theories, practices, and agents of anti-imperialism (Anghie, 2005, p. 6). This debate was part of a critical and complex attempt fostered by the "Third World" during the 1960s and 1970s to broaden and deepen the meaning of the laws of war, to make them more responsive to and reflective of the experiences of decolonization and national liberation, and to acknowledge the devastation wrought by imperialism and sanctioned by the law.[1]

The participation of newly decolonized states and national liberation movements in the Diplomatic Conferences also illuminates a moment when, in Jacques Rancière's words, "the natural order of domination is interrupted by the institution of a part of those who have no part" (Rancière, 1999, p. 11). Prior to this moment, in the codification and development of international humanitarian law, colonized peoples appeared only as *subjects to* the laws of war as possessions of imperial states, a formal "juridically organized exclusion" constitutive of the laws of war itself (Chemillier-Gendreau, 1995, p. 153).[2] The preparatory meetings were a place and a moment in which "a given order of domination and a regime of hierarchy … (was) … radically called in to question by the emergence of a political subject" (Chambers, 2013, p. 8). In this way, the preparatory conferences were indeed an event – "an occurrence that transcends or disrupts the normal course of affairs" – during which formerly colonized peoples previously objects of administration and regulation, and targets of violence and domination emerged as subjects of their own making (Totschnig, 2016, p. 1).

In approaching the development and debates over superfluous injury and unnecessary suffering in the codification of the laws of war, I situate my work in what is known as Third World Approaches to International Law (TWAIL). In his address to the American Society of International Law, in 2001, Professor Makau Mutua defined TWAIL as a "response to decolonization and the end of direct European colonial role over non-Europeans," which actively recognizes the role of political events and organizations, specifically the Bandung Conference and the Group of 77, as its inspiration and heritage (Mutua, 2000b, p. 31). These scholars begin with the premise, as articulated by the Mohamed Bedjaoui in 1955, that classical international law is "a set of rules with a geographical bias (European law), a religious-ethical aspiration (Christian Law), an economic motivation (mercantilist), and political aim (imperialist)" (Mutua, 2000a, p. 849). Thus, TWAIL provides a critical theoretical purchase on the development of the concept of superfluous injury and unnecessary suffering recognizing "that colonialism is central to the formation of international law" (Anghie & Chimni, 2003, p. 79), which requires, in turn, making "the story of resistance an integral part of the narration of international law" (Chimni, 2006, p. 22). Although TWAIL scholars have generally not, with the notable exception of Anthony Anghie, turned their attention to international humanitarian law with the same focus as other elements of international law, this article contributes to the "vibrant ongoing debate around questions of colonial history, power, identity and difference, and what these mean for international law" (Gathii, 2011, p. 27).

The article proceeds in three parts. I first offer a brief overview of the development of the concepts now known as superfluous injury and unnecessary suffering in the laws of war, highlighting the 1899 and 1907 Hague Conventions in which the prohibition was first codified. I then turn to its subsequent rearticulation in the 1977 Protocols Additional to the 1949

Geneva Conventions, setting forth how the debate over its definition was marked by the participation of newly decolonized states and national liberation movements. Claiming equality of presence, these participants insisted the meaning of superfluous injury and unnecessary suffering, address the effects of imperialism and the extent of its violence. Finally, while the successes of newly decolonized states and national liberation movements in altering other elements of the positive laws of war, notably expanding the definition of combatant and defining the scope of its application (in Protocol I), may appear more immediately influential, I argue that attention to superfluous injury and unnecessary suffering can help deepen our understanding of the complexity of their concerns and the breadth of their political agency, while also offering a resource for responding to injury and suffering in contemporary wars.[3]

HISTORY OF THE CONCEPT

In the histories of the laws of war, the concepts of superfluous injury and unnecessary suffering evolve from restrictions on reasons to go to war (*ius ad bello*) and restrictions on the use of means and methods of warfare (*ius in bello*) that would indiscriminately and unduly cause more harm than necessary to accomplish the purpose of war – to right a wrong and to render the enemy unable to fight. In his work on moderation in regard to the use of force, the 17th-century publicist Hugo Grotius commented, "all Combats which are not for the obtaining of Right or concluding a war, but merely for a vain ostentation of strength ... are wholly repugnant to the duty of a Christian and Humanity itself" (Grotius & Tuck, 2005, p. 1456). According to the 18th-century jurist Emer de Vattel, who was also referring to reasons for war, "those who run to arms without necessity are the scourges of the human race, barbarians, enemies to society and rebellious violators of the laws of nature, or rather of the law of the common father of mankind" (Vattel & Chitty, 2011, p. 288). Further, he continues, the use of violence in war should be as restrained as is possible for any use that is in excess transgresses the laws of humanity for although necessity justifies going to war, "Let our valour preserve itself from every stain of cruelty, and the lustre of victory will not be tarnished by inhuman and brutal actions" (Vattel & Chitty, 2011, p. 362). Although these early scholars disagreed in significant ways as to the precise relationship between *ius ad bello* and *ius in bello*, each held the unfettered resort to and the use of force was contrary to particular hierarchies of standards homologous with Christianity, humanity, and civilization (cf. Boucher, 2012). Temperance in war was taken to be a hallmark of civilization and excess one of barbarism and inhumanity (Gong, 1984; Kinsella, 2005, 2011; Lorca, 2010). The St. Petersburg Declaration of 1868, which outlawed inflammable or explosive projectiles of less than 400 g, encapsulated this general sentiment stating:

> Considering that the progress of civilization should have the effect of alleviating as much as possible the calamities of war ... the only legitimate object ... is to weaken the military forces of the enemy ... that this object would be exceeded by the employment of arms which uselessly aggravate the sufferings of disabled men, or render their death inevitable ... the employment of such arms would, therefore, be contrary to the laws of humanity.

Yet, discourses of Christianity, civilization, and humanity equally set limits on to whom and among whom the restraints apply, act to justify unfettered violence against those excluded and determine who is able to formulate the scope and reach of laws of war (Anghie, 2005; Kinsella, 2011; Pemberton, 2013). It has been well established that the histories of the laws of war are inextricably intertwined with histories of imperialism and colonization, as the laws of war were conceived of within what Rey Chow refers to as a Eurocentric "hierarchizing frame of comparison," which was, in turn, reflected and institutionalized in its regulations (Chow, 2006, pp. 80–81; Jouannet, 2007; Lorca, 2010; Pitts, 2012). The discussions and debates, primarily during the 1899 Hague Conference, reveal the manner in which this occurred, while also illuminating the complexities of its occurrence. For while the laws of war claimed a putatively universal reach, historically, constitutive differences always allowed distinctions to be defended.

The 1899 and 1907 Hague Conferences codified the prohibition against superfluous injury and unnecessary suffering in the Regulations annexed to the 1907 Hague Convention IV, Article 22: "the right of belligerents to adopt means of injuring the enemy is not unlimited" and in Article 23(e): "it is forbidden to employ arms, projectiles, or material of a nature to cause unnecessary suffering."[4] In the meetings of those who gathered to formulate the 1899 and 1907 Hague Conventions, there was a clear demarcation between strategies and weapons to be allowed in wars against the civilized and those in wars against the uncivilized. Significantly, representation at both Conferences was limited to recognized sovereign states at the time (1908). Thus, while Persia, China, and Siam were in attendance in both 1899 and 1907 and, in 1907, 19 Latin American states attended, in 1899 only Mexico attended, and no African states were independently represented at either Conference. Accordingly, even with an increase in representation from 26 states in 1899 – of which only six were non-European and none of the six sovereign African states were invited – to 43 in 1907, the states in attendance were almost all the major powers who still possessed colonies or territories, and Africa was entirely excluded (Eyffinger, 2008).

During the two conferences, the means and methods of war held to cause superfluous injury and unnecessary suffering were evaluated according to the identity of those who were targeted. The most infamous example of this is the debate on the use of the dumdum bullet at the 1899 Conference, a weapon whose use would exceed "justifiable limits" and result in "useless cruelty" for it did more harm than was necessary to render its object hors de combat (Hague-Peace-Conference_1899.pdf, pp. 79, 82). In an oft quoted statement, the delegate from England "demand(ed) the liberty of employing projectiles of sufficient efficacy against savage races" (p. 287).[5] Further, any expectation for moderation "as regards to wars with savage peoples ... will be solely to the detriment of civilized nations" (p. 295). For, as another delegate continued, it would place the civilized in a "dangerous situation in a war with less civilized nations or savage tribes" (p. 293). The Russian delegate, somewhat bitingly, reassured those so concerned that even in "the St. Petersburg Declaration of 1868, the contracting Powers decided not to employ these bullets in wars *among* themselves. It is evident that there is a gap in the St. Petersburg Declaration, a gap which enables not only dumdum bullets but even explosive bullets to be used against savages" (italics added, p. 287). In other words, even as he argued "it is not proper to make distinction between civilized and savage tribes," and "both are men who deserve the same treatment," he was well aware that the development of the laws of war was predicated upon (and produced) such a distinction and differential treatment (83). His words brought to the fore that even as the entire conference was permeated – from invitation to participation – with discourses and differences of civilization and barbarism, not all participants held that it was an equally defensible demarcation for assessing harm of particular weapons. However, in no case was the comparison itself deemed wholly irrelevant or false. Rather, these statements convey a profound "imperial ambivalence" and an epistemic uncertainty as to what precisely was the substance of the difference (Berman, 2011, p. 411).

For example, the President of the conference stated that, "There can be no distinction established between the projectiles permitted and the projectiles prohibited according to the enemies against which they fight *even in case of savages*" (italics added, p. 287). For one, such a distinction would "necessarily induce complications of equipment" as militaries would have to be prepared with two separate arsenals – to "have two kinds of projectiles, one for savages and the other for civilized peoples would be complicating the armament" (p. 343). More disquietingly, such complications of equipment exposed the supposed naturalness of order as highly contingent and easily mistaken. The preservation of the distinction between civilized and savage would be threatened if, as a delegate extemporized, one contemplated "the case of soldiers stationed outside of Europe and armed with bullets for use against savages, who would be called upon to fight against the regular troops of a civilized nation" (p. 343). In other words, to contemplate the possibility, much less to risk, that the civilized could or would use the same bullets against their brethren as against savages was by far too great to accept. It was too great to accept not simply because it would complicate the armament, but also because it would render the ostensibly civilized savages in both treatment and behavior, contaminating and complicating the putative (and, at that point, supposedly inherent and characterological) hierarchy of comparison between the two.

Moreover, the measurement of needlessly cruel would always have to be evaluated against the efficiency of the weapon, and the caliber of the enemy. As the delegate from the United States noted that while having a "keen desire" to "render war more humane" it would be foolish to give up a means of warfare that they might be later "usefully employed" (Cassese, 2008, pp. 222–224, 296). Considering that the United States was just beginning to face a colonial "insurrection" in the Philippines, his statement takes on greater significance, as does the refusal of the United States and Britain to sign on to the prohibition (for further discussion of the futility of prohibitions, cf Hay & Root, 1913). In the end, the Hague Conferences embodied the vision of its preamble: an "empire of law," confirming the "general and profound sentiment of the solidarity which more and more animates the civilized world,"[6] both proscribing and defining a set of practices said to be universal, but rooted in a deeply particular collective – "that charmed circle ... which, by grace of race, religion and, more to the point, economic and military preponderance brazenly predicated itself as representing 'civilization'" (Eyffinger, 2008, p. 8; Hicks, 1908).

The principle elaborated in the Hague Conventions – "[T]he right of belligerents to adopt means of injuring the enemy is not unlimited" – was all but falsified during the colonial and interstate wars that followed, especially with the use of chemical, biological, incendiary, and nuclear weapons in violation of specific bans upon them (e.g., Protocol for the Prohibition of the Use of Asphyxiating, Poisonous, or Other Gases, and of Bacteriological

Methods of Warfare, 1925). Weapon development, and superfluous injury and unnecessary suffering were inextricably connected and, consequently, efforts to further address inevitably stalled in debates over state security and sovereignty, and the configuration of threat (Levie, 1981). Further, at the next major opportunity to codify the laws of war, during the Diplomatic Conferences on the four 1949 Geneva Conventions, the nuclear geopolitics of the Cold War hardened the insistence that any discussion of harm from particular weapons be reserved for law making in regards to the conduct of hostilities (colloquially known as Hague law) and not included in law making for the protections of victims of war (colloquially known as Geneva Law) (Barak, 2010; Baxter, 1980). This made any further codification of superfluous injury and unnecessary suffering all but impossible, with the result that the updated IV Geneva Conventions "said little about the precautions and limits belligerents had to observe ... while planning and deploying armed attack or using certain weapons with 'uncontrollable effects'" (Mantilla, 2013, p. 163). It was not until the Diplomatic Conferences for the 1977 Protocols that superfluous injury and unnecessary suffering became, almost a century later, a subject of renewed debate.

NATIONAL LIBERATION MOVEMENTS

The decades preceding the Diplomatic Conferences, held from 1974 to 1977, were rife with wars of decolonization and national liberation, and representatives from national liberation movements and newly decolonized states skillfully utilized the United Nations to stage their struggles, articulating the essential importance of self-determination and respect for human rights and testifying to the legitimacy of their claims. The membership of the United Nations had changed dramatically from its founding and by the 1960s almost half of its members were newly decolonized states. This transformation of international politics was both a consequence of and impetus for the opprobrium with which efforts to prevent self-determination and to maintain colonial rule were treated. Along with the 1960 Declaration on the Granting of Independence to Colonial Countries and Peoples and the 1970 Declaration on Principles of International Law Concerning Friendly Relations and Cooperation Among States – the United Nations General Assembly passed a bold series of resolutions declaiming against racist and colonial regimes – "ruthless and blatant colonialist and racialist repression" – directly linking international peace and security, and the flourishing of human rights, to the abolishment of apartheid and colonialism (G.A. Resolution 2908 [XXVII], 1972, p. 2). The International Conference on Human Rights, held in Tehran in 1968, adopted a Declaration on Human Rights in Armed Conflict which drew especial attention to this link, stating "peace is the underlying condition for the full observance of human rights and war is their negation," and noted that the Hague Conventions, prohibitions on means and methods of war were sorely outdated.

More specifically, the wars of decolonization and national liberation were internal wars, and the manner in which they were fought underscored the startling lack of laws of war pertaining directly to internal armed conflicts, while the use of weapons – nuclear to napalm – underscored the weakness of the prohibitions on superfluous injury and unnecessary suffering. This was a concern that the International Committee of the Red Cross (ICRC) had expressed for years, leading to a three-year effort to formulate a protocol, "Draft Rules for the Limitation of the Dangers Incurred by the Civilian Population in Time of War" (1956), which sought to identify "Prohibited Methods of Warfare" (Article 14). However, due to their explicit mention of nuclear weapons in the context of the Cold War, the Draft Rules were ignored, as was the ICRC's 1967 effort to encourage states to discuss "new weapons [such] as napalm and high velocity rockets" as inflicting "needless suffering" (Kalshoven, 1985, p. 79). The ICRC's efforts to address this lacuna were facilitated by the International Year for Human Rights, its Tehran Declaration, and the adoption of a resolution by the General Assembly inviting the Secretary General to study what would be necessary, feasible, and desirable to update the laws of war, specifically including "the prohibition and limitation on the use of certain methods and means of warfare" (UNGA Resolution 2444 (XXIII), December 16, 1968). The Secretary General produced three detailed reports which were shared with the General Assembly.[7] While the ICRC had already sought to gather expert opinions on "prohibition of 'non-directed' weapons or weapons causing unnecessary suffering," such as napalm, and fragmentation bombs, it was the Secretary General's report on the precise effects of the use of napalm and other incendiary weapons on "human beings and the living environment" which informed its description of the "cruel and barbarous war" waged in Vietnam, and other atrocities attributed to "imperialist" states committing "criminal, inhuman acts" (Napalm and Other Incendiary Weapons and All Aspects of their Possible Use, UN Doc. A/8303, October 9, 1972).[8] The General Assembly kept the issue of armed conflict on its agenda in its session from 1968 to 1973 and encouraged the Secretary General to consult with the ICRC at every available turn.

National liberation movements, newly decolonized states and their supporters, whose histories of organization and efforts can be traced in part to the Bandung Conference of 1955, insisted on the recognition of human rights in armed conflicts, prohibitions on certain weapons, and the rewriting of laws of armed conflict because each was central to the defense and pursuit of self-determination, understood not only in legal terms but also in terms of personhood. The history is too complex and rich to be more than acknowledged here, but two examples illuminate the extent to which newly decolonized states and national liberation movements networked and negotiated a collective (although not wholly consensual) position which informed the tenor and framing of these changes.

First, national liberation movements and newly decolonized states had already been actively organizing independently of the United Nations, developing comprehensive programs of action and consolidating strategies for formal recognition through solidarity conferences (e.g., The Non-Alignment Movement and the Conferences on Afro Asian Peoples) and the establishment of permanent Secretariats (Plummer, 2013, pp. 20, 106). In an effort to expand their campaigns and to deepen the "transnational idiom" already in circulation, the historic first conference of "African, Asian, and Latin American peoples," the Tricontinental Conference, was held in Havana, Cuba in 1966 (Chakraborty, 2016, p. 110). This deployment of the "name of the people and of the space of the grievance to which that name gives substance," actively sought to disrupt and undo "the supposed naturalness of orders," in which colonized peoples were subject to violent prior disregard and dismissal as actors in and of their own right (Rancière, 1995, pp. 33, 98).

This particular conference drew luminaries such as Fidel Castro, Salvador Allende, and Amilcar Cabral, and was attended by more than 500 representatives of 82 countries representing independent governments, guerilla groups, and national liberation movements. Dedicated to building transnational solidarity among Afro-Asian-Latin American movements, the conference explicitly articulated a common political, economic, and social program of liberation and support for independence and self-determination. Its objective was to provide an ongoing forum, through yearly gatherings and national organizations, to develop and refine a global strategy informed by each national liberation movement's successes – an "internationalist nationalism" (Prashad, 2008, p. 12). In this regard, there were two simultaneous efforts at work, to not only transform institutions of rule, such as the United Nations and international law, but also to claim their right and recognition to do so – to act and speak – independent of, and in spite of, such distributions of rule.[9]

Of particular interest, considering his role as the founder and leader of a national liberation movement, the African Party for the Liberation of Guinea and Cape Verde and as a consummate diplomat at the United Nations and other gatherings, is Amilcar Cabral – one of "Africa's most significant" revolutionaries (Chilcote, 1984, p. 3; Westad, 2007, p. 211). His opening speech at the Conference, entitled "The weapon of theory," was a highly complex analysis of the rise of and need for national liberation, which exhorted the delegates to continue to conceive of national liberation as both an internal process (of the self) as well as an external process (of the collective). Situated in, but not beholden to, Marxist theories of production, Cabral connected armed struggle to the recuperation of national culture, identity, and self-knowledge for, as he extrapolated in his other writings, the rebirth of historical and contemporary identities of the peoples is a necessary element in restructuring the economic and the political. Imperialism destroys both the existence of and the capacity for self and collective knowledge, which is why national liberation was not "only a cultural fact, it is also a factor of culture," and national liberation must mean "regaining not only one's historical personality as a free people but also one's own initiative as a maker of history" (Chabal, 1981; McCulloch, 1981, p. 44). The harm done by colonization and imperialism, as all the resolutions of the conference iterated, was comprehensive in scope – underdevelopment was but an "ill-disguised euphemism" for the "concrete and dramatic" destruction of a people (Organization of American States, 1966a, 1966b, p. 33). Drawing attention to the irony of a civilization which was built upon their oppression and exclusion, he queried what was a more "striking manifestation of civilization and culture if not that shown by a people which takes up arms to defend its right to life, to progress, to work and to happiness?" (Cabral, 1970, p. 65).

Consequently, as the General Declaration of the conference asserted, "the right of the peoples to obtain their political, economic and social liberation" is to be defended by "any means necessary" until achieved (Organization of American States, 1966a, 1966b, p. 39). Singled out for consistent condemnation was US action in Vietnam, not as a discrete case of imperialist aggression but as the most "recent manifestation" of it, while nuclear arms and napalm were identified as the most barbarous of weapons (Organization of American States, 1966a, 1966b, p. 116; Prashad, 2008). The work of the conference was substantial – deeply contentious, but conducted in common – as it began a process of strengthening and expanding the relationships, regional and otherwise, and the "transnational body of work" of Third World liberation.[10]

Second, these networks helped to inform the tack taken within the United Nations, with General Assembly Resolutions on Friendly Relations and the New International Economic Order attributed to their advocacy, and insisted that napalm remain under debate in the General Assembly. Moreover, documenting a comprehensive understanding of the harm done by imperialism, these actors collected evidence of a systematic injustice incommensurable with the essential equality of all states and peoples. For example, in 1973, at the International Conference of Experts in Support of the Victims of Colonialism and Apartheid in Southern Africa, the United Nations Special Committee on Decolonization organized a meeting of the leaders of national governments, inter- and nongovernmental organizations, and regional national liberation movements to develop a comprehensive economic, political, and social agenda for action which acknowledged the extensive harm constituted by the very system of states and rule said to prevent it. Within the United Nations, this same committee also allowed "representatives of national liberation movements in Africa (as recognized by the O.A.U.) to participate in their meetings as observers whenever their respective territories are being considered," which gave status to those movements and leaders and, eventually, led to the granting of formal UN observer status to national liberation groups, such as the PLO, which were recognized by the League of Arab states and/or Organization of African Unity (El-Ayouty, 1972; Mittelman, 1976, p. 2). The fight for acknowledgment, of both harm and of agency, was not simply a request for an allocation of, or assimilation to, rule, but also a profound and transformative demand for recognition. As Cabral underscored, "to co-exist one must first of all exist," which meant asserting the right and presence to do so (Prashad, 2008, p. 103).

Assassinated on the eve of independence in January 1973, Cabral did not live to witness official recognition of his country, but the opening act of the first Diplomatic Conference on the Reaffirmation and Development of International Humanitarian Law Applicable in Armed Conflict (Diplomatic Conference) was to issue a formal invitation to the newly independent Guinea Bissau to participate fully. And, out of the 11 national liberation movements invited to the conference, more than half of those that had not yet achieved independence had been in Havana in 1966. The complexity of the approaches to national liberation, constructed "outside the state but within empire," and the comprehensive harm of imperialism, both fundamental to the transnational idiom of national liberation, continued in the conference debates (quoted in Plummer, 2013, p. 23).

DIPLOMATIC CONFERENCES

At the start of the Diplomatic Conferences in 1974, the ICRC was under the illusion that since the draft protocols had already been circulated among states, experts, and organizations, the actual Diplomatic Conferences would proceed rather smoothly. Originally conceived of as only one meeting to last six weeks, the disagreements and discussion over some of the formal procedure as well as substantive issues derailed this assumption. For one, newly decolonized states and others wished that the formal offices of representation within the Conference be distributed representatively according to region and, for another, the question of participation by states and others who had not received an official invitation to attend by the Swiss government loomed large. Thus, the Conference "opened with a bang" as the President of Islamic Republic of Mauritania declaimed his support for national liberation movements and excoriated the Zionists and imperialists who sought to suppress their claims (Baxter, 1975, p. 9). This "set the tone of the conference" and, although the United States and other Western countries sought to block it, it was agreed that national liberation movements recognized by the Organization of African Unity and the Arab League be invited to participate in the work of the Conference (Aldrich, 1977; Baxter, 1975, p. 9). While national liberation movements were not permitted to formally vote, their contributions had the authority and force of official Conference documents (RC-records_Vol-1.pdf, p. 55). Moreover, they were invited to sign the Final Act of the Conference, on June 10, 1977, an indication of the renegotiation and transformation of the politics of law making over the three years of meetings (although Israel refused to sign the Final Act, as the PLO had done so).

Prior to the start of the Diplomatic Conference, the ICRC held two preparatory meetings, the *Conferences of Government Experts*, in 1971 and in 1972. The first conference was attended by 69 experts and the second by 77, and representatives from the Secretary General participated in both. In fact, the second session was expanded to include all signatories to the 1949 Geneva Conventions, after participants at the first conference expressed concern at the lack of representation from the Third World. At both conferences, the United States, the Soviets, and other Western states sought to remove the questions of weapons from debate, insisting that they lay outside humanitarian law and should be considered in a disarmament forum. It was finally agreed after the second conference of the Government Experts, where the ICRC was further tasked with hosting experts on "the problem of the use of certain conventional weapons that may cause unnecessary suffering or have indiscriminate effects," that the ICRC could continue to address the issue of weapons without prejudicing the work on international humanitarian law. This led to yet two more separate meetings of *Conference of Government Experts on the Use of Certain Conventional Weapon*, the first in Lucerne (1974), in which 49 states and six national liberation movements participated, and the second in Lugano (1976) in which 43 states and no national liberation movements participated. As one expert to the Lugano conference reminded the participants, "the Third World, although less well represented at this session than at the previous one ... expected positive results of this Conference," while, notwithstanding their reduced numbers, those who were present "took a most active part in the proceedings" (RC-conf-experts-1976.pdf, p. 5, Kalshoven, 2007, p. 172).[11] Further, during the first session of the Diplomatic Conference, after a tense vote, Sweden along with Egypt, Mexico, Norway, Sudan, Switzerland, and Yugoslavia formed the *Ad Hoc Committee on Conventional Weapons* (with occasional participation by other states, such as Nigeria, Sudan, Algeria, Lebanon, Mauritania, Venezuela, and Mali), which held parallel discussions, sharing delegates with and relying consistently on the Government Experts' reports.

In many ways, the contour of the debate outlined in 1899 at the Hague – the implementation of the prohibition of a weapon as potentially dependent upon the identity of the enemy, the hesitation to outlaw weapons that may of particular use to particular nations in particular wars, the belief that few weapons were inherently indiscriminate, a debate over the true point of international humanitarian law (to regulate war or to humanize it) and the split between powerful nations and less powerful nations in their support for outright bans – was found in 1977.[12] Consequently, as put by the Soviet delegate (in agreement with the United States and France), "it was impossible to approach the matter from a purely humanitarian point of view leaving aside political and military considerations and matters of State security" (RC-records_Vol-7.pdf, p. 19). In response, the delegate from Norway assured him that the "balance of terror" was not going to be directly affected by the work of the Conference, referring not so obliquely to nuclear weapons and the Cold War, while other states (Tunisia, Cameroon, and Sudan and others) insisted upon the complete competence of the Diplomatic Conferences and the Experts Meetings to debate prohibitions on weapons of a nature to cause superfluous injury or unnecessary suffering. To argue against such competence was to "mark a distinction between the powerful States and those who believed in humanitarian law" (RC-records_Vol-7.pdf, p. 31). Or, as put more directly by the delegate from Mozambique,

> With these examples before us of the terrible destruction suffered by the peoples of Indochina and these who were subjected to fascist colonial domination; we can see the urgent need to put an end to the arms race, and particularly the race in arms whose use is a crime against humanity. Unfortunately, we note that whenever we wish to crystallize a known principle which has already been adopted, there are countries which vigorously object, saying that we are straying outside the confines of humanitarian law. (RC-records_Vol-7.pdf, p. 45)

The first meeting of the Ad Hoc Committee was described as a debate:

> between the 'haves' and the 'have-nots'. Itself a power of high military technology, the Soviet Union could not welcome placing restraints on weapons, but at the same time as the steadfast ally of Third World states, it found it difficult to take a hard line against the technologically-deprived developing states. (Baxter, 1977, p. 51)

The Soviet delegate was worried that any prohibitions on weapons might also put smaller nations at a disadvantage because "a small country would become unable to defend its territory and would be in a position of weakness vis-à-vis large countries which produced costlier and more efficient weapons" (Cassese, 1976, p. 162). This debate was to be rehearsed throughout the entire conference, with Sweden leading the effort to address conventional weapons and the Soviets steadily entrenched as the main vocal opposition to prohibitions on weapons. Commenting on the first three sessions, a US observer noted the "Soviets appear as the 'bad guys', and in the process the United States is relieved of the need to take a stand on napalm" and other weapons (Forsythe, 1977, p. 137; Parks, 2006). Throughout both the Diplomatic Conferences and the Expert meetings, napalm and other incendiary weapons were described as a particular "abhorrence" which should be outlawed as affronts to the "public conscience" and, before the Diplomatic Conferences concluded, the Non-Aligned movement had specifically requested that all its members pursue its abolition (RC-conf-experts-1974.pdf, p. 12).[13]

It was this attitude that the United States, in particular, was keen to undermine. According to a diplomatic transmission from its delegate, "the United States had to approach this Conference with caution and concern ... we had seen in other contexts the risk that conferences of one hundred or more countries would be dominated by a majority of developing countries, a majority which all too often seems to be led by radical states bearing grudges against the wealthy countries in general and against the United States in particular" (Boyd, 1978). At various points in the discussions, he encouraged the delegates to keep an open mind about the viability of weapons, and expressed his deep concern that a conclusion had already been reached on which weapons were to be outlawed.

However similar the contours of the debate might be to that of the Hague, they should not be overdrawn. For what is significantly different is who participated in these debates and the context in which it took place. First, it was the largest and most diverse conference on the laws of war. There were some 155 state delegations as well as 11 national liberation movements, and 51 intergovernmental organizations. Out of those 155 states, approximately 40 had recently achieved independence, including those like Mozambique who gained sovereignty during the Diplomatic Conferences: "Yesterday, we were freedom fighters; today, we are the representatives of a sovereign State" (RC-records_Vol-7.pdf, p. 277). The degree of transformation in structure and authority in the international order was marked and ongoing. Second, there was a concerted attempt to clarify the entirely "too vague" provision of Article 23(e) of the 1907 Hague Regulations (Kalshoven, 2011, p. 30). Third, and most strikingly, this attempt was led by, and with recognition of, those most injured by wars of imperialism. After all, "they were the people who really had first-hand knowledge, although mostly as victims, of the effects of modern conventional weaponry" (Kalshoven, 2007, p. 158). Delegates from newly decolonized states, most often led by the Democratic Republic of Vietnam, insisted on the "atrocious reality" of what they had experienced as balancing or even contradicting, the work of "certain experts," who wished to pontificate upon the injuries of war (RC-records_Vol-16.pdf, p. 108). The delegate from Mozambique foregrounded the disjuncture, noting that "while this conference is meeting here, the people of Mozambique are being bombed by illegal and racist regimes ... using napalm and other materials causing superfluous injury" (RC-records_Vol-6.pdf, p. 303). In response to an impassioned description of the harms suffered by the Vietnamese people, the delegate from Mongolia praised the delegate from Vietnam's intervention, stating that it was "far closer to the realities of life than were the theories of experts and it made an indispensable contribution to humanitarian law" (Levie, 1981, p. 261). Unlike earlier conferences, those subjects of and to the laws of war were also to be its creators and its agents, marshaling an expertise of experience.

Finally, the presumption of the inevitability or necessity of imperial war – to bring civilization to the savages – was overturned, with newly independent states and national liberation movements claiming that these wars – colonial, racist, imperialist – betrayed the humanitarian promise of the laws of war upon which civilization was said to depend, and revealed the savagery of the imperialists. As put by the delegate from Nigeria, "The wars of liberation now being waged in Africa, the Middle East, Southeast Asia and elsewhere were being fought with conventional weapons, with the weaker side, particularly the freedom fighters, as the exclusive targets of lethal and indiscriminate weapons" (RC-records_Vol-16.pdf, p. 19). Thus, it was those states that would reduce "human suffering" which would bear the mantle of "civilized" (RC-records_Vol-16.pdf, pp. 26, 28, 147).

Although the delegates disagreed on a large number of issues, in the Ad Hoc Committee and the Experts meetings the delegates were able to agree more or less to the Swedish proposal that the "philosophy which underlay the concept 'unnecessary suffering' was that, if two means of weakening the adversary's military forces were roughly equivalent for the purpose of placing an adversary hors de combat; the less injurious must be chosen" (RC-records_Vol-16.pdf, p. 16). However, even once this agreement was reached, its reasoning still failed to confront these questions: What was less injurious said to be? What was superfluous injury or unnecessary suffering? How is, and who is, one to distinguish and measure expected or necessary suffering and injury against excessive or unnecessary suffering and injury?

The difficulties of answering such questions were acknowledged from the start, but the parameters of inquiry were restricted by its relationship to that of military necessity.

> There was widespread agreement among the experts that this involved some sort of equation between ... the degree of injury suffering inflicted and ... the degree of necessity underlying the choice of a particular weapon (T)he equation would often be a particularly difficult one, as neither side ... could easily be reduced to precise figures ... and were so different that they were hard to compare. (RC-conf-experts-1974.pdf, p. 9)

The challenges of comparison are made all the more difficult by the inherent privileging of military necessity – "a balancing ... between the force dictated by military necessity to achieve a legitimate objective vis a vis injury that may be considered superfluous to the achievement of the stated or intended objective (in other words, whether the suffering caused is out of proportion to the military advantage to be gained)" – which rigs any evaluation in its favor, and limits its scope (Parks, 1997, p. 18). Only a few experts argued that the place to begin was not with a comparison, or a balancing test, but with an absolute claim: "all suffering caused by war was, in a sense, unnecessary" and "all weapons were cruel" (RC-conf-experts-1974.pdf, p. 7; RC-records_Vol-16.pdf, pp. 16, 178).

In an attempt to answer these questions in more "objective" terms, there were hours and days spent on the quantification of suffering in both the Experts' meetings and in the Ad Hoc Committee. In the 1974 Lugano Conference, possible indices of degree of pain, duration of effect, and the number of casualties were proposed (and scientific, medical and humanitarian experts debated the terms and metrics of the three). However, it was soon realized that such measurements were inherently subjective and complexly related, with extreme variance across individuals more than likely, and the vulnerability of individuals connected to their status (rich, poor, rural, urban), age, health, etc. Thus, there were no truly objective or accurately measurable indices that could be created for international use. Further, the sociopsychological response was a factor in all and "cannot reasonably be quantified" (RC-Weapons.pdf, p. 27). Nevertheless, during the Diplomatic Conferences there were often slightly absurd exchanges, as when the delegates from Sweden and the United States traded opinions as to whether death from fragmentation or blasts was worse physically and psychologically, and lamented that "an unsatisfactory feature of the experiments carried out at the Goteberg Symposium had been that the pigs used had wound channels" which were insufficient for evaluation (RC-records_Vol-16.pdf, pp. 311, 333–335, 356). Third World delegates also drew attention to the inherent subjectivity in the use of the terms superfluous injury and unnecessary suffering, for they "all were too manipulable and could potentially justify genocide, as the irony was technical advances in certain imperialist countries enabled them to justify using arms which were said to cause less unnecessary suffering by killing more quickly" (RC-records_Vol-4, p. 184). Further, as the delegate from the Democratic Republic of Vietnam explained: "to prohibit or restrict certain categories of weapons would give the impression that they alone were dangerous. In fact, by the large-scale use of permissible weapons, or even of industrial equipment such as the bulldozers used in Vietnam, the aggressor could produce effects that were just as dangerous and cruel, if not more so" (RC-records_Vol-7.pdf, p. 345).

Over a period of meetings, in which the technical data "proved to be debatable and frequently contradictory," and with growing acceptance of the impossibility (due to the geopolitics of the time) of identifying more weapons to be prohibited, much less attempting to quantify the meaning of superfluous injury and unnecessary suffering, the delegates returned to methods of war to provide conceptual purchase (RC-records_Vol-7.pdf, p. 46; RC-conf-experts-1974.pdf, p. 10).[14] A focus on methods would highlight the use to which a weapon is put as potentially unlawful, irrespective of the lawfulness of the weapon and its properties. This shift in emphasis, from means to method, also reflected the continuing influence of newly independent states and national liberation movements who insisted upon the specificity of the wars against them – those "methods of combat" that were purposely employed by "colonial and racist regimes to crush liberation movements" (Levie, 1981, p. 186). Or, as the delegate from Algeria suggested, those "used in highly uneven conflicts" (RC-records_Vol-16.pdf, p. 156). The delegate from the Democratic Republic of Korea went so far as to ask for a prohibition against the "cruel means of warfare" in use in the "colonies," while a few African countries wished to approach the debates about methods even more specifically with a "regional" focus, highlighting apartheid as "typical of imperialism" (Organization of American States, 1966a, 1966b, p. 124; RC-records_Vol-7.pdf, p. 41; RC-records_Vol-16.pdf, p. 21). For these delegates, the methods to be prohibited were those capable of "destroying means of life" (RC-records_Vol-14.pdf, p. 241).

Means of life, in this context, pushed the conversation to encompass the entire population and its subsistence, not simply those who were specifically targeted. For example, the delegate from Democratic Republic of Vietnam wanted the specific method of pacification to be outlawed, because its purpose was "to subdue an entire people" (RC-records_Vol-14.pdf, p. 236). Third World delegates, supported by the ICRC, insisted upon broadening the discussion beyond individual physical and psychological suffering, to include harm done to a people and to the environment, namely injury and suffering should also be conceptualized in terms of "genocide, biocide, and ecocide" (RC-conf-experts-1974.pdf, p. 13). Unsurprisingly, the emphasis on damage to the environment as fundamentally damaging to ways of life was iterated frequently in regards to the effects of defoliation and the use of herbicides for which "Vietnam had become a testing ground" (Aldrich, 1985; RC-records_Vol-16.pdf, p. 344; Sandoz, 1994, p. 93). Introduced also throughout these debates was the temporality of harm with the insistence that it be evaluated according to scope (widespread), degree (severe), and duration (long lasting) (see Protocol I, Article 35(3)). As Cabral and others had argued, the harm was comprehensive, generational, historical, and imperial.

CONCLUSION

Notwithstanding the success of national liberation movements, newly decolonized states, and their supporters in effecting great changes in the laws of war in other areas, the work of the two Experts Meetings, the Ad Hoc Committee, and the Diplomatic Conference on the question of superfluous injury and unnecessary suffering was deemed to have been less than satisfactory by many of the participants (Kinsella, 2011; Mantilla, 2013). The blame was attributed to the politics of national security, the unwillingness of States to compromise, and the radical inequalities of power and economics of weapon development and implementation. The difficulties in defining the concepts were also caught in the geopolitics of the time, in which "there was also an implied linkage between advanced technology in weapons with increased inhumanity: a notion which had considerable appeal to certain developing States and groups involved in guerrilla war-fare and wars of national liberation," but which did little to promote consensus among all states (Mathews, 2001, p. 995). Additionally, national liberation movements and newly decolonized states were hobbled by a lack of expertise in international humanitarian law and, while certainly skilled at UN diplomacy, these movements and states were less fluent in (and well-funded for) the process of international treaty making (Adler-Nissen & Pouliot, 2014; Forsythe, 1975, p. 82).[15] For all these reasons, as Richard Baxter put it at the time, "many delegates from developing countries are thus still engaged in reading themselves into this body of law" (Baxter, 2013, p. 252).

And, yet, what Baxter identifies – the very act of reading themselves into this body of law – calls any conclusion as to simple success or failure into question for this act is itself emancipatory. By reading themselves into the body of law, newly decolonized states and national liberation movements were not seeking to adapt to it. Rather, they asserted themselves as authors and "maker(s) of history," projecting their self-constitutive understanding of liberation to demand that the laws of war, predicated on their very exclusion and degradation, instead "protect the overall physical and moral well-being of human beings and to create all the legal conditions necessary to enable them *fully to develop* their personality, even under the difficult conditions of war, when weapons are being used to destroy them" (Democratic Republic of Vietnam, RC-records_Vol-4, p. 178; McCulloch, 1981, p. 44).

The quantification of harm, which began in totally technical, limited, and individual terms was expanded and deepened to consider the complexity and nuances of suffering and injury encompassing entire ways of life. Importantly, this was not acceptance of or an identification as pure victims of imperialism, but an effort to disrupt the "distribution of the sensible" and make visible and make evident the suffering and injuries of imperialism (Rancière, 2004, p. 12). These discussions, led by newly decolonized states, national liberation movements, and their supporters verified the falsity of limiting or believing it possible to empirically quantify suffering and injury, and identified the specificities of the wrongs done in the name of imperialism. This move, in turn, required a transformative grasp of history, and of the histories of the laws of war through which the colonized and the wars against them were governed – a position that challenged the separation of *ius ad bello* and *ius in bello* and, moreover, a position that aspired to change the bases of contemporary laws of war. Thus, the participation of newly decolonized states and national liberation movements at the Diplomatic Conferences both enacted and produced different "ways of doing, ways of being, and ways of saying," influencing the formal substance of the laws of war and confirming, in Cabral's words, that while "the colonialists usually say that it was they who brought us into history: today we show that this is not so" (McCulloch, 1981, p. 44; Rancière, 1999, p. 29).

To pay attention to the debate over superfluous suffering and unnecessary injury, and the politics of the debate, is also to recognize that this moment of politics – the claiming of the injustice of imperialism which, unto itself, forces a new stage and results in new distribution of the sensible – is contingent and never fully realized. We are reminded of this by those "living under the drones" who demand, against all insistence that the drones are a legal means of war, a full registering of the suffering and injury to which they are subject.

NOTES

1. I use the term "Third World" in recognition of its use and circulation during the period under discussion as highlighting a history of colonization and imperialism, foregrounding economic and political inequalities, and referring to a self-identified group of states and national liberation movements – a "revolutionary network" (Chamberlin, 2011, pp. 11, 270).

2. Some newly decolonized state representatives, such as Algeria, participated in the expert meetings leading up to the Diplomatic Conferences. However, this form of participation was not as a recognized or official representative of the state itself, but in a "private" role, and delegates at these meetings could not bind their states to agreed upon language. I say more about the contests over participation in the Diplomatic Conferences below.

3. I do not have sufficient space to fully detail the changes to combatant status and the radical definition of Protocol I's scope of application, both of which were a result of advocacy and agitation on the part of newly decolonized states and national liberation movements. Somewhat ironically, newly decolonized states and national liberation movements also disrupted attempts to expand the scope of Protocol II, notwithstanding the conventional (and recently imperial) understanding

of state sovereignty it confirmed. For longer discussion of the politics of both moves, see Mantilla (2013), Kinsella (2011), Suter (1984).

4. The 1899 Hague Conference concluded with two Hague Declarations Concerning Asphyxiating Gases and Expanding Bullets, both of which were "inspired by the sentiments which found expression" in the St. Petersburg Declaration (Hague-Peace-Conference_1899.pdf).

5. "Sir John Ardagh, in accord with the Austrian delegate, adds that there is a difference in war between civilized nations and that against savages. If, in the former, a soldier is wounded by a small projectile, he is taken away in the ambulance, but the savage, although run through two or three times, does not cease to advance" (Mégret, 2006; Orford, 2006).

6. Preamble to Article 1 of the 1907 Hague Conventions reads: "Recognizing the solidarity uniting the members of the society of civilized nations; Desirous of extending the empire of law and of strengthening the appreciation of international justice" (Hague-Peace-Conference_1907-V-1.pdf, p. 347).

7. Respect for Human Rights in Armed Conflicts: Reports of the Secretary-General, UN Docs. A/7720 (1969), A/8052 (1970), A/8370 (1971).

8. This was followed by the UN SG's two volumes of analysis on "Existing Rules of International Law Concerning the Prohibition or Restriction of Use of Specific Weapons," UN Doc. A/9215 (November 7, 1973) (Vol. I, II). The instructions from the GA were that the UNSCG was to focus on the "prohibition of the use of weapons and methods of warfare which indiscriminately affect civilians and combatants, and the prohibition or restriction of the use of specific weapons which are deemed to cause unnecessary suffering" (Baxter, 1977, p. 47). The writing of the reports was done almost entirely without experts from the "Western Alliance" (Blix, 1974, p. 23).

9. As Havercroft and Owen (2016, p. 746) explain, these efforts effected a "double-movement" composed of: "(1) a dis-identification of 'the part of those with no part' with the existing order and (2) the exemplification of a world in which the distinction between those who have a part and those who have no part is erased."

10. It also founded a journal titled *Tricontinental* in which the writings of Cabral, Sartre, Guevara, Ho Chi Minh, Fanon, and others helped to depict national liberation "not as a single political and theoretical position, but as a transnational body of work with a common aim of popular liberation – political, economic, material, cultural – for the countries of the South" (Chapman & Young, 2006, p. 201).

11. The cost of attendance at these multiple conferences, as well as the number of delegates required to be in attendance at all of the various conferences, was well beyond that which most national liberation movements and newly independent states could afford.

12. This was made most evident in the exclusion of nuclear weapons entirely from the debates, and in the signing statement of the United States which expressly noted that the rules of Protocol I did not have "any effect on ... regulate or prohibit" the use of nuclear weapons (Aldrich, 1981, p. 781).

13. "The heads of State of Government of Non-Aligned Countries ... urged all States to pursue their negotiations at the Diplomatic Conference with a view to the prohibition of certain cruel weapons, particularly napalm and other incendiary weapons" (RC-records_Vol-7.pdf, p. 381).

14. That it does not ban specific weapons is a result of diplomatic and state maneuvering. "It is apparent … that the primary reason for the failure … lies in the non-cooperative attitude and the delaying tactics of two groups of States: those of NATO (minus Norway) and those of the Warsaw Pact (minus Romania). This strong coalition succeeded in nullifying all the generous efforts of a group of States, made up of some Afro-Asian countries, a few Latin American countries and some Western States such as Sweden and Norway" (Cassese, 1981, p. 184).

15. The delegate from Nigeria "regretted that his delegation had not the resources to enable it to participate fully in the work of the Ad Hoc Committee" (RC-records_Vol-16.pdf, pp. 182, 356). The work of the Diplomatic Conference was divided into four commissions, in addition to the Ad Hoc Committee and the ICRC meetings. Smaller delegations, often made up of only one or two individuals outside of those from the Western and Soviet delegations, were unable to fully participate, while attendance was subject to availability of national funding – two months of annual meetings for four years was an exorbitant cost (Baxter, 1975; Forsythe, 1977, p. 141).

ACKNOWLEDGMENTS

With gratitude to Tarak Barkawi, Sam Chambers, George Lawson, Arnulf Becker Lorca, Tor Krever, and Patricia Owens who encouraged me to do more, and less.

REFERENCES

Adler-Nissen, R., & Pouliot, V. (2014). Power in practice: Negotiating the international intervention in Libya. *European Journal of International Relations*, *20*(4), 889–911.

Aldrich, G. H. (1977). Establishing legal norms through multilateral negotiation – The laws of war. *Case Western Reserve Journal of International Law*, *9*, 9–16.

Aldrich, G. H. (1981). New life for the laws of war. *American Journal of International Law*, *75*, 764–783.

Aldrich, G. H. (1985). Progressive development of the laws of war: A reply to criticisms of the 1977 Geneva protocol I commentary. *Virginia Journal of International Law*, *26*, 693–722.

Anghie, A. (2005). *Imperialism, sovereignty, and the making of international law*. Cambridge: Cambridge University Press.

Anghie, A., & Chimni, B. S. (2003). Third world approaches to international law and individual responsibility in internal conflicts. *Chinese Journal of International Law*, *2*, 77–104.

Barak, E. (2010). *Deadly metal rain the legality of Flechette weapons in international law: A reappraisal following Israel's use in the Gaza Strip (2001–2005)*. doi:10.1163/ej.9789004167193

Baxter, R. (2013). Humanizing the laws of war: Selected writings of Richard Baxter.

Baxter, R. R. (1975). Humanitarian law or humanitarian politics – The 1974 diplomatic conference on humanitarian law. *Harvard International Law Journal, 16*, 1–26.

Baxter, R. R. (1977). Conventional weapons under legal prohibitions. *International Security, 1*(3), 42–61. doi:10.2307/2626654

Baxter, R. R. (1980). Geneva conventions of 1949, The the use of force, human rights and general international legal issues. *International Law Studies Series. US Naval War College, 62*, 220–232.

Berman, N. (2011). *Passion and ambivalence colonialism, nationalism, and international law*. Leiden: Brill.

Blix, H. (1974). Current efforts to prohibit the use of certain conventional weapons. *Instant Research on Peace and Violence, 4*(1), 21–30.

Boucher, D. (2012). The just war tradition and its modern legacy: Jus ad bellum and jus in bello. *European Journal of Political Theory, 11*(2), 92–111. doi:10.1177/1474885111425115

Boyd, J. A. (1978). Contemporary practice of the United States relating to international law. *The American Journal of International Law, 72*(2), 375. doi:10.2307/2199962

Cabral, A. (1970). *Revolution in Guinea; selected texts*. New York, NY: Monthly Review Press.

Cassese, A. (1976). Means of warfare: The present and the emerging law studies. *Revue Belge de Droit International/Belgian Review of International Law, 12*, 143–165.

Cassese, A. (Ed.). (1981). *New humanitarian law of armed conflict*. Napoli: Oceana Publications.

Cassese, A. (2008). *The human dimension of international law: Selected papers*. Oxford: Oxford University Press.

Chabal, P. (1981). The social and political thought of Amilcar Cabral: A reassessment. *The Journal of Modern African Studies, 19*(1), 31–56.

Chakraborty, A. (2016). The peasant armed. In *Cultures of decolonisation* (pp. 109–125). Manchester University Press.

Chamberlin, P. (2011). The struggle against oppression everywhere: The global politics of Palestinian liberation. *Middle Eastern Studies, 47*(1), 25–41. doi:10.1080/00263201003590300

Chambers, S. A. (2013). *The lessons of Rancière*. New York, NY: Oxford University Press.

Chapman, M., & Young, R. J. C. (2006). Robert J. C. Young in South Africa: Interview. *English in Africa, 33*(2), 199–208.

Chemillier-Gendreau, M. (1995). *Humanité et souverainetés. Essai sur la fonction du droit international*. Quoted in Koskenniemi, M. (2011). Histories of international law: Dealing with eurocentrism (Vol. 19, pp. 152–176). *Rechtsgeschichte*.

Chilcote, R. H. (1984). The theory and practice of Amilcar Cabral: Revolutionary implications for the third world. *Latin American Perspectives, 11*(2), 3–14.

Chimni, B. S. (2006). Third world approaches to international law: A manifesto. *International Community Law Review, 8*, 3–28.

Chow, R. (2006). *The age of the world target: Self-referentiality in war, theory, and comparative work*. Durham, NC: Duke University Press.

Cole, A. (2015). The function of theory at the present time. *PMLA, 130*(3), 809–818.

El-Ayouty, Y. (1972). Legitimization of national liberation: The United Nations and Southern Africa. *Issue: A Journal of Opinion, 2*(4), 36–45. doi:10.2307/1166492

Eyffinger, A. (2008). Caught between tradition and modernity: East Asia at the Hague peace conferences. *Journal of East Asia and International Law, 1*, 7–46.

Forsythe, D. P. (1975). The 1974 diplomatic conference on humanitarian law: Some observations. *The American Journal of International Law*, 69(1), 77–91. doi:10.2307/2200192
Forsythe, D. P. (1977). Three sessions of legislating humanitarian law: Forward march, retreat, or parade rest? *The International Lawyer*, *11*(1), 131–142.
Gathii, J. T. (2011). TWAIL: A brief history of its origins, its decentralized network, and a tentative bibliography. *Trade, Law and Development*, *3*, 26–64.
Gong, G. W. (1984). *The standard of "civilization" in international society*. Oxford: Clarendon Press.
Grotius, H., & Tuck, R. (2005). *Rights of war and peace*. Indianapolis, IN: Liberty Fund.
Hague-Peace-Conference_1899.pdf. (n.d.). Retrieved from http://www.loc.gov/rr/frd/Military_Law/pdf/Hague-Peace-Conference_1899.pdf
Havercroft, J., & Owen, D. (2016). Soul-blindness, police orders and black lives matter. *Political Theory*, *44*(6), 739–763. doi:10.1177/0090591716657857.
Hay, J., & Root, E. (1913). Instructions to the American delegates to the Hague conferences, 1899 and 1907 comments. World Peace Foundation Pamphlet Series, 1913–1914, pp. 1–28.
Hicks, F. C. (1908). Equality of states and the Hague conferences. *American Journal of International Law*, *2*, 530–561.
Jouannet, E. (2007). Universalism and imperialism: The true-false paradox of international law? *European Journal of International Law*, *18*(3), 379–407.
Kalshoven, F. (1985). Arms, armaments and international law. *Recueil des Cours*, *191*, 183–342.
Kalshoven, F. (2007). *Reflections on the law of war: Collected essays*. Leiden: Brill.
Kalshoven, F. (2011). *Constraints on the waging of war: An introduction to international humanitarian law* (4th ed.). Cambridge: Cambridge University Press.
Kinsella, H. M. (2005). Discourses of difference: Civilians, combatants, and compliance with the laws of war. *Review of International Studies*, *31*, 163–185.
Kinsella, H. M. (2011). *The image before the weapon: A critical history of the distinction between combatant and civilian*. Ithaca, NY: Cornell University Press.
Levie, H. S. (1981). Humanitarian restrictions on chemical and biological weapons international regulation of chemical and biological warfare symposium. *University of Toledo Law Review*, *13*, 1192–1202.
Lorca, A. B. (2010). Universal international law: Nineteenth-Century histories of imposition and appropriation. *Harvard International Law Journal*, *51*, 475–552.
Mantilla, G. (2013). *Under (social) pressure: The historical regulation of internal armed conflicts through international law*. Ph.D. Dissertation, University of Minnesota.
Mathews, R. J. (2001). The 1980 convention on certain conventional weapons: A useful framework despite earlier disappointments. *Revue Internationale de La Croix-Rouge/International Review of the Red Cross*, *83*(844), 991–1012.
McCulloch, J. (1981). Amilcar Cabral: A theory of imperialism. *The Journal of Modern African Studies*, *19*(3), 503–511.
Mittelman, J. H. (1976). Collective decolonisation and the U.N. Committee of 24. *The Journal of Modern African Studies*, *14*(1), 41–64.
Mutua, M. (2000a). Critical race theory and international law: The view of an insider-outsider symposium – critical race theory and international law – keynote address. *Villanova Law Review*, *45*, 841–854.
Mutua, M. (2000b). What is TWAIL? *American Society of International Law Proceedings*, *94*, 31–38.

Organization of American States. (1966a). *The "First Tricontinental Conference," another threat to the security of the inter-American system*. Pan American Union, Washington, DC.

Organization of American States. (1966b). *The tricontinental conference of African, Asian, and Latin American Peoples: A staff study*. U.S. Govt. Print. Office, Washington, DC.

Parks, W. H. (1997). Joint service combat shotgun program. *Army Lawyer, 1997*, 16–24.

Parks, W. H. (2006). Means and methods of warfare. *George Washington International Law Review, 38*, 511–542.

Pemberton, J.-A. C. (2013). So-called right of civilisation in European colonial ideology, 16th to 20th centuries. *The Journal of the History of International Law, 15*, 25–52.

Pitts, J. (2012). Empire and legal universalisms in the eighteenth century. *The American Historical Review, 117*(1), 92–121. doi:10.1086/ahr.117.1.92

Plummer, B. G. (2013). *In search of power: African Americans in the era of decolonization, 1956–1974*. Cambridge: Cambridge University Press.

Prashad, V. (2008). *The darker nations: A people's history of the third world*. New York: New Press.

Rancière, J. (1995). *On the shores of politics*. London: Verso.

Rancière, J. (1999). *Disagreement: Politics and philosophy*. Minneapolis, MN: University of Minnesota Press.

Rancière, J. (2004). *The politics of aesthetics: The distribution of the sensible*. London: Continuum.

Sandoz, Y. (1994). Three key questions. *International Review of the Red Cross, 299*, 93–98.

Stoler, A. L. (2009). *Along the archival grain: Epistemic anxieties and colonial common sense*. Princeton, NJ: Princeton University Press.

Suter, K. (1984). *An international law of guerrilla warfare: The global politics of law-making*. New York, NY: St. Martin's Press.

Totschnig, W. (2016). What is an event? Probing the ordinary/extraordinary distinction in recent European philosophy. *Constellations*. doi:10.1111/1467-8675.12204

Vattel, E. de, & Chitty, J. (2011). *The law of nations, or, principles of the law of nature applied to the conduct and affairs of nations and sovereigns*. Cambridge: Cambridge University Press.

Westad, O. A. (2007). *The global cold war: Third world interventions and the making of our times*. Cambridge: Cambridge University Press.

THE SOVEREIGN SOCIETY: HISTORICAL RUPTURE AND THE EMERGENCE OF THE "DOMESTIC" IN 17TH CENTURY EUROPE AND EAST ASIA

Aleksandra Thurman

ABSTRACT

If moments of historical rupture create spaces for social change, what emerges to fill those gaps? This article approaches this question by exploring the creation of the "domestic" in 17th century Europe and Asia following the decline of the Spanish Habsburgs in the West and the Ming Dynasty in the East. Two events will serve as lenses through which that process will be explored. The first case centers on arguments for the legitimacy of the 1603 Dutch seizure of a Portuguese carrack in what would serve as the basis for Hugo Grotius's defense of the free seas. The second debate focuses on the appropriate mourning ritual following the 1659 death of King Hyojong, the 17th ruler in Korea's Choson dynasty. I argue that, in the process of responding to the crises they faced in their environments, social elites in both cases defined and articulated a

International Origins of Social and Political Theory
Political Power and Social Theory, Volume 32, 233–252

ISSN: 0198-8719/doi:10.1108/S0198-871920170000032009

conception of themselves as sovereign societies, creating a political space and corporate identity distinct from the extant institutional apparatus of the state and cultural framework of the nation.

Keywords: Methodological nationalism; Choson Korea; United Provinces; history; international relations

INTRODUCTION

In February 1603 Dutch captain Jacob van Heemskerck captured a Portuguese carrack, the *Santa Catarina*, in the straits of Malacca off the coast of what is now Singapore. The subsequent defense of the seizure provided the occasion for Hugo Grotius's 1609 *Mare Liberum* and the free seas debate that ensued following its publication. Grotius's argument against papal donation as the basis for title echoed a broader conversation that took place within the United Provinces on the rights of both the individual and the polity to structure their lives in accordance with principles they themselves determined – an argument that stood in sharp contrast to what the Dutch viewed as top-down pronunciations by the Catholic clergy. In the wake of the Protestant Reformation and during the United Provinces' war of independence against Spain, the seizure and surrounding discussion provided what would become the central Dutch argument for recognition of their union as a state.

Half a world away in 1659, Korean scholars and bureaucrats engaged in a heated debate on the proper mourning ritual to be followed by a deceased king's surviving stepmother. At the heart of the ritual's minutiae – the length of mourning and the clothing to be worn – lay questions of identity and legitimacy, in particular the source of legitimacy. The collapse of the Ming dynasty and establishment of the "barbarian" Manchu invaders as the ruling Qing dynasty 15 years prior had raised questions within Korea as to its future relationship with a political and cultural unit that had been regarded as the center of world civilization. Would Korea remain a sincere tributary of a now-corrupted Confucian order or the last bastion and ultimate protector of true Confucian learning? While participants in the debate on mourning ritual could and did reference the traditional intellectual lodestones that had been situated in China under the Ming, the discussion also created space for the articulation of a set of principles that were entirely self-referential in that they claimed authority – and therefore legitimacy – based on their local origins.

These seemingly disparate events provide a snapshot of two societies navigating moments of profound political upheaval in which the epistemic frameworks that actors had previously relied on to orient themselves in their sociopolitical worlds had been demolished. Where institutions might ordinarily be seen as providing a guide during these periods of change, when institutional collapse is the catalyst for change then new approaches to those discredited social and political structures are required. The Dutch and Korean cases shed light on the ways in which polities respond to moments of significant external change by turning inwards and, in so doing, redefining themselves and the worlds they inhabit.

This article argues that, in the process of responding to the crises they faced in their environments, 17th century political and social elites in both the United Provinces and Korea defined and articulated a conception of themselves as sovereign societies, creating a political space and corporate identity distinct from the extant institutional apparatus of the state and cultural framework of the nation. The intellectual orientations provided by the emergence of these sovereign societies – defined here as an independent community recognized as such by its members that claims the power to act politically as one body – served not only as anchors in periods of change, but also contained the foundations of the political institutions that would develop in both regions from the second half of the 17th century.

This comparison between the Dutch and Korean cases through the lens of sovereign societies is particularly instructive for the insights provided on the importance of ideas in the creation of the political institutions that emerge in the wake of periods of social change. Both polities exhibited a shift in their understandings of the locus of sovereignty, and in the United Provinces and Korea this shift entailed the rejection of external sources of law and the development of legal justifications that solely referenced local laws and customs. Yet, turning inwards alone could not provide these actors with the epistemic anchor required to resolve the tension created by the social change taking place around them. Neither the cultural identity of a nation nor the political institutions of the state offered a clear response to the questions presented by changing external circumstances. A new social structure in the form of a self-consciously autonomous body, however, could.

The article begins by framing the article in the context of a broader literature on the limits of methodological nationalism in the social sciences. I argue that a cross-cultural comparison of state institutions obscures meaningful differences and important similarities in the Korean and Dutch cases. As an alternative I draw on Pierre Bourdieu's work on social spaces as a resource for thinking about the importance of ideas and beliefs held by individuals. I then turn to the Dutch and Korean cases and explore the debates and the ways in which the arguments presented illustrate deeper philosophical concerns that indicate a shift in understanding on the locus of sovereign authority from outside to inside the policy. I conclude with a brief discussion on the ways in which the conceptions of the domestic presented in the Dutch and Korean cases may illustrate the emergence of the two polities as sovereign societies.

METHODOLOGICAL NATIONALISM AND THE LIMITS OF STATE-CENTRISM

By pointing to the problem of methodological nationalism in the social sciences, scholars have underscored and problematized the naturalness with which the state is regarded in contemporary research (Chernilo, 2006, 2007; Wimmer & Glick Schiller, 2002, 2003). The state is not only the primary political unit of analysis, but it also serves to demarcate all other political actors. In this framework politics is bound by territory rather than by mental constructs. An actor's understanding of self or the world around him/her is secondary to his/her geographic placement. The boundaries that frame the state may change, but the understanding that those boundaries matter for defining the unit of analysis does not.

This domestic/international bifurcation that relies on territorial boundaries raises a number of concerns when looking beyond the specific temporal and geographic limits of early modern Europe, particularly with the case of the 17th century United Provinces and Choson Korea. Go (2011, p. 239) argues in his work on the American and British empires that state-centric accounts rely on internal factors to explain outcomes, ignoring transnational processes. In turning to transnational processes in the Dutch and Korean case, we find that a similar argument can be made with respect to the role played by ideas – the concepts, opinions, and attitudes that resist the geographic boundaries of the nation-state. In the Dutch case, the same notions of individual autonomy promulgated during the Protestant Reformation are echoed in the defense of the *Santa Catarina*'s seizure. In the case of the Korean discussion on the legitimacy of their own, local legal codes, placing native traditions on par with those promulgated by what was understood to be the center of the civilized world could not have been conceived of outside the collapse of the Ming dynasty.

If the ideas contained within the Dutch and Korean debates served as a link to transnational processes that resist the international/domestic binary inherent in methodological nationalism, the two cases also show how those same ideas proved their resilience despite challenges. Individual beliefs withstood criticism as well as threats. One of the more predominant features of both the free seas discussion in the United Provinces and the debate on mourning ritual in Choson Korea was the all-or-nothing nature of the positions adopted by the participants. Actors took the rightness of their conceptualization of reality as given and that rightness accommodated no compromise: of course the Pope has no authority to donate portions of the sea to states; of course the United Provinces is an independent state; of course Korea's indigenous legal code is as valid a source of law as the Confucian classics; and of course Korea is part of the Confucian universe. One of the greatest obstacles to reaching agreement in the debates was precisely the self-evident character of the arguments being made to those who were making them. These were not conversations about how to apply a certain framework or which rules best encapsulated a particular understanding of reality – two scenarios that would possibly accommodate strategic rhetorical decisions to emphasize one point over another or attempt to mislead an audience. These were conversations about the very nature of reality. As such, the actors could no more change their position in an effort to find a solution to a problem than they could declare the sky to be chicken.

Just as their assumptions about the "truth" of their reality took on a fixed quality, so too were the same actors entirely unaware of what they did not know. For example, while early Choson Korea possessed what contemporary audiences would consider the external markers of sovereign power, the idea of an accompanying set of sovereign rights would arguably have been problematic to a 16th century Korean audience. Even with its formal status as a tributary, the Korean polity in the early Choson period would have met objective criteria for political centralization and autonomy; however, the idea of a set of rights belonging to an autonomous organization would not have been coherent. A Confucian polity understood its place in the world only through the absence of autonomy. An analysis of the 15th century Iberian powers from the perspective of the audience of the day would encounter similar difficulties (Albaladejo, 1989). Similar to the Korean case, the crowns of Castile and Aragon in the 15th century Iberian peninsula possessed formally centralized, autonomous political structures, yet the conception of an identity independent of a pan-European body of the Catholic faithful did not exist.

If methodological nationalism were to limit our attention to the state aspect of the Dutch and Korean polities, that analysis would obfuscate the transnational processes that make the comparison an illustration of how societies respond to moments of significant external change. Individual actors in both the Korean and Dutch cases possessed clear, fixed understandings of the nature of their reality. They formed opinions and passionately defended their beliefs. While it is certainly possible that audiences would have been receptive to different framing devices for the arguments being presented, that set is finite and limited by individual beliefs. Confucian scholars could no more have made a case for natural rights than Dutch politicians could have made an argument based on divine revelation. Possibilities that exist in some temporal and cultural contexts are absent in others.

Were we to look at those 17th century institutions through the lens provided by methodological nationalism, we would focus on the presence of the external signs of sovereign power and find a clear outline of what we would now call the modern state. The meaning those historical actors ascribed to their own political institutions is significantly different, as one may find in the distinctively nonmodern sensibilities inherent in a conversation about Korea's status as a tributary state or in the invitation made in the early years of the United Provinces to be ruled under a British protectorship.

This distinction between state institutions and the set of ideas that actors draw on to assign meaning to and navigate those institutions suggests a separation between the state and the domestic. The existence of social cohesion and group affiliation based on shared ideas points to the presence of a dynamic beyond an arithmetic aggregation of individual beliefs. Instead, the Dutch and Korean cases suggest the existence of a social "self," a collective identity capable of creating and sustaining those independent values. This distinction – between actors' social and political self-understandings and the institutions they inhabit, between sovereignty in its lived and codified forms – allows for the possibility of a social unit that exists alongside the cultural practices of the nation and the institutions of the state.

Drawing on Pierre Bourdieu's work on social classes, one way of thinking about the dynamics found in the Dutch and Korean cases is as a social space. Bourdieu approaches social space as multidimensional sets of properties. Different properties are salient in different social spaces based on the ability of these properties to "confer strength, power within that universe, on their holder" (Bourdieu, 1985, p. 724). The positions occupied by individuals in these sets of properties allow for differentiation among individuals. Groupings of individuals in these spaces form the basis of social classes, defined as "sets of agents who occupy similar positions and who, being placed in similar conditions and subjected to similar conditionings, have every likelihood of having similar dispositions and adopting similar stances" (Bourdieu, 1985, p. 725).

If Bourdieu's sets of properties can be extended to include ideas, this framework allows actors to share beliefs and values across territorial boundaries. This is most clearly seen in the Dutch and Korean cases through the scholarly and social networks that had developed in Europe and Asia by the beginning the 17th century. The Dutch and their Korean counterparts enjoyed participation in rich, active intellectual communities. Merchants, diplomats, priests, and scholars trafficked ideas that created social groups based on beliefs that were not necessarily linked to national identity.

Bourdieu's social world possesses an existence independent from the actors who populate it, yet at the same time these actors also contribute to its construction and change through the performance of their social identity. Power is manifested in the durability of these social relations but also in the creation of new categories, "the power to make groups by making the common sense, the explicit consensus, of the whole group" (Bourdieu, 1985, p. 729). The social system that is created by a specific set of properties and the individuals distributed across them is symbolic, but the power of what Bourdieu calls the "imposition of the legitimate vision of the social world" (Bourdieu, 1985, p. 731) has profound consequences for the material world. From property rights to educational titles, the formal and informal structures of society originate in this space of social relationships.

It is in this context that the salience of the Dutch and Korean debates becomes clearer. The grouping of individuals into social spaces based on their beliefs does not account for the vehemence with which they argue the claims that stem from those same beliefs. Yet, if we accept Bourdieu's argument that those relationships potentially grant individuals the ability to confer and remove benefits, what is at stake in these debates becomes exponentially more significant than booty from a ship or whether a surviving stepmother wears untrimmed or trimmed linen skirts in mourning. The competing visions of social worlds reflected in the debates not only have material consequences, they illustrate the emergence of new understandings of what constitutes the legitimate social world that extend well into the future. The same principles that are contained in successful arguments for one course of action become the basis for successive debates. In the case of the Dutch, the argument made by van Heemskerck justifying his seizure of the *Santa Catarina* served as the foundation for the Dutch negotiating position vis-à-vis the Spanish for what would become the Twelve Years' Truce. In the Korean case, the debate on mourning ritual illustrates a significant moment in the development of substantive legal constraints on the monarch's power (Ginsburg, 2012).

While Bourdieu provides a way to think about the transnational forces that draw on ideas to shape the content and ideas of social groups, his work is more limited in providing a theoretical account of the emergence of sovereign societies. Ideas may allow for the crystallization of group affiliations, but it does not necessarily follow that those groups merge as independent communities recognized as such by their members that claim the power to act politically as one body. Although quite a departure from Bourdieu's work, one may think about this creation of a sovereign society through John Locke's account of the origins of political societies. Reflecting the concern with an ontological separation of political institutions from sovereign society, Locke's understanding of the creation of political community is distinct from the institutions of the state and views the latter as designed to achieve the goals of that political community:

> Men being, as has been said, by nature, all free, equal, and independent, no one can be put out of this estate, and subjected to the political power of another, without his own consent. The only way whereby any one divests himself of his natural liberty, and puts on the bonds of civil society, is by agreeing with other men to join and unite into a community for their comfortable, safe, and peaceable living one amongst another, in a secure enjoyment of their properties, and a greater security against any, that are not of it. (Locke, 1980, p. 52)

This distinction between the institutions of the state, the social dimensions of nation, and the voluntarism of participation in political society forms the basis of the domestic: the idea that ultimate sovereignty resides within the community. That same movement away from a sovereignty held by the "other" is seen in the Dutch and Korean debates. In both cases, the turning inwards rather than outwards for the legal authority to adjudicate disputes marks the subtle yet meaningful genesis of sovereign societies.

Locke's is not an automatic grouping based on an intrinsic or social identity but one based on choice. That same dimension of choice can be found in the arguments presented for and against this shift in legal authority. The Spanish and Portuguese provided ample precedent in their own disagreements between each other for a Dutch argument that drew on the same legal principles that would also have justified continued Spanish dominion over the prerevolt Spanish Netherlands. Korean scholars could and did make a case for the legitimacy of the Qing dynasty as the new center of the Confucian universe; however, the argument based on local legal sources found favor with the Choson monarch. The details of each of those choices will be presented in the following sections.

THE DUTCH CHALLENGE TO SPANISH AUTHORITY

While Spain's fortunes continued to thrive with its colonial endeavors outside the continent, within Europe the Spanish monarchy faced increasing challenges to its authority. The Protestant Reformation had given rise to a radically new way of conceptualizing the individual's relationship with the divine and the subsequent fragmentation of faith gave rise to an equally dramatic set of political transformations, including the revolt of the Habsburg Netherlands and creation of the United Provinces. The same war between France and Spain that had given rise to the Treaty of Chateau-Cambrésis – the document permitting French exploration in Spanish waters – had also aggravated Spanish relations in the Low Countries. After a series of revolts beginning in 1566 and a brief period as a protectorate of England, the United Provinces emerged as a cohesive, functioning state by 1590. How the Dutch reoriented themselves intellectually during this period of transformation can be seen through the lens of the Amsterdam Admiralty Court's defense of the 1603 seizure of the *Santa Catarina*.[1]

Focused Dutch efforts to extend their maritime trading reach beyond Europe's boundaries began in 1592 when nine Amsterdam merchants sent Cornelis de Houtman and his brother Frederik to Lisbon to steal information on the Portuguese spice trade. The two were caught, convicted, and imprisoned. In the interim, the nine merchants had formed the *Compagnie van Verre* (Long Distance Company) in 1594. When the de Houtman brothers returned to Amsterdam in 1595, Cornelis was appointed captain of the first fleet of four Dutch ships that set sail for the East Indies. Out of 249 men who set sail in 1595 only 89 returned in 1597 on three ships with a small cargo of pepper (Israel, 1995, p. 319). In economic terms, this first expedition is regarded as an unmitigated disaster. As a rallying point for growing Dutch nationalism and as evidence of the viability of long distance trade, however, the trip was regarded as a tremendous success. The *Compagnie van Verre* made its second expedition to the East Indies in 1598, led by Admiral Jacob van Neck and Vice Admiral Jacob van Heemskerck. van Heemskerck returned to the United Provinces in 1600, while van Neck and a portion of his crew remained in the Indies. Their 1601 execution by Portuguese authorities in Macao provided the central justification for what would become an international debate on the freedom of the seas.

Van Heemskerck departed for the East Indies in April 1601 as part of the third wave of Dutch trading missions to the East Indies. Upon the arrival of the eight ships off the coast of Java in February 1602, the expedition spent the following year trading and establishing Dutch posts at various ports in the region. Like many Dutch traders before him, van Heemskerck encountered a number of obstacles to his efforts. Inclement weather made some ports impossible to reach and the presence of the Dutch fleet triggered dramatic price inflation in some of the markets that could be accessed. Other ports had their spice stocks exhausted. The Sultan of Demak detained 12 of van Heemskerck's crew to serve as gunners in his war against the Mataram of Java. For all intents and purposes, it would be difficult to characterize the first half of van Heemskerck's expedition a success (Van Ittersum, 2003, pp. 7–20).

Following many military exchanges with the Portuguese, van Heemskerck learned of the execution of 17 Dutch sailors – van Neck and his men – by the Portuguese in Macao in November 1601. The historical account presented by Blussé (1988) paints a picture of violent acts of retribution by both parties. Upon his arrival in the region in 1601, van Neck learned that Dutch sailors had been taken by surprise and "dismembered and hacked into pieces one by one in front of each other" (Blussé, 1988, p. 651) by their Portuguese hosts after receiving a misleadingly friendly welcome in Tidore. Van Neck took revenge by (unsuccessfully) attacking Portuguese ships. After continuing his travels and facing inclement weather, van Neck docked at the Portuguese settlement of Macao. Eleven members of his crew were captured by the Portuguese during an attempt to make contact on shore. A second set of six sailors sent as envoys were likewise promptly captured. The Dutch ships were isolated in the bay and prevented from making contact with either the Chinese or Portuguese. Van Neck and his remaining crew left the area shortly thereafter, leaving the captured sailors behind without knowing whether or not the prisoners were still alive. Van Heemskerck learned of the execution from letters discovered in the June 1602 capture of a Portuguese frigate and it was these executions which served as a rallying cry against the Portuguese for van Heemskerck and his crew.

To avenge what he believed to be the wrongful deaths of those Dutch sailors and to punish the Portuguese for their attacks against Dutch traders, van Heemskerck ordered his crew to lay in wait off the eastern coast of the Malay Peninsula for Portuguese merchants. Van Heemskerck found a local ally in the Sultan of Johore. The Sultan had been attacked by the Portuguese for his decision to engage in trade with the Dutch. In retaliation, the Sultan provided van Heemskerck with information on the location of Portuguese ships in the region (Borschberg, 2002, p. 45). On February 25, 1603, the tensions came to a head with van Heemskerck's capture of the *Santa Catarina*. As an isolated incident, the event is spectacular in its banality. When judged by its ramifications, however, the event is genuinely remarkable.

The financial impact of the seizure and its importance to the VOC were enormous and unprecedented. Accounts describe the cargo as consisting of: "1,200 bales of raw Chinese silk; chests filled with coloured damask, atlas (a type of polished silk), tafettas and silk; large amounts of gold thread or spun gold; cloth woven with gold thread; robes and bed canopies spun with gold; silk bedcovers and bedspreads; linen and cotton cloth, thirty last (approximately 60 tons) of porcelain comprising dishes 'of every sort and kind'; substantial quantities of sugar, spices, gum, musk (also known as bisem); wooden beds and boxes, some of them beautifully ornate with gold; and a 'thousand other things, that are produced in China'." The ship also carried approximately 70 tons of gold and "a 'royal throne' that was inlayed with precious stones" (Borschberg, 2002, p. 38). At auction, the cargo was valued at roughly £300,000 (using 17th century exchange rates) (Van Ittersum, 2003, p. 36). To provide some basis for comparison, England's total revenue for 1600 amounted to approximately £170,000 (O'Brien, 2006, p. 56). England's income from direct taxes in 1600 totaled approximately £75,000 (O'Brien, 2006, p. 76).

The value of the prize made it an opportune target for privateers and the Estates General placed its navy in the North Sea and English Channel on high alert. When the Dutch fleet intercepted the *Santa Catarina* in June 1604, eight out of eighteen sailors had survived the return voyage. The *Santa Catarina* docked in Emden (Germany) and van Heemskerck and his crew on the *Witte Leeuw* (White Lion) arrived in Amsterdam in July 1604. Not surprisingly, a number of contending claims to the *Santa Catarina*'s cargo arose. The Holland and Zeeland trading companies had merged in March 1602 to form the United Dutch East India Company or VOC (*Verenigde Oostindische Compagnie*): the inheritor of van Heemskerck's commission. The VOC's directors appealed to the Amsterdam College of the Admiralty Board for access to the *Boshuis* – a storage area for the most valuable cargo. The request was granted under the condition that two of the Board's members be present to ensure an accurate inventory of the ship's cargo. Dutch sailors guarding the *Santa Catarina* in Emden were said to have appropriated part of the cargo, selling Chinese porcelain on the city's streets. The Frisian College of the Admiralty Board seized four Dutch ships involved in transporting the *Santa Catarina*'s cargo from Emden to Amsterdam. The Estates General instructed the Amsterdam College of the Admiralty Board to allow the VOC's directors to auction off the cargo's perishable goods. Amsterdam's sheriff immediately tore down the handbills announcing the sale, arguing that the Admiralty Board had encroached on his municipal jurisdiction. Amsterdam's burgomasters adjudicated the dispute, siding with the Admiralty Board, and the cargo was sold in two auctions in August and September 1604 (Van Ittersum, 2003, pp. 115, 116).

The sale of the cargo did not, however, solve the question of who possessed rightful ownership of the prize. Three plaintiffs presented their cases to the Admiralty Court: Holland's Solicitor General on behalf of the County of Holland; Van Heemskerck and his crew; and the VOC's directors. During its deliberations the Admiralty Court issued bimonthly summons for other claimants to the cargo which remained unanswered. On September 1, 1604, the Estates of Holland relinquished all claims to the cargo, leaving only the VOC and van Heemskerck as the plaintiffs. The Admiralty Court ruled the carrack and its cargo to be good prize – property legitimately seized in war – and that the proceeds of its sale should be divided between van Heemskerck and his crew and the VOC directors (Grotius, 2006, pp. 510–514).

Rather than turn to any existing set of treaties or bulls defining international boundaries, the Amsterdam Admiralty Court's justification for the seizure of the *Santa Catarina* was entirely self-referential in the sense that the Court considered no law not promulgated by the Dutch themselves. Their first line of argumentation centered on the status of Spain and Portugal as enemies of the Dutch Republic. In the context of the Low Countries' revolt against their Hapsburg rulers, the Dutch Estates General passed a resolution on April 2, 1599, authorizing Dutch privateers to consider all Spanish and Portuguese ships open targets. This declaration was reinforced by Article 37 of the Dutch East India Company's charter (1602), which declared the Portuguese and Spanish enemies of the Dutch people.

The Court also grounded their approval of the *Santa Catarina*'s seizure on the basis of van Heemskerck's commission. In the commission granted him by Prince Maurice of Nassau, Lord High Admiral of Holland, van Heemskerck received permission for "the use of force in self-defense and ... in order to obtain reparations for damages sustained"

(Van Ittersum, 2003, p. 521). The Board failed to comment on how this commission would allow for an attack on a Portuguese vessel when van Heemskerck had not been harmed. Nor did it elaborate on how a calculated capture could be described as something other than piracy. Grotius elaborated upon the Admiralty's ruling and argued that Prince Maurice's commission had made van Heemskerck an agent of the Dutch Republic. Here, Grotius incorporates a discussion on the right to revolt and the independent nature of the body politic as something distinct from that body's ruler. The Dutch people were within their rights to declare war on Spain and, by association, Portugal. Having established the Dutch as an independent nation, Grotius (*De Iure Praedae*, Chapter 13) then continues to elaborate upon van Heemskerck's role as an agent of the state in his support of the war against the Spanish. As an agent of the state, van Heemskerck's actions were perfectly consistent with the Dutch Estates General's 1599 policy on war against Spain's Philip III (who also ruled Portugal at the time) (Van Ittersum, 2003, p. 28). Although no direct order to seize the *Santa Catarina* had been given, "the lack of such authorization would nevertheless have been counterbalanced by the execution of a publicly advantageous enterprise, and by retroactive approval, so to speak" (Grotius, 1950, p. 305). Van Heemskerck was neither a pirate nor a privateer. In his attack on the Portuguese, van Heemskerck acted as an extension of the Dutch state.

Finally, the Amsterdam Admiralty Court supported the capture based on the decision made by the fleet's Broad Council[2] while in port in the East Indies (Van Ittersum, 2003, p. 23). On December 4, 1602, the Broad Council unanimously agreed to remain in the port of Pulau Tiuman to lie in waiting for Portuguese merchant ships. The policy document which emerged from that meeting justified an attack against the Portuguese for three reasons: (1) any attack on Portuguese trade would ultimately weaken the Habsburg efforts to quell revolt in the Netherlands; (2) the "ravenous Portuguese" had encouraged indigenous rulers to prohibit Dutch merchants from their markets and harbors; and (3) the Portuguese would continue to try and eradicate the Dutch presence in the East Indies and the only option remaining was to "attack and harm [the Portuguese] wherever we can or may" (Van Ittersum, 2003, pp. 520, 521).

CRISIS OF THE CONFUCIAN WORLD

The fall of the Ming dynasty in 1644 precipitated a crisis of meaning in the neo-Confucian universe. China under the Ming had stood at the center of the civilized world – a status recognized by Korea as a tributary state. Through the lens of this Confucian order the conquest of the Ming by Manchu "barbarians" and the institution of the Qing dynasty went beyond a transferral of power from one set of rulers to another. For Korea it represented the collapse of civilization, a "whirlwind of disorder, [in which] they had to construct a new episteme with which they could understand and conceptualize the changed world order" (Haboush & Deuchler, 1999, pp. 68, 69). The death of the Yi dynasty's seventeenth monarch, King Hyojong (효종, 1619–1659) in 1659 and the ensuing debate on the mourning ritual to be followed provided one site upon which several of these new frameworks for understandings would be contested.

The debate centered on the type of mourning ritual to be followed by Hyojong's stepmother, Queen Dowager Jangryeol (장렬, also referred to as Chaŭi, 1624–1688) – the second wife of Hyojong's father King Injo (인조, 1595–1649). The scholars and advisors who developed policy in the neo-Confucian polity could find precedents specifying the formal rituals for almost all public occasions, yet Jangryeol's case was the first of a stepmother surviving a stepson who had also succeeded her husband to the throne. The mourning ritual performed by Jangryeol – specifically the length of the mourning period and the type of clothing worn – reflected particular understandings of Hyojong's status as a son and monarch and, thereby, would be an unambiguous, public statement on the legitimacy of Hyojong's rule. To a 17th century Korean audience, the ritual chosen would speak volumes and play a significant part in the shaping of Hyojong's legacy and perceptions of his son and successor, Hyeonjong (현종, 1641–1674).

Court scholars and bureaucrats had anticipated the issue and began discussing possible solutions immediately after Hyojong's death. The lines drawn in the debate largely reflected the period's political divisions between the *Namin* (western) and *Soin* (southern) factions. These factions emerged as the product of power struggles in the 15th and 16th centuries between the *Hungu*, political elites based in the capital, and the rural, neo-Confucian scholars in the provinces known as *Sarim*. While the *Sarim* would eventually come to dominate the *Hungu*, internal disputes among the *Sarim* themselves would lead to the emergence of additional factions.

A more general discussion of factional politics and the philosophical positions staked out by the different groups is beyond the scope of this article. For the purposes of understanding the debate on the mourning ritual and situating it in a broader political and intellectual context, however, two points are noteworthy: (1) the centrality of Confucian thought in Choson Korea's social, political, and economic life and (2) the flexibility with which

Confucian thought could accommodate multiple, occasionally contradictory, interpretations and prescriptions.

One way to characterize the transition from the Koryo (918–1392) to the Choson (1392–1910) dynasty in Korea is by tracing the shifts in intellectual orientation from a combination of indigenous and Buddhist traditions to one solidly rooted in Chinese neo-Confucianism. By the mid-17th century, neo-Confucianism possessed an undisputed ideological hegemony and neo-Confucian officials and scholars occupied a central position in Korean culture at the heart of political, economic, and intellectual life (for a discussion on the role of the scholar-official in Choson Korea, see Kim 2009). To be a politically engaged Korean meant to be a Confucian and to be a Confucian in this context meant to be a student of the neo-Confucian scholar Zhu Xi (朱熹, 1130–1200) (Haboush & Deuchler, 1999).

In the context of Zhu Xi's broader influence on Korean thought, his commentaries on *qi* (氣) and *li* (理) are of particular salience for illustrating the differences between the factional politics that formed the basis of the mourning ritual debate. *Qi* could be interpreted as physical or material force, the action that takes place within the world. *Li*, in contrast, may be seen as the basic underlying principle of the universe. The *Namin*'s philosophical focus on *qi* translated politically into a policy focus that reflected active individual engagement with the external world – reforms that would strengthen the government and improve the lives of citizens. The *Sarim*'s interpretation of *li* as the source of *qi* led to an emphasis on *li* and the fostering of an inward, spiritual orientation. Politically, this meant a policy emphasis on the moral purification of rulers and the removal of corruption from public life.

While both groups drew on the Confucian classic *Ceremonials and Rites* as their primary reference texts, the differences in emphasis and interpretation reflected complex differences in interpretations of monarch's function, the source of his legitimacy, and the means by which that legitimacy is granted. The *Namin* position, as articulated by scholar Yun Hyu, proposed that Hyojong be mourned by the queen dowager as a king by his subject with three years of untrimmed mourning. The term untrimmed refers to type of clothing to be worn during the mourning period. In this case untrimmed mourning would have displayed the greatest solemnity. Other types of mourning dress included, for example, trimmed, thick hemp, and loosely woven. In adopting this position, the *Namin* abstracted the throne as an institution from its specific occupant, assigning the ruler a purely public identity even in the relationships with his own family members.

The *Soin* position relied on Hyojong's filial rank, more specifically his status as a second son. Referencing passages in *Ceremonials and Rites*, the

Soin framed the queen dowager's role as that of a mother mourning the loss of her son. What made the *Soin*'s interpretation controversial was their view of Hyojong as a second son rather than as the eldest son. His elder brother, Crown Prince Sohyeon (소현, 1612–1645) had died shortly after returning from his nine-year imprisonment as a hostage at the Manchu court in Shenyang where Hyojong was also being held hostage. Sohyeon's release came shortly before Hyojong's and the elder brother died under mysterious circumstances shortly after his return to Korea (but before Hyojong's return). Were Hyojong seen as having taken Sohyeon's place as the family's (second) eldest son, a three-year period of mourning would have been called for. The *Soin*'s advocacy of a one-year mourning period reflected their view that Hyojong was to be mourned as a second son.

While the *Soin* did not directly challenge Hyojong's legitimacy through their advocacy of a one-year mourning period, the implications would have been clear to those following the proceedings. The *Soin*'s interpretation of filial rank reflected common practice among Korea's sociopolitical elite, the *yangban*. The *yangban* adhered to a custom of strict patrilineal descent in which the line of succession passed from a father to his *eldest* son. In the event of that eldest son's death, inheritance passed to the eldest son of the eldest son. At the time of Hyojong's death Crown Prince Sohyeon had one surviving son. Mourning Hyojong as a second son rather than as an eldest son implied that the correct succession would return the monarchy to Crown Prince Sohyeon's line (Haboush, 1999).

The day after Hyojong's death the Ministry of Rites sent a memo to King Hyeonjong. The Ministry alerted Hyeonjong to the absence of a clear mourning ritual to be followed by Queen Dowager Jangryeol and recommended that the State Council meet to discuss the issue. The State Council met later that same day. Given the ramifications of the *Soin*'s argument, Prime Minister Chong presented Hyeonjong with a third position. Chong also advocated a one-year period of mourning; however, rather than echo the *Namin*'s and *Soin*'s reliance on the *Ceremonials and Rites*, Chong instead turned to Korean legal code. Chong pointed out that the *National Code* prescribed a one-year period of mourning for a mother mourning one of her husband's primary sons.[3] Having noted that the *Ming Legal Code* contained the same provision, the *Soin* agreed. Following the State Council's recommendation, Hyeonjong determined that Queen Dowager Jangryeol would adopt a one-year period of mourning.

Expressing their concerns with the challenge to the Korean monarchy's legitimacy presented by the one-year period of mourning, the *Namin* raised the issue of the mourning ritual again shortly before the queen dowager's one-year period of mourning was set to end. In this second debate, the *Namin* agreed with the *Soin*'s insistence on the primacy of Hyojong's filial rank over his status as monarch. Where the two factions differed was in their understanding of how that rank was determined.

As previously mentioned, the *yangban* class – the class to which the *Namin* and *Soin* belonged – followed strict patrilineal descent, a Confucian practice also practiced by the Chinese and advocated by the *Soin* in their argument for the one-year mourning period. In the context of the royal family, however, a much looser set of principles had been followed in the practice of dynastic succession. For example, the sons of *yangban* concubines faced severe social stigma and were not accepted into the *yangban* class despite the status of their fathers. Yet, it would not have been inconceivable to consider a son of one of the king's concubines the heir apparent absent a more suitable candidate. The distinction, so the *Namin* argued, lay in the nature of the monarchy itself. The office of the monarch performed its own legitimizing function, transforming individuals who in other circumstances would not have qualified for an inheritance. The *Namin* recognized Hyojong's birth as a second son, but according to their argument he became the (second) eldest son by virtue of having ascended the throne.

While the discussion surrounding the State Council's original recommendation took place among a comparatively small group of people, the *Namin*'s appeal drew a much larger audience and dealt with the question of political legitimacy head on. The *Soin* adhered to their original position, with scholar Song Siyol defining it in even starker terms by explicitly stating that there could not be "two right lines" (Haboush & Deuchler, 1999, pp. 57, 58). In response Yun Sondo, a prominent *Namin* poet and scholar/official, accused Song of challenging Hyeonjong's legitimacy – an unusually direct reference to the central issue at stake in the discussion. After confirming the clarity and appropriateness of the Korean legal code, Hyeonjong reaffirmed his decision for a one-year period of mourning. The most visible *Soin* participants in the debate retired or left the capital. Yun Sondo was banished to a province known for its inhospitable climate.

The death of Queen Inseon (1619–1674), Hyojong's widow, raised the issue once again. According to Confucian custom, the ritual to be followed by a surviving stepmother for her daughter-in-law would be dependent on the status of her daughter-in-law's husband – in this case King Hyojong. The existence of precedent clarified the decision. Confucian tradition prescribed that the wife of an eldest son be mourned for one year while the wife of other primary sons would be mourned for nine months. The Ministry of Rites decided that Queen Dowager Jangryeol would be required to engage in a nine-month mourning ritual for Queen Inseon; however, Hyeonjong intervened and reversed the decision, requiring Jangryeol to engage in one full year of mourning.

CONCLUSIONS

The discussion on methodological nationalism began with an observation on the limits such a framework presents for understanding cases that fall outside the early modern European context, in particular the Dutch and Korean cases. By stepping away from that framework and shifting our focus from state institutions to the ideas contained in the debates on the *Santa Catarina* and mourning ritual, I hope to draw our attention to the ways in which ideas can function to (1) serve as orienting points that allow actors to form social groups and (2) form the basis of sovereign societies to the extent that they articulate a conception of an independent community that claims the power to act politically as one body.

With reference to the first point, the argument presented here points to the role to be played by social groups in the development of sovereign identities. While this article focused on a narrow aspect of single debates, it is important to note that these discussions did not happen within a vacuum. The debate on the *Santa Catarina*'s seizure took place within a broader public debate on continuing the war with Spain as well as discussion among elites on the evolution of the new republic's economic, religious, and political institutions. A flourishing network of academies in the provinces and engaged discussions among scholars working outside the capital served as the backdrop to the debate on mourning ritual in Korea.[4] The debates discussed in this article were embedded within contexts that underscore the significance of debates that cross political and social boundaries. While scholarship grounded in a state-centric approach can point to the use of the "other" as one factor in the development of a sovereign awareness, it may not be the sole, or even primary, dimension of the conversations taking place within polities.

The second point revisits the idea that the distinction between sovereign society and state may be reflected in the choices made by actors to make the ideas of their own social group the ultimate source of legitimacy for their view. The rejection of Spanish authority by the Dutch did not necessarily entail embracing the notion of a sovereign Dutch republic. One could be Dutch in both cultural and political terms without being autonomous and self-governing. In 1584 local leaders invited both France's Henry III and Britain's Elizabeth I to assume sovereignty over the revolting provinces. The 1585 Treaty of Nonsuch established the United Provinces as a British protectorate which would be governed by the Earl of Leicester until 1588. Only 15 years later with the defense of the seizure of the *Santa Catarina* do we find a shift in consciousness that indicates the emergence of an independent community recognized as such by its members that claims the power to act politically in terms of self-governance as one body. The collapse of the Ming dynasty in 1644 likewise did not precipitate a change in Korea's status as a tributary state to China. The Yi dynasty continued to send diplomatic missions to the Qing imperial court, yet did so with the "overwhelming sense that Korea was the last bastion of Confucian civilization and that it should fulfil this mission in the best way possible" (Haboush, 1999, pp. 69, 70). This appropriation of Confucian authority combined with a self-validation of the legitimacy of such a move was reflected in the equal status granted to Korean and Ming legal code in the adjudication of the mourning ritual dispute.

In complicating this idea of a single, "domestic" space that is equated with the state and situated as the alternative to the "international," the comparison between the Dutch and Korean cases illustrates the theoretical potential of moving beyond the state as the primary form of political organization. By uncoupling political societies from the institutions they inhabit potentially allows for a more theoretically complex treatment of ideas in political life and may serve as an alternative to the state for comparative work across temporal and geographic boundaries.

NOTES

1. The Spanish and Portuguese crowns were united under Philip II of Spain following the 1580 Portuguese succession crisis. In that context, the Dutch seizure of a Portuguese carrack would also have been an act of aggression against Spain.
2. The Broad Council was a body composed of all naval officers in the fleet and held responsibility for decision-making while at sea.
3. There is a distinction to be made between primary sons (i.e., those born to a man's legal wife) and *sŏja*, sons born to a man's concubines. The term *sŏja* may also be used to refer to younger primary sons when making a distinction between the eldest son and his younger brothers.
4. For more on the growth of Korean civil society, see Koo (2007).

REFERENCES

Albaladejo, P. F. (1989). Cities and the state in Spain. *Theory and Society*, *18*(5), 721–731.

Blussé, L. (1988). Brief encounter at Macao. *Modern Asian Studies*, *22*(3), 647–664.

Borschberg, P. (2002). The seizure of the Sta. Catarina, revisited. The Portuguese empire in Asia, VOC politics and the origin of the Dutch-Johor alliance. *Journal of Southeast Asian Studies*, *33*(1), 31–62.

Bourdieu, P. (1985). The social space and the genesis of groups. *Theory and Society*, *14*(6), 723–744.

Chernilo, D. (2006). Social theory's methodological nationalism: Myth and reality. *European Journal of Social Theory*, *9*(1), 5–22.

Chernilo, D. (2007). *A social theory of the nation state: The political forms of modernity beyond methodological nationalism*. London: Routledge.

Ginsburg, T. (2012). Constitutionalism: East Asian antecedents. *Chicago-Kent Law Review*, *88*(1), 11–33.

Go, J. (2011). *Patterns of empire: The British and American Empires, 1688 to the present*. Cambridge: Cambridge University Press.

Grotius, H. (2006). *Commentary on the law of prize and booty*. Indianapolis, IN: Liberty Fund.

Haboush, J. K. (1999). Constructing the Center: The Ritual Controversy and the Search for a New Identity in Seventeenth-Century Korea. In J. K. Haboush & M. Deuchler (Eds.), *Culture and the state in Late Choson Korea* (pp. 46–90). Cambridge: Harvard University Asia Center.

Haboush, J. K., & Deuchler, M. (Eds.). (1999). *Culture and the state in Late Choson Korea, Asia Center*. Cambridge: Harvard University.

Israel, J. I. (1995). *The Dutch Republic: Its rise, greatness, and fall 1477–1806*. Oxford: Clarendon Press.

Koo, J.-W. (2007). The origins of the public sphere and civil society: Private academies and petitions in Korea, 1506–1800. *Social Science History*, *31*(3), 381–409.

Locke, J. (1980). *Second treatise of government*. In C. B. Macpherson (Ed.). Indianapolis, IN: Hackett Publishing Company, Inc.

O'Brien, P. K. (2006). Contentions of the purse between England and its European rivals from Henry V to George IV: A conversation with Michael Mann. *Journal of Historical Sociology*, *19*(4), 341–363.

Van Ittersum, M. J. (2003). Hugo Grotius in context: Van Heemskerck's capture of the Santa Catarina and its justification in De Jure Praedae. *Asian Journal of Social Science*, *31*(3), 511–548.

Wimmer, A., & Glick Schiller, N. (2002). Methodological nationalism and beyond: Nation-state building, migration and the social sciences. *Global Networks*, *2*(4), 1470–2266.

Wimmer, A., & Glick Schiller, N. (2003). Methodological nationalism, the social sciences, and the study of migration: An essay in historical epistemology. *International Migration Review*, *37*(3), 576–610.

ABOUT THE EDITORS

Tarak Barkawi is a Reader in the Department of International Relations, London School of Economics. He earned his doctorate at the University of Minnesota and specializes in the study of war, armed forces, and society with a focus on conflict between the West and the global South. He is the author of *Globalization and War*, *Soldiers of Empire* and many scholarly articles.

George Lawson is an Associate Professor in the Department of International Relations at LSE. His theoretical work focuses on the interface between International Relations and Historical Sociology; his empirical work concentrates on processes of radical change, particularly revolutions. His books include *Negotiated Revolutions* (2005); *The Global 1989* (2010, co-edited with Chris Armbruster and Michael Cox); *The Global Transformation* (2015, with Barry Buzan); and *Global Historical Sociology* (2017, co-edited with Julian Go).

INDEX

www.ingramcontent.com/pod-product-compliance
Lightning Source LLC
Chambersburg PA
CBHW050341270326
41926CB00016B/3554
* 9 7 8 1 8 3 8 6 7 9 2 2 4 *